W9-DCC-956

117457

LIVABLE CITIES

Livable Cities

A GRASS-ROOTS GUIDE TO REBUILDING URBAN AMERICA

BY
Robert Cassidy

HOLT, RINEHART AND WINSTON • NEW YORK

To the memory of my brother,
William Andrew Cassidy,
1934–1971

Copyright © 1980 by Robert Cassidy

All rights reserved, including the right to reproduce
this book or portions thereof in any form.

Published by Holt, Rinehart and Winston,
383 Madison Avenue, New York, New York 10017.

Published simultaneously in Canada by
Holt, Rinehart and Winston of Canada, Limited.

Library of Congress Cataloging in Publication Data

Cassidy, Robert, 1946–
    Livable cities

    Bibliography: p.
    Includes index.
    1. Urban renewal—United States.   2. Community
development—United States.   I.   Title.
HT175.C37   307.7′6′0973   79-3446
ISBN Hardbound: 0-03-042951-X
ISBN Paperback: 0-03-056291-0

First Edition

Designer: Helene Berinsky
Printed in the United States of America
10 9 8 7 6 5 4 3 2 1

Grateful acknowledgment is made to the following authors and publishers for permission to reprint excerpts from their publications.

Charles Abrams, *The Language of Cities: A Glossary of Terms*, copyright © 1971 by the Estate of Charles Abrams; reprinted by permission of Viking Penguin Inc.

Saul D. Alinsky, *Rules for Radicals*, copyright © 1971; reprinted by permission of Random House, Inc.

T. S. Eliot, "Murder in the Cathedral," in *The Complete Poems and Plays 1909–1950*, copyright 1930, 1939, 1943, 1950, © 1958, 1962, by T. S. Eliot; copyright 1934, 1935, 1936, 1952, by Harcourt, Brace & World, Inc.; used by permission of Harcourt Brace Jovanovich, Inc.

Nora Ephron, *Scribble Scribble: Notes on the Media*, copyright © 1975, 1976, 1977, 1978 by Nora Ephron; reprinted by permission of Alfred A. Knopf, Inc.

Dennis E. Gale, *The Back-to-the-City Movement . . . Or Is It?*, Occasional Paper, Department of Urban and Regional Planning, The George Washington University, Washington, D.C., 1976.

Andrew M. Greeley, *Neighborhood*, copyright © 1977 by The Seabury Press, Inc. Used by permission of the publisher.

Richard Harris, "A Nice Place to Live," *The New Yorker*, April 25, 1977. Reprinted by permission of *The New Yorker*.

James W. Hughes and Kenneth D. Bleakly, Jr., *Urban Homesteading*. Copyright © 1975 Rutgers, The State University of New Jersey. Reprinted by permission of the Center for Urban Policy Research.

Independent Community Consultants, Inc., *A Guide to Funding Sources Research*, copyright © 1974 by ICC, Inc., Box 141, Hampton, Arkansas 71744. Information on other ICC publications of interest to community development/organization projects can be obtained from ICC.

Jane Jacobs, *The Death and Life of Great American Cities*, copyright © 1961 by Jane Jacobs; reprinted by permission of Random House, Inc.

Joan Kennedy, Earl Anthes, Jerry Cronin, Carolyn Strong, *A Guide to Fundraising and Proposal Writing*, written by Independent Community Consultants, Inc., and the Design and Planning Assistance Center, copyright 1975, ICC, Inc.

Peter Libassi and Victor Hausner, *Revitalizing Central City Investment* (Columbus, Ohio: Academy for Contemporary Problems, 1977); reprinted by permission of the publisher.

Martin Mayer, *The Builders: Houses, People, Neighborhoods, Governments, Money*, copyright © 1977 by Martin Mayer; reprinted by permission of W. W. Norton & Company, Inc.

Richard S. Morris, *Bum Rap on America's Cities: The Real Causes of Urban Decay*, copyright © 1978 by Richard S. Morris; reprinted by permission of Prentice-Hall, Inc.

Oscar Newman, *Defensible Space: Crime Prevention through Urban Design*, copyright © 1972, 1973 by Oscar Newman; used by permission of Macmillan Publishing Company, Inc.

Vance Packard, *A Nation of Strangers*. Copyright © 1972 by Vance Packard. Reprinted by permission of the David McKay Company, Inc.

Leslie Shipnuck, Dennis Keating, and Mary Morgan, *The People's Guide to Urban Renewal and Community Development Programs*. Copyright © 1974 by Leslie Shipnuck, Dennis Keating, and Mary Morgan. Reprinted by permission of the Berkeley Tenants Union.

Roger Starr, "How to Make New York Greater: Make It Smaller," *The New York Times Magazine*, November 14, 1976; © 1976 by The New York Times Company. Reprinted by permission.

Morton and Lucia White, *The Intellectual Versus the City: From Thomas Jefferson to Frank Lloyd Wright*, copyright © 1962 by the Joint Center for Urban Studies of M.I.T. and Harvard University.

They shall rebuild the ancient ruins,
 the former wastes they shall raise up
and restore the ruined cities,
 desolate now for generations.

—ISAIAH 61:4

CONTENTS

PART FOUR:

Special Considerations

PREFACE

Early in 1975, my colleague Sylvia Lewis and I were sitting in our office at the American Society of Planning Officials (now the American Planning Association), dreaming up ideas for *Planning* magazine. I was particularly concerned that so many of our stories were negative in tone, and that they read like autopsies for failed programs and ideas. Surely, I thought, there must be a few cases of successful revitalization of American cities. "Why don't we do some stories about the winners for a change?" I asked. Sylvia agreed.

At about the same time, the Field Newspaper Syndicate asked me to write several articles about city improvement, focusing on neighborhoods. From my previous work as a planner in the Neighborhood Conservation Program in Arlington, Virginia, I was aware of at least a few success stories, and I was confident there must be more.

As it turned out, there was more than enough material to document many such stories, for America's neighborhoods were in the midst of a rebirth of spirit, physical improvement, and citizen involvement. The articles I wrote for *Planning* and the Field Newspaper Syndicate became the basis for this book, which is an attempt to codify the practical experience of successful neighborhood revitalization efforts into one volume for the layman.

While there is not enough room here to thank everyone who

helped in the writing of this book, I would like to express my appreciation to the following: Bill Toner and Frank Popper, for their review of early drafts of the manuscript; the staff of the Merriam Center Library, under the direction of Patricia Coatsworth, for their help in obtaining research materials; my agent, Dominick Abel, for sticking with the idea; my editors, Donald Hutter and Keri Christenfeld, for helpful advice; Ernest D. Langley, known to his friends in the Arlington County Planning Division as Skeeter, for supplying certain illustrations, and Sally Hughes for drawing others; Elsie Phalen, for typing the manuscript, with some help from Liz Coggs and Lottie Kearns; and Marsha Cassidy, my wife, who not only typed part of the manuscript but virtually lived with it for four years.

I would like to give special thanks to Louis Winnick and Robert Chandler of the Ford Foundation, without whose generous support this book could not have been written.

ROBERT CASSIDY
Chicago, Illinois

LIVABLE CITIES

INTRODUCTION

THE NEIGHBORHOOD RENAISSANCE

What is the city but the people?

—CORIOLANUS, III, i

Since the end of World War II, our cities have been on a rapidly downward course. As millions of families left for the green fields of suburbia, it began to seem that except for a small group of incurable urbiphiles, anyone who could, was leaving. Industries and businesses followed the middle-class masses for the wide open spaces beyond the city limits, taking with them the jobs, tax revenues, and wealth of the cities. The cities were becoming a dumping ground for the residue of society—the racial minorities, the poor, and the elderly.

Today, a glimmer of light is falling on this bleak picture. Against the general pattern of despair, there are more and more cases of civic regeneration, cases where the people of a neighborhood, refusing to believe that their city is dying, have joined together to upgrade the quality of life for themselves and others. In city after city, pockets of renewal activity are sprouting up. House by house, block by block, once-desolate neighborhoods are bouncing back to life. Using the strength of their numbers to form neighborhood organizations, allying with progressive business leaders and public officials, broadening their bases of power by cooperating with similar groups in other areas, the citizens of these neighborhoods are pulling together to reverse three decades of urban decay. In short, we are witnessing a neighborhood movement that may indeed restore the health of our beleaguered cities.

Revitalization is already taking place in all 30 of the nation's largest cities and in three-fourths of the 260 cities with fifty thousand or more population. One-third of the big-city respondents in a 1977 Gallup Poll said they had participated in a neighborhood-improvement effort of some kind and felt that their involvement had contributed to solving a problem. City homeowners in the mid-1970s have reinvested more dollars in their homes than have suburban homeowners, and the percentage of money from savings and loan institutions loaned for housing rehabilitation (which goes mostly to city housing, as opposed to new suburban construction) will quadruple in the next few years to $320 billion. Much of this activity is new, occurring within the last few years, and therefore has not yet been recorded. It is likely that the neighborhood movement is even bigger and more widespread than we think it to be.

While skeptics may point out—quite accurately—that the movement to rebuild urban neighborhoods accounts for a relatively small proportion of the nation's total housing, examples from around the country abound. In St. Louis, a citizens' group led by a Roman Catholic priest has fought off state highway officials and land developers who threatened to destroy the Italian district known as The Hill. The civic group has also provided local citizens with numerous community services—at no cost to the city or the residents themselves.

In Pittsburgh, the predominantly black Central North Side has been turned around from an area where 90 percent of the homes were on the verge of becoming slum properties to one where 90 percent of the homes are sound. The program that brought about this remarkable turn of events is now being replicated in dozens of other cities.

In Toledo, the residents of a Hungarian neighborhood prevented the closing of their library branch, stopped a road-widening project that would have split the community in two, got heavy trucks off their main street, and pushed the city to go after slumlords who refused to keep up their buildings.

In Baltimore, citizens in thirty neighborhoods are saving the city millions of dollars by performing their own housing-code inspections. Through peer pressure, the community groups have achieved a high level of compliance with city codes, thereby helping to assure the stability of their neighborhoods.

In Brooklyn, New York, residents of the Northside neighborhood, aided by architects and planners from Pratt Institute, have implemented a plan that permits local industries to expand, while providing replacement housing for uprooted families.

These are just a few examples from an accumulating body of evidence indicating that farsighted neighborhood groups are taking decisive steps to improve the quality of life in urban America. Apparently, too, there is an untapped reservoir of support for saving cities. A 1977 Gallup Poll shows that a majority of city residents not only don't want to leave their neighborhoods, but also are willing to take direct action to defend or maintain them. At the same time, thousands of young married couples, living-together singles, enlightened suburbanites, and artists of all types are rediscovering the joys of living in the city. Becoming aware of the distinctiveness and potential of old neighborhoods, they are returning and rebuilding them with their own sweat and initiative. Call them the urban pioneers, if you will.

Tom and Sally Hughes are typical members of this new breed of urban pioneers. Both grew up in the Rogers Park section of Chicago. Tom, forty-one, is an architect; Sally, thirty-five, is an artist and design teacher. They met at the University of Illinois in Champaign, were married, and in 1967 moved to an apartment in Pilsen, a predominantly Mexican-American neighborhood on Chicago's Near West Side.

"We had no financial game plan," said Tom. "We just played it by ear. We lived here for about six years and had a lot of friends in the neighborhood. We had a sense of belonging in the area. We had every intention of living in our rented place. But then some friends bought a house west of Halsted Street. At that time, west of Halsted was very bad, but we thought it had potential. We found a house two doors from them."

"We were going to buy it, no matter what the condition," recalls Sally. "We could have afforded the suburbs. We just wanted to stay in Pilsen."

The house, a nondescript two-story brick structure on a small lot, was a mess, physically and financially. "We had to pay $3,000 in owner's liens to get the building," said Tom. "Legally, we could have bought it for $744 in back taxes, but morally we just couldn't do that. We even found a place for the original owner and his wife, a little bungalow, and we fixed that place up for them before we started working on our own place."

It was late in the fall of 1973 before they could get started. "There were fifteen years of newspapers in there and hundreds of empty kerosene cans," said Tom. "We filled ten of those five-ton dumpsters. Then there was the basement. The previous owner had broken the waste stack, so that sewage ran under the basement floor. We had to dig up the basement floor, dig up the sewer pipes, re-lay the entire sewer, and backfill the whole thing— five hundred gallons of waste and sewage, all carried by hand, plus the dirt and concrete.

"We thought we had a roof, but we found out we had to tear it down," he continued. "Two weekends in a row, we had a roof-removal party. The neighbors cooked for us and helped us take the roof down. Luckily, we got the new roof on before winter."

With the building closed in, they were able to start work on the major systems. "I learned to do a lot of things, how to cut and thread pipe, for example," said Sally. "I stained all the overhead beams, and Tom put in the plumbing and electricity. About the only people we hired were contractors to put in the new roof, a sandblaster to clean the brick, a guy who poured concrete for the basement floor, and an electrician to bring service into the house. We saved money by buying things second-hand. We got our sinks, our range hood, the plumbing fixtures, and the metal insert for the fireplace that way."

For that matter, they nearly got a divorce, too. "We were laying brick, thirteen thousand of them, for the back wall," Sally recalled. "I mixed the mortar, and Tom laid the brick. That's the point where we went to a marriage counselor. Tom wanted to prove that he could do all the work, but *I* wanted a house to live in—and I wanted to lay brick. So, I got to do the wall in the basement." How did the job turn out? "The wall's kind of serpentine, even though it wasn't meant to be that way," says Sally Hughes, her eyes glinting in a smile, coupled with a hearty laugh.

The whole job cost them $7,000 for the building, $17,000 in materials, and $5,000 in new furniture. "If we paid ourselves eight dollars an hour, we'd have fifty thousand dollars in the house," Tom calculates. Counters Sally, "It would have been easier to build from scratch than to do what we did."

I visited the Hugheses on a warm spring night in 1978, shortly after they had moved in, some 250 weekends after they had started. The house was perfect—exposed beams in the ceilings, beautiful cabinetry in the kitchen, an exquisitely designed bathroom, Sally's six-by-eight glass mural hanging over their bed. As we sat on the steps of their new home drinking beer and watching the kids play basketball in the playground across the street, I could sense the great feeling of accomplishment that my friends Tom and Sally had about their new home. A year later, they were awarded a plaque for "excellence in rehabilitation" by the city of Chicago.

The Hugheses are not alone in their quest to restore the quality of life in the cities. There are thousands of these urban pioneers in neighborhoods across the country. People like Ruth Kamphoefner, a St. Louis widow with five children who, in 1970, decided to change her life. "I was sick of sitting around doing nothing," she recalled. "So I took a course at the Missouri Botanical Gardens, and they talked about ecology, and how hopeless certain neighborhoods were, particularly Lafayette Square."

At the time, Lafayette Square was a crime-ridden, run-down slum of boarding houses and abandoned buildings, full of prostitutes and alcoholics, with less than one-fifth of the houses occupied by their owners. Yet, when originally built in the late nineteenth century, Lafayette Square was the most fashionable neighborhood in St. Louis, its ornate Victorian homes occupied by the families of doctors, bankers, lawyers, even the mayor. But in 1896 a tornado destroyed many of the houses, and the neighborhood rapidly lost its previous elegance.

"Two days after I heard about Lafayette Square, I sold my house in the suburbs and bought an eight-room mansion on Mississippi Street for $2,750," Mrs. Kamphoefner continued. "You couldn't get near it, it smelled so bad. You'd peel off the old wallpaper, and the cockroaches would come crawling out by the thousands. People thought I was a little crazy." With months of backbreaking work, Mrs. Kamphoefner and her children, who then ranged in age from seven to sixteen, got the building into the condition it would have been in during the last century—resurfaced plaster walls, a country kitchen with stone floor, a completely restored "parlor," working fireplaces, polished woodwork—all the fineries of Victorian high society.

But Ruth Kamphoefner and her family went beyond fixing up their own home. They looked at the larger community, and saw that it needed fixing, too. "We came to restore old houses, but we wound up restoring the neighborhood," she said.

Since then, the group she helped found, the Lafayette Square Restoration Committee, has grown to more than two hundred members. They have saved more than half the old homes in the neighborhood, sometimes by purchasing a home that comes on the market and then reselling it to an interested purchaser. In cooperation with the city, they have set up an "urban homesteading" program to help families restore abandoned or tax-delinquent properties, and they have refurbished the neighborhood park, turning an old police station into a museum and information center. They have convinced lending institutions to grant home improvement loans and mortgages at conventional rates, something the lenders were once afraid to do. Most important, they were able to have Lafayette Square named a historic landmark; in so doing, they were able to prevent state highway officials from routing a new road through the neighborhood, probably destroying it in the process. In short, through the efforts of Ruth Kamphoefner, her children, and her neighbors, a neighborhood that the experts once thought beyond redemption has been restored to a new grandeur.

The efforts of these community groups and individuals like the Hugheses and the Kamphoefner family point to a new direction for our cities. Clearly, a new ethic is capturing the imagination of millions of Americans, an ethic which holds that "old" is not necessarily "useless," an ethic which states that we as a nation cannot discard the tremendous physical, financial, and social investment we have made in our cities; an ethic which says that we must think twice before tearing down what we already have—the houses, the schools, the parks and playgrounds, the streets, the shopping areas—and instead build upon them whenever possible. In so doing, we will conserve and strengthen a most precious resource, our neighborhoods.

What exactly *is* a neighborhood?

"A neighborhood," said the National Association of Real Estate Boards in 1938, "is an entity hard to define but easily understood." More recently, the writer Murray Kempton has said that "a neighborhood is where, when you go out of it, you get beat up." In a less waggish sense, we can say that a neighborhood is a place where people live. It is a single block or dozens of blocks, linked by some unifying element—a park, or a church, or a school, or the ethnic or social characteristics of the residents.

In classic city-planning terms, a "neighborhood unit" is an area compact enough for its residents to be able to walk to their vital services—shopping, recreation, medical care. At the center of the neighborhood unit, according to Clarence Arthur Perry (who developed the concept in 1929 in his *Regional Survey of New York and Its Environs*), is the neighborhood grade school.

A neighborhood, then, can be looked upon as pure geography, as "a local area," according to the late Charles Abrams, the lexicographer of cities, "whose residents are generally conscious of its existence as an entity and have informal face-to-face contacts and some social institutions they recognize as their own."

Yet to many people, "neighborhood" implies more than just a geographical area. A neighborhood *is* its people—the neighbor from whom you borrow a cup of sugar, the families of the children who go to school with *your* children, the people you can count on in an emergency. These "neighbors" are also the people who provide you with a reference group, who give you some of your status, and who create part of your identity. Thus, because I live in a politically conservative, heavily European, largely Catholic neighborhood of Chicago, people have a certain image of me quite different from what it would be if I lived in ultra-hip Old Town or "academic" Hyde Park (although any such image would hardly be a full representation of my character and values).

It is in this sense of identification with people, not mere geography, that the concept of neighborhood begins to take on aspects of the term "community." The terms neighborhood and community are often used interchangeably, but they actually have quite different meanings. To quote Charles Abrams again, a community is "a group of people living together in some identifiable territory and sharing a set of interests embracing their lifeways." In these terms, "community" connotes a group of people who share not only the same turf, but the same set of guiding principles, goals, and beliefs as well, such as the Amish communities of Pennsylvania, or the Hasidic communities of Brooklyn.

Most neighborhoods are not communities in the sense that Abrams speaks of. That is because few Americans feel compelled to live near their friends or family or the people with whom they share a "set of interests embracing their lifeways." Most Americans can live wherever they want—in a neighborhood that feeds their egos, or has good schools, or is close to work—and still find their friends, their "community," elsewhere—at the office, in their professions, perhaps in other cities. Our society is so mobile that we can live one place and carry on our social lives in entirely different sets of communities. Indeed we seem to like the idea of separating these two parts of our existence in order to guarantee our privacy. As Nora Ephron, the columnist for *Esquire*, puts it, "I like neighborhoods, you see, but I worry about neighbors."

Yet there comes a time when even the most aloof neighborhood begins to assume the unified identity of a true community—although that may not have been the original intention behind the neighborhood organizing. The situation often occurs when a neighborhood is threatened by a crisis—an outbreak of muggings, arson in the vacant building on the corner, a scheme to run a highway through the middle of the neighborhood. Neighbors then band together to fight the problem, thereby laying the foundations upon which a true community can be built.

In this book, I shall focus on such neighborhoods that are moving in the direction of community. They are, for the most part, neighborhoods in which the residents, confronted with a crisis, have learned to overcome their individual hesitations, suspicions, and fears to join in common cause against an enemy or outside force threatening to destroy them.

I shall concentrate mainly on neighborhood empowerment

brought about by the community itself, at the grass-roots level, rather than cases where city government has been decentralized by partially restoring administrative, political, or economic functions to the neighborhood. In some cities, for example, administrative decentralization is used to break down the delivery of public services to the nieghborhood level, such as by establishing "little city halls" in the neighborhoods to distribute food stamps, process building permits, and take complaints about trash collection. Other cities use political decentralization, whereby the city grants specific powers to neighborhoods; New York City, for example, has established sixty-two community planning boards to review planning and zoning matters within their respective boundaries and make nonbinding recommendations to the City Planning Commission. Economic decentralization involves the capture of economic markets by neighborhood-controlled, decentralized businesses and industries; examples include worker-controlled food cooperatives, neighborhood-run credit unions, and community-based farming and food processing. Not that these forms of "neighborhood power," to borrow a phrase from David Morris and Karl Hess, are invalid—they indeed deserve support from all concerned with saving neighborhoods. But in my experience the community-organizing mode of neighborhood empowerment has proven to be the most practical approach to neighborhood-based problem solving. It does not require an act of Congress to create a neighborhood organization, only the will of the people in the neighborhood. Nor are community organizations limited by a mandate handed down from above: They can put *any* problem on their agendas—housing, pollution, traffic, crime, schools. And because community organizations can deal with virtually any issue that is likely to affect a neighborhood, they stand the best chance of developing the kind of political punch necessary to produce the greatest results for their respective neighborhoods. In effect, strong community organizations can become the de facto government of their neighborhoods. And that is what neighborhood empowerment is all about.

But how did this new wave of interest in neighborhoods spring up? What is the background of today's neighborhood movement? Actually, there has been a long history of interest in preserving neighborhoods in this country. As far back as 1938 the National Association of Real Estate Boards called for the passage of a federal "Neighborhood Improvement Act." In 1951 Baltimore became the first major city to establish a neighborhood conservation program. Shortly thereafter, the Hyde Park–Kenwood neighborhood in Chicago became the nation's first residential urban renewal project. In 1959 Mayor Robert F. Wagner formally established a Neighborhood Conservation Program for New York City.

Most of these early neighborhood programs had serious defects. In those days, neighborhood conservation was really a poor cousin of the more grandiose federal slum clearance and urban renewal programs. The philosophy behind these programs was that any job worth doing had to be done big; if that meant tearing down a whole neighborhood to rebuild it, so be it. "Conservation" became a euphemism for wholesale destruction of neighborhoods. Few of the programs had been developed by neighborhood people; most of them were conceived by Washington bureaucrats, with the result that they were mired in government red tape and inefficiency. Overblown, overpromised, and overregulated, these programs were doomed. And fail they did.

The intellectual watershed in these matters came in 1961, with the publication of *The Death and Life of Great American Cities*. The author, a New York City housewife, mother, and sometime architecture critic named Jane Jacobs, was at the time the guiding force behind the effort to prevent the construction of a highway through her West Village neighborhood. It is hard to exaggerate the importance of Jacobs's book. In many respects, it turned city planning on its ear. If the planners of her day believed that massive projects were the only way to build, Jacobs showed how small-scale projects could be both socially *and* economically feasible. If planners advocated building at the "superblock" scale, Jacobs advocated chopping up city streets and subdividing neighborhoods. If planners said that areas should be confined to one use—housing only, shopping only, industry only—Jacobs demonstrated that mixing land uses could provide a vitality too often missing in the sterile atmosphere of the planners' single-use neighborhoods. Certainly there is much to dispute in *The Death and Life of Great American Cities*, and some of the author's conclusions are too broad for the evidence given. But its sheer genius of intellect, intuition, and insight make it a cornerstone in the literature of cities. With its publication, a whole new generation of city planners started questioning the traditional teachings of their profession.

The current neighborhood movement is built upon the foundation laid by Jane Jacobs. Yet it is vastly different from the so-called neighborhood conservation efforts of the past. Today's neighborhood conservation movement is bigger, more widespread, and more popular than any such movement in the past, as the figures cited previously show. Nor is the movement limited to the United States. Canada has a neighborhood effort in progress, as do England and several European countries.

The redevelopment of city neighborhoods takes two forms, "incumbent upgrading" and "gentrification." Incumbent upgrading occurs when the current residents and property owners take on the task of revitalizing their own neighborhoods. One example would be the handyman homeowner who closes in his back porch to make a new room, thereby increasing the value of his home. Incumbent upgrading prevails in working-class and middle-class neighborhoods where the real estate market is healthy but not necessarily robust—homes are being resold, apartments rented. Property owners sense that they will get their investment back, but they probably won't make a killing. The other kind of neighborhood reinvestment, gentrification, occurs when a new group of families, usually more affluent or socially prestigious, moves into a lower-class or working-class neighborhood, more often than not pushing out the original residents. We'll take a closer look at this problem of "displacement" in Chapter 10.

Within the context of these two basic forms of revitalization, there is considerable diversity in the actual type of renewal. Urban revitalization aimed at historic preservation, for example, is very popular. The large majority of the thousand or so registered historic districts already have undergone or currently are undergoing revitalization. (See Chapter 11.) Many more neighborhoods not on the National Register, but possessing what Lawrence O. Houstoun, Jr., calls "urban charm," could be added to this list. Another group includes stable neighborhoods where only minor public investment, such as for neighborhood cleanup and beautification programs, or enforcement of housing codes is needed. A step below are those neighborhoods where a heavier investment is required to upgrade the quality of housing and neighborhood amenities, perhaps low-cost loans for home repair, city-sponsored public investments, or urban homesteading programs. In the very worst neighborhoods, those where housing deterioration, unemployment, crime, and other indicators of social pathology run high, a comprehensive approach is required. In such hard-core neighborhoods, the community development corporation, which ties together programs for manpower development, drug rehabilitation, child care, housing construction, mental health, and so on, faces a panoply of urban problems. Yet even those community development corporations with the most impressive records—the Bedford-Stuyvesant Restoration Corporation in Brooklyn, Southeast Development, Inc., in Baltimore, The Woodlawn Organization in Chicago—know that they are touching only the tip of the iceberg.

Today's neighborhood revitalization movement is distinctive in yet another way: It is being fueled by dramatic demographic changes. To understand the impact of these changes, it is necessary to see what has happened in the past. Broadly speaking, housing patterns in America have been explained by two theories. The "concentric-ring theory" depicts the city as a core surrounded by a set of concentric rings. At the center of the city are the poor, packed into low-rent tenements. As one moves into the outer rings, one finds the housing to be of higher quality, less dense (that is, more space between buildings), more expensive, and occupied by more affluent citizens. The "filtering theory," actually a corollary of the concentric theory, posits that, as a family gains wealth, it will continually upgrade its housing, moving farther and farther out along the rings at each step. Theoretically, the housing each family leaves behind will then be available for a new, upwardly mobile family to occupy. Thus, a family filters up in housing quality when it moves out from the city center—a broad statement, to be sure, but more accurate than not.

Implicit in the concentric-ring and filtering theories is the average American family's preference for a single-family home on its own plot of land. A small percentage of families might prefer to live in a townhouse or a high-rise apartment building, but most want a single-family detached home; in fact, 97 percent of those responding to a survey of current home-seekers said so. Since high land prices make it uneconomical to build a ranch house in the middle of, say, Times Square, those seeking the American dream house historically have found it in the outer rings of the metropolis. Hence, the great exodus from the cities to the suburbs.

Patterns of movement worked fine as long as new, affordable housing was built in the suburbs. What has happened in recent years, however, is that suburban housing costs have gone through the roof, so to speak. The median sales price of new houses in 1977 was $57,500. The 20 percent down payment on that house would be $11,500. Add three or four thousand dollars in closing and moving costs, and it should come as no surprise that three-quarters of United States families are priced out of the new housing market. If the great majority of home-seeking families can't find houses in the suburbs, where will they look next? The answer is obvious: in the cities.

But the situation is even more complicated, and there are other reasons why the simple concentric-ring filtering theory is no longer adequate to explain all the changes taking place in our metropolitan areas. For example, not only have most older *cities* been losing population (as they have steadily since the end of World War II), but whole *metropolitan areas* (cities plus their suburbs) in the Northeast and Middle West are shrinking in population. "We're going from the exploding metropolis of the sixties to the imploding metropolis of the seventies," says Patrick Hare, a planning consultant in Hartford, Connecticut. Much of the shift is from the so-called Frost Belt or Snow Belt of the North and East to the Sun Belt of the South and West. Moreover, while the rate of growth of both the total U.S. population and the population of other urban areas is declining, the total number and rate of growth of *separate households* are increasing. There are many more single- and two-person households than ever before, adding to the housing crunch. And although today's families are smaller (in 1940, the average household contained 3.67 persons; by 1976, the average was only 2.89 persons), they demand the same, if not more, housing than in the past. Thus, while it would seem logical that we would need less housing in cities today, we actually need more.

Yet another demographic fact is contributing to the housing crunch: We are also feeling the reverberations of the postwar baby boom. All those babies who were born in the early fifties have been marrying and forming families. They want houses, too, and it is certain that their very presence will increase the demand for housing throughout the market. True, the baby-boom generation is not having as many children as families have had in the past, but this fact alone is an indication that they may behave quite differently from past generations in other ways. For example, many of the women of the boom generation have chosen to work, even if they are married and have children. This fact has an important bearing on housing choice. For a working couple with a pre-school-age child, access to and distance from their jobs, child-care services, and other necessary services (laundry, shopping, medical care) become vitally important. They may buy a second car, move to an area equidistant between their workplaces and the child's day-care center, or find housing served by mass transportation. For such a family the logical choice might be a city neighborhood—irrespective of their actual income.

Still other sociological and economic changes are affecting population patterns. The energy crisis, for example, has prompted people to think about living close to their workplaces. With the cities now primarily centers of white-collar employment, families with professional, managerial, or clerical skills will be attracted to the city.

To summarize, we have shrinking cities and metropolitan areas in the Frost Belt, yet more demand than ever for housing in these areas because of the increasing number of families seeking housing. But does this mean that there is a "back-to-the-city" movement?

The answer is No, if by "back to the city" one implies a complete reversal of population trends, with more families leaving the suburbs and moving into the city than vice versa. On the contrary, the trend is still outward. "There is not any significant [overall] return to the city," said Franklin J. James, a researcher with the Urban Institute. But while people are not deserting the suburbs in vast numbers to move downtown, considerable numbers of those who are already in the city, particularly that curious group in the baby boom, *are* fueling the neighborhood revitalization movement. Dennis Gale, a planning professor at George Washington University, studied two such revitalizing neighborhoods in the District of Columbia and found that "most newcomers are established city dwellers, not recent suburbanites." Thus it would be more correct to say that the current neighborhood movement is a "stay-in-the-city" rather than "back-to-the-city" phenomenon. The encouraging thing, however, is that the neighborhood revitalization movement, while small and nascent today, apparently will continue to grow. Housing economics, changes in the style of living, and demographic patterns all point in that direction.

The contemporary neighborhood movement differs in still another way from previous urban revitalization: Its emphasis is from the grass roots up, not from the top down. In the past, federal officials *forced* citizen participation upon people seeking to improve their neighborhoods. Every program had to have a "citizen participation component," or risk the loss of federal money. But the overarching fact is that citizens had no real control over these programs—the functionaries in city hall ran them, with Washington wielding a veto over funding. By contrast, today's neighborhood movement is generating its strength from the grass roots, starting from the needs and wishes of the people in the neighborhoods and working its way up through the various levels of government.

Perhaps the best way to illustrate this final point, and to give an indication of the general tenor and approach of this book, is to tell briefly about one such group of citizens in Southeast Baltimore. Their story is more than just a case history of a ragtag bunch fighting the government bureaucracy. It is the story of working-class people who short-circuited plans by outsiders to destroy their community and in the process built one of the most powerful and effective community organizations in the country.

Baltimore has always had a reputation for being a rawboned, blue-collar, highly industrialized city with close ties to the sea. The area around the port, one of the oldest and most heavily industrialized sections of the city, is really a conglomeration of old neighborhoods, many of them originally independent towns before they were consolidated into the city of Baltimore—places with names like Highlandtown, Fell's Point, Canton, and Little Italy. About one-tenth of Baltimore's 900,000 people live in the Southeast section, and they are a diverse lot—Ukrainians, Poles, Greeks, Italians, Germans, Finns, Irish, Czechs, Appalachian whites, some Orientals, a group of Lumbee Indians from North Carolina, and blacks (about ten thousand of the latter)—some three dozen ethnic groups in all. They have, on the average, a junior-high-school education and make less money than the rest of the people in Baltimore ($9,800 median family income versus $13,000 for the city)—a lot less if you include the people in the suburbs ($15,700). Twenty percent are poor. Many are old. Their housing is the typical thirteen-foot-wide Baltimore row house, built cheap enough for working-class families to afford, yet sturdy, even though the brick of which they are made can dry up and crumble if it's not painted regularly.

In 1966 the Baltimore City Council passed an ordinance permitting the demolition of hundreds of homes in Southeast Baltimore to make way for Interstate 83, a federally assisted state highway. Within two years, 350 homes in the Canton portion of the right-of-way had been torn down. Meanwhile, a small group of leaders in Canton and Fell's Point, the old area abutting the waterfront, decided to do something about the road. Among them was Jack Gleason, a widower who moved to Fell's Point from New York in the winter of 1966, encouraged by his son to "give Baltimore a try." Gleason chose to live in Fell's Point because he and his roommate, Bob Eney, were early-American architecture buffs, and Fell's Point had some of the oldest buildings in Baltimore.

"We had not been here a week before we got a phone call from someone saying, 'Could you come to a meeting? We're trying to save some buildings in Fell's Point from being destroyed for a highway,' " recalls Gleason. That meeting led to the founding of the Society for the Preservation of Federal Hill and Fell's Point. "The idea of community activism was alien to me. My major outside interests were my church [Episcopalian] and old buildings. I'd never been a joiner or an advocate."

At first, only a few people, never more than eight, led the fight, a tiny coalition who called themselves SCAR, the Southeast Council Against the Road. They seemed to be butting their heads against a wall. They failed to prevent passage of the ordinance allowing the city to destroy the houses. They failed to defeat a bond referendum that the city needed to finance its share of the highway costs. They failed to convince a design-study team, which was being paid $9 million to disguise eight lanes of concrete, that the highway had to go. "In those early days," says Gleason, "we just had one defeat after another."

But luck and the United States Congress were on SCAR's side. At a conference in Richmond, Virginia, Bob Eney learned that historic districts enjoyed special protection from demolition under a 1966 federal law. If Fell's Point could be named to the National Register of Historic Places, it would be practically impossible for the state highway department to use federal dollars to build a highway through the neighborhood. "Bob and I put together a committee of preservationists and local people, and we did a survey of the historic buildings and prepared the nomination papers to place Fell's Point on the National Register," says Gleason. "Virtually overnight, we put that application through, and Fell's Point was the first entry from Maryland on the National Register. The road people and the city never forgave us for that."

The highway barons gave up. In December 1977, papers rescinding the demolition orders were signed, and the city started releasing the remaining intact houses for sale. Interstate 83 was stopped dead. If it ever gets built, it will run in a tunnel under the harbor.

While the victory over Interstate 83 was greeted with a communal sigh of relief, it was apparent that the road was only one part of a scheme to reshape Southeast Baltimore. As people became familiar with the city's plans for the highway, they could see a larger pattern developing. "They found that the city had literally written this area off," notes Joe McNeely, a one-time Marist seminarian and later a neighborhood organizer. "No new capital improvements were planned because the city had a twenty-year projection of declining population. No new school had been built here in thirty years." Existing services were in jeopardy of being cut off: for example, the trustees of the branch library in Canton threatened to close it. Worst of all, the city's planners had a new zoning map in their back pockets, which showed most of Southeast Baltimore planned for industry, not houses.

So to the antihighway coalition were added a group fighting to keep the Canton library open, another group challenging city hall over the revised zoning plan, still others working on setting up a recycling center and a youth council. It was becoming clear to local leaders that the way to get things done in Southeast Baltimore was not in one-shot stabs, but to take a comprehensive approach by forming an areawide coalition. Thus, the idea of an umbrella organization to serve Southeast Baltimore was conceived.

It poured the evening of April 17, 1971, but that could not keep away the more than one thousand people who crowded into an auditorium for the founding of what was about to become the Southeast Community Organization. Over ninety organizations were represented. Ralph Nader gave the keynote address. Jack Gleason was elected president, much to his own surprise and that of others who expected a blue-collar, non-WASP native to be elected. "If anything ever changed my life, that did," Gleason said seven years later.

With Gleason as president of the Senate, the representative body that was to run the new organization, and with Joe McNeely as staff director, SECO was off and running. Shortly after the SECO Congress, Baltimore City Hospital announced plans to close D Building, a long-term-care facility for the aged, within two weeks. The closing would put the city's chronically-ill elderly out on the streets. Clearly, here was an issue with widespread appeal. Two SECO activists, Sirkka Lee and Elaine Lowry, pulled together a coalition of the elderly, doctors, nurses, hospital staff, and other volunteers. They held a mass meeting at the Civic Center and picketed Governor Marvin Mandel's residence in Annapolis. Finally, hospital officials capitulated: D Building would be kept open. SECO had its first victory; its credibility as an organization was firmly established.

In short order, it won other victories: keeping the Canton Library open, knocking down the planned industrial rezoning, getting the city to put more services and improvements into the area, including two new schools. A newly formed group, Citizens for Washington Hill, joined SECO to get help in preventing the city from destroying a three-block area of their neighborhood. "We wanted to stop the city from even *planning* to demolish anything," said Betty Hyatt, a social worker for the Methodist Church. In the end, they convinced the city and the federal government to rehabilitate more than two hundred housing units instead of tearing them down.

Similar efforts began to be made throughout the SECO area. In Patterson Place and Upper Fell's Point, neighbors organized cleanup committees and housing-inspection teams. Others started a health cooperative. A group of parents, concerned about the low reading scores of children attending the local grammar school, developed a tutoring program for students with dyslexia and other learning problems. The children jumped whole grades in reading ability, and their attendance at school increased remarkably. Another program, the Youth Diversion Project, which combines jobs with recreation activities such as canoeing and sporting events, cut the recidivism rate among delinquent youths who participated in the program from 50 percent to less than 3 percent.

Clearly, SECO was headed in a new direction, forming partnerships with government, business, and other institutions. These efforts have culminated in the creation of Southeast Development, Inc., a community-controlled development corporation whose purpose is to create jobs and economic opportunities for local residents. In its brief history, SDI has made quite a record of achievement for itself. It has established its own version of a housing services program that originated in Pittsburgh which, in its first three years of operation, has helped 245 families become homeowners and another 100 to renovate their properties. With a loan from the Ford Foundation, an SDI subsidiary created a "land bank" for those SECO neighborhoods threatened by real estate speculation. By mid-1978, 110 houses had been purchased for the community.

SDI created Southeast Arts and Crafts, a community-controlled company that produces and markets the work of some forty elderly and handicapped residents, mostly hand-sewn items and ethnic crafts. Southeast Baltimore Artisans, Inc., which provides jobs for eleven persons, has used SDI's services to market its metal products—wind chimes, plant stands, mirrors—to outlets in the Washington, D.C. area. Another offshoot, Baltimore Homes, Inc., provides low-cost services and maintenance to homeowners in the SECO area, while creating jobs for local residents. The health cooperative has evolved into a primary-health-care facility serving three thousand patients a month. The Highlandtown Revitalization Corporation has been serving more than one hundred businesses in the Highlandtown commercial district, offering merchants technical help on architectural and urban planning, widening sidewalks, renovating store façades, improving parking, and sponsoring cooperative events and promotions. And this is only a sampling of programs sponsored by SECO, SDI, and their various subsidiaries.

The story of the Southeast Community Organization shows how a neighborhood that had been written off by the experts can be given a new life, provided the people who live there care enough to take action. That, in a nutshell, is the theme of this book. Its purpose is to offer practical advice and information, distilled from the experiences of community groups around the country, on how to organize the citizens of a neighborhood so that they can be effective partners in the social and physical rehabilitation of their communities. It is directed at people who are concerned about improving our neighborhoods—urban pioneers, community activists, historic preservationists, property owners, local merchants, city planners, public officials, students, academicians, and all those who are eager to make life in our cities more livable.

PART ONE

The Dynamics of Neighborhood Decline

A successful city neighborhood is a place that keeps sufficiently abreast of its problems so as not to be destroyed by them. An unsuccessful neighborhood is a place that is overwhelmed by its defects and problems and is progressively more helpless before them.

—JANE JACOBS,
The Death and Life of Great American Cities

1

THE MONEY DRAIN

In *The Death and Life of Great American Cities*, Jane Jacobs refers to cities as "problems of organized complexity." A problem of organized complexity has more than two, and perhaps dozens, of variables, but unlike certain other kinds of problems, all the variables are interrelated: change one and you change them all. Most of the problems of the life sciences are problems of organized complexity. For example, the problem of how to describe aging in terms of biochemistry might include an analysis of changes in tissue composition, mineral content in the blood, bone structure, heartbeat and respiration, and a dozen other factors. But changes in the mineral content of the blood might have an effect on tissue composition, which in turn might affect bone structure, heartbeat, and respiration. All the factors are interrelated. It's impossible to analyze one factor without considering all the others.

Cities work in much the same way. Healthy cities have all their constituent parts functioning together as an interrelated whole. The variables are many, but they are not helter-skelter; change one and the urban ecosystem will be forced to adapt to new conditions. Take the example of a neighborhood that contains a block of rundown houses. A developer proposes to tear down the houses and build a high-rise office building. He presents an analysis showing how the construction of his building will, in his estimation, affect the city's tax base, the circulation of traffic in the neighborhood, the number of jobs available, parking, landscaping, and so on. The proposal may seem straightforward, but it is never quite that simple. What, for example, will happen to the land across the street? Will another developer ask to tear down more houses there to build another office building? What then will happen to all the people living in those houses? Will they move to adjacent neighborhoods, perhaps causing overcrowding? Will the increased traffic going to and from the office building generate a need for more automobile-related services, such as gas stations and drive-in restaurants, in the neighborhood? Will that make the neighborhood less desirable? Will there be an increase in air pollution? Will sunlight to adjacent houses be cut off? What happens if the developer lowers the height of the proposed building but spreads the building over a greater portion of his land? Wouldn't that affect the landscaping plans and the amount of open space? It is obvious that what seems like a simple problem is a complex one in which all the variables are related to one another.

Where we usually go wrong in trying to solve problems of organized complexity is when we think of them as simple problems. Take the matter of housing costs. It would seem logical that if we could find a way to cut the cost of construction, say in half, housing prices would fall commensurately. In fact, that was the idea behind Operation Breakthrough, a government-sponsored program to test new building materials and designs in order to cut construction costs. What the government learned from this experiment, however, was that it is difficult to cut construction costs without running into other problems—building-safety codes, for example. Then there was also the matter of people's taste: The average homebuyer did not like the "space-age" houses the experiments produced. Finally, it was learned that construction cost is only a small portion of the final price of a house; land prices, taxes, and most important of all, finance charges, have the greatest effect on what the consumer pays. Even if the cost of construction were cut in half, it would reduce the final purchase price by only a fraction. Moreover, if cheap houses suddenly did become available, there would be such a rush for them that land prices would go up, credit availability would be tightened (meaning that interest rates would increase), and the savings might be negated.

Most problems neighborhood activists are likely to encounter unfortunately are problems of organized complexity. For the urban revitalization movement to succeed, neighborhoods must be viewed as complex ecosystems. As with a delicate coastal wetland, altering any one of the many variables that are functioning as an interrelated whole can either make a neighborhood a healthy place for people to live or a stagnant environment that reeks of decay.

In this and the following chapters, the many interrelated factors that go into the neighborhood equation will be discussed and analyzed. The rest of this chapter focuses on governmental and institutional forces at work in city neighborhoods—how, for example, the federal government plays a role in the decline and fall of neighborhoods, and how banks and other financial institutions play their part. In the next chapter, the emphasis is on "social" factors, such as crime, poverty, and race. This is not to say that governmental and institutional factors do not have a social aspect, or that "social" factors do not influence government and institutions. Quite the contrary. Again, they are all part of the ecology of a city and its neighborhoods.

Before going into these factors, let me mention an additional factor, one that distinguishes cities and neighborhoods from other problems of organized complexity. That factor is human perception. Often the way people subjectively view a city or a neighborhood is more important than what the facts reveal to be the truth. Let me give an example. Hyde Park, the neighborhood where I once lived, is one of the safest in Chicago. It is certainly one of the most heavily patrolled, with numerous private guards supplementing the efforts of the city police. Yet I was always shocked to hear of people from outside the neighborhood who were afraid to go to a university function or a late party simply because Hyde Park once had a reputation as a high-crime area. Statistically, Hyde Park is safe; but it is hard to convince people with facts and figures when they have long perceived it as an area where crime is high.

People with options don't just buy a house: They buy a neighborhood. They weigh all the variables—the condition of the surrounding houses, the maintenance of the area, the general amenities, and the characteristics of the people who already live there—before making a decision. If they see the neighborhood as a place that seems to be "holding steady" or "moving up"—whether or not that is in fact the case—they, too, will be encouraged to invest in that neighborhood. Conversely, if they lack confidence in a neighborhood, if they perceive it as beginning to show signs of decay—trash in the streets, abandoned houses, lack of maintenance—they will hedge on making an investment there. Thus people ultimately decide where to live on the basis of their subjective perceptions, which may or may not be "correct."

"Community rebuilding is, in many ways, a confidence game," says Saul Klibanow, the director of RESCORP, a Chicago housing development corporation. He means "confidence" in both senses: To create investor confidence in a community, it is often necessary to play a confidence game with their perceptions. Making people see a neighborhood in a different light is often the key to getting them to invest time, money, and effort not only in their own property, but also in that neighborhood as a whole. And once the ball starts rolling, it picks up speed and size.

Besides the individual property owner or tenant, there are bigger, wealthier, more powerful players in the neighborhood game. Government is one. The decisions emanating from Washington ripple through the federal system, influencing the actions of the states and cities and profoundly affecting where and how people live. Local governments, too, set policies that affect the provision of services, programs, and public improvements to each neighborhood and the allocation of city dollars among neighborhoods. Financial institutions are immensely important to neighborhoods as well, for they supply the lifeblood of housing—money. Thus, public- and private-sector actions, such as the construction of a highway through a healthy neighborhood or the refusal of banks to give loans in certain neighborhoods, requires careful scrutiny. In considering these institutional forces, let's first focus on the federal government.

"Many of our urban policies and programs have contributed to the very problems they were supposed to cure." That statement comes, not from an archcritic of the system, but from President Carter's own Urban and Regional Policy Group, a cabinet-level commission charged with developing urban policy. It is no news to anybody that one federal policy often undoes the good work of another. The income tax is a case of one hand dirtying the other. "We pay people to do the wrong things," says Allen E. Pritchard, Jr., executive vice-president of the National League of Cities. "Although the figures are difficult to analyze, for every dollar of federal grant money spent to solve adverse problems, it appears that there is at least an equal amount of federal tax subsidies [tax expenditures] acting to encourage investment decisions which reinforce the adverse condition." Thus, we spend billions for urban renewal to revitalize declining downtown shopping areas (destroying tens of thousands of small businesses in the process), and at the same time the tax laws encourage developers to put up new shopping centers in the suburbs—and billions more in highway funds go to build the roads to those suburbs. Or consider housing. The federal tax laws favor subsidizing the *new*, single-family suburban home, as opposed to subsidizing rehabilitation of older, multifamily buildings—the kind likely to be found in cities. The same goes for office buildings, shopping centers, and factories. "New buildings . . . can be depreciated for tax purposes at much faster rates than old buildings," notes economist George E. Peterson. The rate of return on investment, in fact, is about half again as much for constructing a new building as for rehabilitating an old one. So, while every administration since John F. Kennedy's has professed concern about "saving the cities," and billions have been poured (often unsuccessfully) into urban renewal programs, the tax laws—the unwritten policy of government—work against the cities.

Even when the government decides to handle a problem directly, it often causes more trouble than it relieves. The federal urban renewal program, for example, destroyed 300,000 more houses than it replaced. In 1968, Congress came up with a subsidy program known as Section 236 of the Housing Act, which makes it 20 percent more expensive to build subsidized housing than comparable construction in the private market. By 1975, 1,600 of the 4,000 or so buildings (containing half a million apartments) constructed under the program were behind in mortgage payments. Another program, Section 235, by that time had proved such a scandal (as we shall see in a moment) that Congress was forced to refashion the housing subsidy laws. The product of that effort, the Section 8 program, has been labeled by Martin Mayer as "a mix of proposals from the libertarian right and the academic left, without much leavening of common sense or input from people actually working on the problem." ("Section 8," coincidentally, is the military designation for "discharged by reason of insanity.") This program has proved the biggest boondoggle of all. At New York's Manhattan Plaza project, for instance, a two-bedroom apartment has to be subsidized to the tune of $1,200 a month. The average subsidy under Section 8 in 1976 was $300 a month per family, more than what most families pay in total housing costs. Mayer puts the total cost of existing housing subsidy programs at $50 billion. That price might even be worth it if the subsidy program helped all the poor, but it reaches at best 15 or 20 percent of those families who qualify. That means that the rest of the taxpayers (including the unsubsidized poor) will pay for years to solve only a small portion of the housing problem.

This is hardly a full accounting of the failure of federal urban policy. The "New Communities" program, for example, was supposed to build new towns on the urban fringe, "garden cities" with self-sustaining economies and life-styles. Most of them have gone bankrupt, with the federal government left holding the bag. The "new towns in town" program was supposed to use surplus federal land as sites for new housing projects. Only one partial project ever got built, thanks to bureaucratic red tape and conflicts with city governments.

One of the notable effects of this failure of federal urban policy is that government's inability to "save the cities" has made the suburbs all the more attractive to the American middle class. But America has been urbiphobic since Jefferson's time.* This historical abhorrence of the city, with its concomitant romanticizing of the countryside, surely distorts people's image of today's cities, no matter what the facts. As one second-generation Chicagoan

---

*Morton and Lucia White have described this anti-urban sentiment best, in *The Intellectual and the City*, where they note that cities historically have been considered "Too big, too noisy, too dusty, too dirty, too smelly, too commercial, too crowded, too full of immigrants, too full of Jews, too full of Irishmen, Italians, Poles, too industrial, too pushing, too mobile, too fast, too artificial, destructive of conversation, destructive of communication, too greedy, too capitalistic, too full of automobiles, too full of smog, too full of dust, too heartless, too intellectual, too scientific, insufficiently poetic, too lacking in manners, too mechanical, destructive of family, tribal and patriotic feeling."

told me, "My parents have always dreamed of living in the suburbs. After all, Dick Van Dyke and Donna Reed live in the suburbs. Who lives in the city? Starsky and Hutch." But instead of *planning* for the effect of increased suburbanization on America's cities, government has adopted a policy of benign neglect. The result, not surprisingly, is that the cities *have* declined, while the suburbs have prospered.

Look at some of the statistics. Jobs and people are shifting to the suburbs. Since 1969, for example, the city of Chicago has lost 212,000 jobs, while its suburbs have picked up 220,000. In the same period, New York City lost 650,000 jobs. Nine of the ten largest cities in the United States have failed to keep pace with the growth in both employment and manufacturing in their suburbs. (The exception is Pittsburgh, where the whole region sagged.)

The *kinds* of jobs the cities have lost also is important. The jobs that are leaving the cities are in manufacturing and other blue-collar areas. The kind that are staying in the cities are primarily highly skilled administrative and white-collar positions— finance, insurance, real estate, the media, and office work. Since the cities continue to play their traditional role as ports of entry for immigrants (albeit new kinds of immigrants—Puerto Ricans, Mexicans, and Asians, for example), it is important to have plenty of low-skill, entry-level jobs for them, as well as for the generally poorer, lower-skilled people left behind in the cities. Unfortunately, the jobs for which these workers are suited have moved to the suburbs; the jobs that remain in the cities require skills that are often beyond the ability or even training potential of many city residents.

Thus, we have a curious flip-flop: The people suited for blue-collar jobs live in the cities, and the white-collar workers live in the suburbs. In Hartford, for example, suburbanites hold more than 60 percent of all city jobs, as well as 70 percent of the total wage income and 90 percent of all jobs paying $15,000 or more. The suburbs also house the professional and managerial elite of our society: In the Newark, New Jersey region, 80 percent of all professional and managerial workers live outside the central city; in Cleveland, it's 73 percent; in Boston and St. Louis, 68 percent, and so on. To the extent that federal policy and funding have contributed to the fostering of these trends, the government is indirectly responsible for the decline of the cities and city neighborhoods.

Sometimes, however, the government's actions are more blatant. The Federal National Mortgage Association, known affectionately as Fannie Mae, is a federally chartered corporation that buys mortgages from lending institutions, freeing cash so the lenders can make more loans. For a long while, Fannie Mae's policy implicitly discriminated against mortgage lending in older areas. If the age of the house plus the term of the mortgage totaled more than sixty years, that mortgage got special attention from Fannie Mae's auditors. Sometimes they bought the paper, sometimes they didn't. The point was clear to the lending institutions, though: If you want to avoid extra paperwork, don't send Fannie Mae mortgages on old properties. Since most old houses in any region are in the cities (in Chicago, two-thirds of the housing was built before 1940), a smart banker would send Fannie Mae only new, suburban mortgages. Thus, another incentive favoring the suburbs over the cities.

The movement of people, jobs, and wealth to the suburbs is a familiar story to most people, and I don't want to belabor it. In part, the movement has been spurred by federal tax policy and public programs. But government actions alone cannot explain the suburban shift. Numerous other economic and social factors contribute to exodus from the cities—the need to build one-story manufacturing plants and warehouses, which require more land than city "loft" structures, is just one reason for the trend to the suburbs. Nor is it necessarily always bad for cities to lose population. Such a situation enabled the mayors of Pittsburgh and Baltimore to cut the budget while avoiding a catastrophic decline in city services.

More significant, perhaps, is the point that our cities have become dumping grounds for the worst-off members of society— the poor, the elderly, and the minorities. Cities have become "reservations" for the outcasts of society, where the emphasis of public policy has been on pouring social services and "transfer payments"—welfare checks, housing allowances, food stamps— into the cities, instead of providing economic development to move people up the income ladder.

There is another trend even more significant than the movement from city to suburb—the shift, alluded to in the Introduction, from the Frost Belt to the Sun Belt. In the last two decades, the warm regions of the South and West have been growing at a superinflated rate, while the older regions of the Northeast and North Central states have been stagnating and declining. In population, the South grew 24 percent and the West 35 percent between 1960 and 1975, while the North grew 11 percent, well below the national average of 19 percent. From 1970 to 1974, cities in the Northeast lost 125,000 people a year; cities in the North Central states lost 142,000 people a year. In terms of jobs, from 1960 to 1975 the Northeast lost 781,000 jobs, for a 13.9 percent drop, while the North Central region gained 234,000 jobs, for a slight gain of 4.2 percent, but still below the 8 percent national average. The West, however, gained 520,000 jobs, a 27.8 percent leap, while the South boomed with 1.5 million new jobs, a 41.0 percent increase.

Part of the reason for these shifts can be explained by subjective factors, such as the desire to live in a warm climate, and even technological changes, such as near-universal air conditioning. But a good part of the reason can be laid at the door of the federal government. Since the end of World War II, the government has spent more money in the South and West than it has taken back in taxes, while it has drained more in taxes from the North than it has spent there. To take just one year, in 1975 the government collected almost $44 billion more in taxes than it spent on government programs in the Northeast states, whereas it spent nearly $36 billion more in the Sun Belt states than it collected in taxes. In the fifteen Northeast states, only the New England states (with the exception of Connecticut) paid less in taxes than they got back in government grants. In the fifteen Sun Belt states, *every* state except Texas got more money back from the U.S. Treasury than it paid in taxes. Thus, while the Frost Belt states (and their beleaguered cities) continue to cry out for help, federal tax and expenditure policies continue to drain money away from the region.

It is one thing for government to harm cities indirectly. It is another matter entirely when government is party to a scandal that destroys whole neighborhoods. Just such a case occurred recently in the Federal Housing Administration (FHA) insurance programs. As Brian D. Boyer notes in his exposé of the FHA fiasco, whole sections of cities were "destroyed for cash" through the shortsightedness of Congress, the ineptitude of the bureaucracy, and the connivance of shady moneylenders. Tens of thousands of poor families were driven out of what was for many the first, and last, house they would own. Most of the foreclosed houses were abandoned, later to become a blight on the neighborhoods in which they stood.

The Sholar family was one of the victims. In 1973, when Clara Sholar had to go into the hospital for surgery, she sent a partial payment of $78 to Bell Federal Savings and Loan, a Chicago lender, on the home she had purchased under one of the FHA insurance programs sponsored by the 1968 Housing Act. She also promised to pay a $31 deficit. But then she had to stay in the hospital for a month and lost her job. Shortly thereafter, she received a foreclosure notice from the lender. The next day, she went to Bell with $144 to cover the $31 deficit and the current payment. Bell informed her that she owed not $144, but $492; the difference was "legal fees." Nor would Bell accept a partial payment of $144. By January 1974, Mrs. Sholar was able to borrow enough money from friends to make a payment of $1,220 to Bell, even though by this time she was on welfare. Bell accepted the payment, but told her that $693 in legal fees was still due. She was never able to pay the legal fees and was subsequently ordered by the court to leave her home.

The Sholar case is by no means an isolated one. By 1976, HUD, FHA's parent agency, owned some 350,000 FHA-insured houses by way of foreclosure. In the so-called Section 235 program (designed to provide single-family housing for poor families), more than 100,000 homes had gone into foreclosure by 1977. Twenty percent of all Section 235 houses were late in payments; for Section 236 houses (multifamily units), the figure was 40 percent. Between April 1972 and March 1977, the foreclosure rate for FHA-insured mortgages was 4.56 percent. A foreclosure rate higher than 1 percent is considered unthinkable in the lending business. The cost to the taxpayer: at least $2 billion, perhaps $4 or $5 billion.

And the cost to neighborhoods? Anyone who has driven

through a neighborhood like Chicago's Roseland or Lawndale and who has seen row after row of boarded-up homes knows the impact of the FHA scandals on neighborhoods. The abandoned houses are open invitations to arson, vandalism, and destruction. They are festering sores, scarring the neighborhood.

Not that anyone intended the FHA insurance programs to run into scandal. Reacting to the riots of 1968, Congress was prompted to help the poor get a slice of the American housing pie. Its new housing law created various programs to permit the FHA to insure 100 percent of the mortgage for poor families that qualified. With the federal government backing these loans, they were virtually risk-free. Unfortunately, that foolproof guarantee paved the way for unscrupulous moneylenders to take advantage of the poor at the taxpayers' expense.

To get to the roots of the FHA scandal, it is necessary to look closely at the mortgage banking industry. Mortgage banking is, as several observers have noted, "an unknown industry." Mortgage bankers make long-term mortgage loans—about one-fifth of all real estate lending in the United States is done through them—but do not accept deposits from customers. Theoretically, mortgage bankers make their money by *originating* loans; that is, they find potential homeowners and get them mortgages. Almost always, the mortgage banker then "sells the paper" to a large commercial bank or savings and loan institution, or to one of two federal corporations—the Federal National Mortgage Association, or Fannie Mae, and the Government National Mortgage Association, or Ginnie Mae. Fannie Mae and Ginnie Mae buy more than half of all loans originated by mortgage bankers. The rest of the mortgage bankers' income is derived from *servicing* loans once they've been sold. For a fee (a percentage, called "points," of the mortgage), the mortgage company collects the monthly mortgage payment and handles the paperwork for the bank or national corporation that holds the actual mortgage.

But the real windfall for many mortgage bankers has been FHA foreclosures. Mortgage bankers have the lion's share—$80 billion, or three-fourths—of the FHA mortgages on single-family homes. Crazy as it seems, they stand to make more—much more!—if the loan goes bad than if it is paid back on time. That's because the FHA's 100 percent guarantee means that HUD will pay up in the end. The following table shows how a typical FHA foreclosure can yield almost a 32 percent return on original investment over a twenty-seven-month period. As the authors of *More Holes than Net* have noted, "FHA-insured lenders can be careless but still reap handsome profits." Careless?—the system practically encourages fraud.

How to Make a Fast Buck on Fast Foreclosure

The following is a breakdown of the profits that a mortgage banker realizes on an FHA-insured loan foreclosed after twelve months.

House value	$19,000
Down payment	500
Thirty-year FHA mortgage at 8.5 percent—Principal and Interest only, $132.19	18,500
"Points"—fee charged to adjust interest rate on loan to meet FHA regulations (10 percent)	1,850
Mortgage company payment to seller	16,650

Twelve months after closing, the owner misses a payment and is in default. After a three-month mandatory grace period, the mortgage company begins foreclosure proceedings. This probably takes another twelve months. HUD then pays off the remaining principal and interest that has accrued over the last fifteen months:

For twelve months, borrower paid:	
Interest	$ 1,521
Principal	148
	$ 1,669
At foreclosure, HUD pays:	
Fifteen months of foreclosure interest	$ 1,892
Principal less $148	18,351
	$21,913
Mortgage company's original cash investment	-16,650
Mortgage company's profit	$ 5,263
Mortgage company's return on investment	31.6 percent

Source: *The American Nightmare* (Chicago: National Training and Information Center, 1976), p. 1. Reprinted by permission.

A high percentage of foreclosures could have been predicted because neither the lenders nor HUD cared about who got the

FHA-insured mortgages. In many cases, a mortgage banking company would set up a field office in a middle-of-the-road or racially changing neighborhood. It would make some cosmetic repairs on a few buildings, then go looking for customers. Many of their targets were welfare families or near-poor families, almost all of them minority-group members. Often the mortgage bankers would falsify the information about the family's income or credit rating to make the loan application flow more smoothly through FHA. Most of these families had never owned a home before. They didn't know to look for signs of a leaky roof or a wet basement; if the inspector from the Federal Housing Administration said the house was satisfactory, that was assurance enough for them. Of course, the inspector had already been paid off or was simply doing shoddy work in passing over the violations. The family would walk into their new home thinking everything was perfect; meanwhile, the mortgage banker had sold the paper to a bank or Fannie Mae and was now "servicing" the loan from some distant office.

Almost any minor catastrophe could start the family on the road to foreclosure—a long illness to the breadwinner, a job layoff, an unexpected bill. The latter would often come as a result of the faulty inspection—the furnace wouldn't work or the water pipes would burst. Unused to budgeting for such disasters, the family would panic, afraid to tell anyone about their plight. They would miss one payment, then two. By the third month, they faced foreclosure. Normal banking practice would call for a "workout plan," whereby the family would be able to make partial payments for a certain period. But the mortgage bankers' computers would spit out any payment that was not in full. A special investigation conducted by HUD found, for example, that in none of the twenty-five sample cases reviewed did the mortgage company attempt to set up a workout plan for the family. Instead, usual procedure was to begin foreclosure proceedings, with legal fees being added on to the mortgage payments, as in Clara Sholar's case. In a high percentage of cases, it would not be long before the foreclosure would be made final.

Even with the mortgage foreclosed and the family evicted, the mortgage bankers would inflict further damage on the house and the neighborhood in which it was located. Since it was known that HUD eventually would take over the property, there was really no incentive to keep the house in good condition. Instead of boarding it up properly, winterizing it to withstand the cold, and maintaining its value for possible resale, the mortgage bankers would again do only cosmetic work and then bill HUD for the work that should have been done. For example, one company, Unity Savings Association, charged HUD hundreds of dollars for boarding up a house, but used plywood that was only one-eighth-inch thick. The house was later vandalized. Advance Mortgage Company charged HUD $120 to clean a house that was occupied at the time by a tenant. Mortgage Associates, Inc., charged HUD for winterizing a house, but did such a poor job that the pipes burst and the floors were ruined.

Almost nothing was done to police these companies, and hardly anything happened in the way of penalties. HUD did suspend Advance Mortgage, the nation's second-largest mortgage banker, in 1975, finding a catalogue of abuses: refusal to accept partial payments, failure to help defaulted homeowners, charging HUD excessive fees for maintenance work (which was sometimes never done), supplying false credit reports, and defrauding the government. The suspension was supposed to apply to all Advance Mortgage operations nationally, for 180 days, but it was later changed to cover the Los Angeles office only, for 30 days. Its own negligence made FHA/HUD a partner in the scandal.

Today, HUD is supposed to be paying back homeowners who were cheated. But who will pay all those thousands of families who lost their homes? Or the neighborhoods that have been saddled with the mess left behind by the FHA scandals?

By now it should be clear that the federal government, both through the indirect effects of its policies and the overt actions of its agencies, has played a major role in the decline of city neighborhoods. As Senator William Proxmire, chairman of the Senate Banking, Housing, and Urban Affairs Committee, has observed, the country "probably would have better neighborhoods today if there had been no [federal] programs at all."

It would be wrong to make the federal government the fall guy for urban decline. The cities and states, not to mention the nation's financial institutions, have also done their share.

Take the case of bureaucratic bungling in New York (the Big Apple is easy to pick on, but instances like this do seem to flourish there). Beginning in 1970, the city started condemning properties in the Park Slope section of Brooklyn where two new schools were slated to be built. It moved out 184 families from some forty buildings and slowly started demolishing a few of them—too slowly, since the city left thirty-six of them for the vandals and arsonists to pillage. Today, the area is piled five feet high in debris; the schools, of course, were never built, after the Board of Education realized that the area's student population had declined to such a level that they were not needed. This should not have come as a surprise to the school board, since they were the ones responsible for moving more than three hundred children out of the neighborhood. The total money cost was nearly $4 million. There is no way to measure the true cost to the neighborhood.

State laws and city ordinances can also present unnecessary obstacles to those who are trying to save the neighborhoods. "In some cases, the laws seem deliberately designed and perpetuated to frustrate any neighborhood-based revitalization effort," notes John McClaughry, president of the Institute for Liberty and Community in Concord, Vermont, and a member of the National Commission on Neighborhoods. In Chicago, for example, it takes at least one year, and usually two, to foreclose on a property for failure to pay taxes. Sometimes it can take as long as ten years to get clear title to property. An owner whose property has been sold in a tax foreclosure then has up to twelve months to buy it back for the cost of the back taxes alone. In short, if the landlord refuses to provide maintenance and services to his tenants and won't pay his taxes, a community group is practically at a loss for anything to do about it.

As far as housing-code violations go, it's almost impossible to get the housing court to do anything about problem buildings, because the landlord's lawyer can almost always get a continuance to another date, or have his client make a few repairs to show "good faith." "We had one landlord in Uptown who had forty-five continuances on one slum building alone," says Gale

Cincotta, head of Chicago's Metropolitan Area Housing Alliance.

In such situations, the landlord simply "milks" the building. He pays only those bills he's forced to pay and forgets the rest. A conscientious landlord of a small apartment building may pay more than $5,000 a year for such expenses as janitorial supplies, repairs to the boiler, the building and individual apartments, management, maintenance, and exterminating fees, miscellaneous costs, plus $6,000 or so in real estate taxes. The result is that the conscientious landlord is lucky to break even, whereas the slumlord pockets more than $11,000.

But the landlord is not always entirely to blame—sometimes he is backed into a corner by the financial institutions. The owner of an apartment building can make money in only three ways: by collecting more in rents than he pays out in expenses; by getting certain tax benefits, such as an allowance on federal taxes for depreciation (decline in value due to aging of the building); and by refinancing or reselling his property, based on a presumed increase in value. When the banks say, "No mortgages in this area," the real estate operator *cannot* refinance or resell his building. Thus, he is left with only a few choices. He can hire an arsonist to burn the building and collect the insurance (more on this later). He can increase the rents, which may drive tenants out of the building. Or he can cut services, not pay taxes, and milk the building for as much cash as it will yield for as long as possible, then abandon the building, sticking the city with the back taxes and the mortgage holder with the unpaid principal. When such landlords cannot obtain adequate financing, the appalling scenario outlined above, which has led to the wholesale abandonment of dozens of neighborhoods across the country, is unavoidable.

The euphemism bankers use to cloak the fiscal starvation that they visit upon city neighborhoods is "disinvestment." Neighborhood people have another name for it. They call it "redlining."

The origin of the term "redlining" goes back to the once-common practice of FHA officials of drawing a red line on a map to indicate those neighborhoods where the FHA would not insure loans. That practice supposedly was ruled out years ago, but redlining, in one form or another, goes on. Here, for example, is the story of a redlining victim in Boston:

> I have owned my house in Jamaica Plain for eleven years. Several months ago, I decided to make some major improvements and went to the bank that held my first mortgage. The mortgage officer declined to even give me an application for the loan. "Why don't you think about moving out of that area?" he said. "We'd be glad to give you a new mortgage somewhere else." I think he saw my request for a couple of thousand dollars as an opportunity to get me to sell off so that they could call in the mortgage they'd made on my house in the first place. . . . Jamaica Plain isn't being abandoned by us [residents]. It's being strangled by our would-be banks. The red line goes right down Center Street, and we're on the wrong side.

In its simplest form, redlining occurs when a lending institution refuses to make a home improvement loan or mortgage on a house simply because of its location. Lenders must, of course, make an evaluation of the risk before granting a mortgage. The customary procedure is to examine the borrower's credit rating and ability to pay, the quality of the building, the general market conditions, and the availability of property insurance (and, sometimes, the availability of mortgage insurance, such as that made by the FHA and the Veterans Administration). Last but not least is the quality of the neighborhood.

What happens in the case of redlining is that the lender decides that a certain neighborhood is a "bad area" and refuses to lend there, no matter what the condition of the particular house or the credit standing of the buyer may be. Lenders rarely acknowledge this as the reason for rejecting an application; they are clever enough to invent other "lending criteria" that produce the same results without being labeled redlining. They can do this by:

1. Requiring a bigger down payment than is required on comparable properties in other areas.

2. Fixing loan interest rates in an amount higher than those set for all or most other mortgages in other areas.

3. Fixing loan closing costs in an amount higher than those charged for loans in other areas.

4. Refusing to lend on a property on the basis of the building's age, no matter what its condition.

5. Granting relatively short-term mortgages, resulting in proportionately higher monthly payments than for mortgages in other areas.

6. Refusing to lend on the basis of the building's presumed "economic obsolescence," no matter what its condition.

7. Setting a minimum loan amount, thereby excluding many low-priced properties likely to be found in older neighborhoods.

8. Charging discount "points" (a percentage of the loan, payable in advance) as a way of discouraging financing.

9. Applying more rigid structural standards than those applied to comparable properties in other areas.

10. Stalling on the appraisal to discourage potential borrowers, or setting the appraisal so low that the borrower has to make a larger down payment than he would for a comparable property in other areas.

Ever since the redlining issue was brought to the nation's attention in the early seventies, there have been dozens and dozens of studies of redlining and related discriminatory practices. Here is just a sampling of their findings.

In Boston, a state study found that "a much lower proportion of the Boston banks' savings deposits are reinvested in urban mortgages than in suburban areas." Almost half the home sales in Boston take place without the aid of bank financing. Moreover, said the report, bank home-mortgage lending appears to be racially discriminatory in effect, if not in intent.

In Dallas, while 48 percent of all home loans went to "outer Dallas" mortgages, inner-city neighborhoods got only 15 percent of the total, and the "core area" got only 1.3 percent.

In Cleveland, an analysis by the *Cleveland Plain Dealer* showed that lenders have "invested heavily in suburban residential mortgages, and placed few dollars in the city," even though suburban mortgages were being financed primarily through deposits made in the city.

In St. Louis, a study of ninety-two lenders showed that banks made only 12 percent of their residential loans in the city, while savings and loan institutions made only 4 percent of their loans in the city. The state's largest savings and loan association, Farm and Home Savings, made only 2.6 percent of its total residential loans in the St. Louis *region* and only 0.05 percent of its loans in the city of St. Louis.

In Michigan, a state task force found a "disturbing" pattern of practices in a test of the Flint lending market: (1) the average mortgage was significantly smaller in black neighborhoods than in white neighborhoods; (2) the average mortgage was smaller in racially changing neighborhoods; and (3) fewer mortgages were given in older neighborhoods, more in newer neighborhoods. Overall, the task force *"assembled convincing evidence that a significant number of lending decisions are influenced by factors which are discriminatory in effect."* [Emphasis in original.]

In Baltimore, a 1975 study showed that lenders would not make loans on houses less than eighteen feet wide, while most Baltimore row houses are less than fourteen feet wide. Lenders refused to make loans for less than $15,000, even though three-fourths of all Baltimore houses are valued at less than $15,000.

Finally, in the District of Columbia, a study found that the heavily white area west of Rock Creek Park, with 14 percent of the population, got 43 percent of the total mortgage loans (and 55 percent of the total dollar value) from 1972 to 1975; but the section east of the Anacostia River, which is largely black, with 27 percent of the population, got only 10 percent of the loans (6 percent of the dollar value). This was not for lack of demand. "To the contrary," notes the report, *"the most significant finding of this report is that there is a large, untapped demand for home mortgage loans through many sections of the city east of Rock Creek Park."* [Emphasis in original.]

The lenders say that these reports are statistical hogwash and are completely out of date. "People who are fighting redlining are fighting a battle that's over," says James Wimberg, president of Cincinnati's Eagle Savings, a lending institution with a good reputation among community groups. Redlining has never been proved to the bankers' satisfaction.* Besides, they say, lenders

---

*The only proven case of redlining, *Laufman* v. *Oakley Building and Loan Co.* (No. C-1-74-153), is extremely limited in scope. The U.S. District Court for the Southern District of Ohio ruled in 1976 that "redlining" had indeed occurred in an integrated area, in violation of civil rights laws. But, as one commentator has noted, *Laufman*'s scope is "unclear because its facts are confined to integrated neighborhoods." See Robert E. Wisniewski, "Mortgage Redlining: The Parameters of Federal, State, and Municipal Regulation," 54 *Journal of Urban Law* 346, Issue No. 2, Winter 1977.

are making loans in city neighborhoods. The lenders have also amassed a number of other arguments in their favor, including the following:

Antiredliners confuse cause and effect. "Certainly no one has proved that refusing to grant loans is the *cause* of neighborhood deterioration," says *The Saver*, a magazine published by First Federal Savings and Loan, the Chicago area's biggest residential lender. "To say that lack of faith by lenders brings about deterioration is putting the cart before the horse. First, neighborhoods deteriorate; then lenders are more cautious about making loans there."

Lenders have no evil intent. "To blame urban decay on private market villains is like blaming bad news on reporters," says Kenneth J. Thygerson and Dennis Jacobe. "The fact is that real estate brokers, appraisers, and mortgage lenders are simply reporters documenting urban housing problems."

There is no demand. Fairfield Savings, a savings and loan institution on Chicago's near West Side, told *Savings and Loan News* that it once offered $1 million in mortgages at favorable rates (20 percent down, no points, 7.9 percent rate on FHA-insured loans) for its home area. Despite announcements at community meetings and letters mailed to every address in the area, only thirty-three applications were made over a seven-month period in 1973–74. None of these applicants signed with Fairfield.

Lenders have been singled out for blame. "For a variety of reasons, the banks and the S & Ls have got this target painted on the back of their suit coats—REDLINERS! That's unfair," says William Plechaty, senior vice-president, Continental Bank, Chicago. "That's not something we have cornered on the market. What about all the national *non*-financial businesses who have their home offices here [in the cities]? What type of responsibility do they have? They close their stores and move to the suburbs."

Lenders cannot take unnecessary risks. "You don't concentrate all your mortgages in one area," says a Chicago lending executive. (This is a reference to the demands of antiredliners that lenders make loans in an area proportional to the percentage of total deposits in that area.) And even if they wanted to make loans in redlined areas, the lenders say, they can't because they have no right to risk the investments of their depositors. (At this point, reference is usually made to widows and orphans.)

Whether or not studies prove beyond a reasonable doubt that lenders engage in redlining, they do contain a preponderance of evidence to show that lenders have favored the new, suburban housing market over the old, inner-city market. But it is precisely those old city neighborhoods that are supplying the bulk of the deposits that the banks are lending as mortgages in the suburbs. By shifting that finite source of real estate investment capital from older areas to the suburban fringe, the lenders are "facilitating the redistribution of significant numbers of people" and putting "added stress on the older neighborhoods," according to Calvin Bradford and Leonard S. Rubinowitz. By draining the "lifeblood of housing"—money—from city neighborhoods, the lenders fulfill their own prophecy that these neighborhoods will decline. Without a steady flow of money being pumped into a neighborhood, the rental industry will decline and investment in private homes is sure to stop.

Moreover, a strong case has been made that bank redlining has gone beyond the neighborhood level to whole cities, thereby precipitating the fiscal crisis that struck first in New York City in 1975 and then spread to the entire Northeast. In *The Abuse of Power: The Permanent Government and the Fall of New York*, Jack Newfield and Paul Dubrul argue that the banks themselves precipitated the crisis by redlining housing in New York City as early as 1973. They did this because there was more money to be made in other forms of investment (real estate investment trusts, for example), and in other areas of the country, notably the Sun Belt. With a shortage of capital for reinvestment and resale, the city's housing industry entered a critical stage, leading to rampant abandonment of buildings. After thousands of buildings had been milked or abandoned, city real estate tax collections fell dramatically; within three years, uncollected property taxes totaled *$300 million*. This shortfall of tax collections in turn cast doubt on the city's ability to borrow on the municipal bond market, because the city was limited by law to borrow money based on a percentage of its total tax base. When it started to borrow more than it could pay back (due to the uncollected taxes caused in part by bank redlining), the city's credit base fell apart. The big investors would no longer accept the city's credit for bond sales, and without the ability to borrow, the city went into a fiscal crisis. Furthermore, the banks not only precipitated the crisis, but they also benefited from it, both through the higher rates now charged on municipal bonds and on account of their gaining control of the Municipal Assistance Corporation, which now in effect runs New York City.

Moneylenders aren't the only redliners—insurance companies also engage in discriminatory practices. Insurance redlining is even more insidious than bank redlining, because without insurance it is impossible to get a mortgage. "Communities without insurance are communities without hope," said a 1968 report of the National Advisory Panel on Insurance in Riot-Affected Areas. "Insurance is essential to revitalize our cities. It is a cornerstone of credit. . . . "

One of the most comprehensive and methodical studies of this subject is a 132-page report by Anton Valukas, a former United States attorney who was tapped by the Illinois insurance commissioner in 1977 to investigate charges of insurance redlining made by a number of citizens' groups. Valukas found a pattern of discriminatory practices, notably:

1.) *Outright refusal to insure* or the imposition of stricter underwriting requirements solely on the basis of the *age of the dwelling*, its *geographical location*, or *subjective evaluations* by insurance agents or inspection companies hired to make reports on buildings. Subjective evaluations used in describing a neighborhood include such terms as "changing," "deteriorating," "high-crime," and "high-vandalism."

2.) *Establishment of artificially high prices* for policies in particular areas of the city (or the whole city), which had the effect of pricing the company out of that location.

3.) *Selective placement of agents* in "acceptable areas" and *removal of agents* from "unprofitable" areas. If an area has no agent, it is all the more difficult for local residents to get insurance from that company. Often, when a company removes an agent from an area, it cancels or refuses to renew his policies, wherever they are held, whether in the "redlined" area or not. This put property owners in a Catch-22 bind. If their insurance was canceled or "nonrenewed," they could not get insurance from most of the other companies serving Illinois because their current practice is to refuse to write insurance for any property when the policy has been canceled or nonrenewed, even by another company.

Nor is Chicago the only victim of insurance redlining. In Detroit, according to a 1977 report to the City Council, it is a regular practice for insurance companies to redline by ZIP code or to refuse to accept new policies at all in the city. A report by the Michigan insurance commissioner found the following practices to be common: (1) refusal to insure homes more than thirty years old or that cost less than $25,000 to replace; (2) refusal to insure homes in which the gap between the market value and the replacement value (the cost to rebuild the structure) exceeds a certain percentage, usually 50 percent; and (3) subjecting homes in the city to more numerous or stricter inspections than suburban homes, including an inspection of the neighborhood.

"The obstacle of being unable to receive insurance at reasonable rates may be a factor in causing neighborhoods to deteriorate," concluded Valukas. The Michigan report was a little stronger. It quotes the underwriting manager of a leading Michigan home insurance company: "Anyone who thinks this industry isn't redlining has his head in the sand."

Both the Michigan and Illinois studies show that insurance companies engaged in these practices without any "actuarial experience." The latter term refers to the very basis of the insurance industry: the knowledge that the average person lives to seventy-plus years allows the insurance companies to set life-insurance premiums accordingly. In home insurance, the companies have made no such studies. Take the restriction against insuring old buildings. None of the insurance company representatives interviewed by Valukas could present any studies to show why a building thirty years old was automatically more of a risk than a newer building. (Allstate Insurance Company *did* have figures on buildings less than five years old, for which it gives a special rate; but none of the companies could present data on buildings more than five years old.) The restriction against writing policies for houses built before 1940 ruled out insurance for 60 percent of the owner-occupied residences in Chicago. "The most insidious thing about all these practices was that there was nothing the homeowner could do," said Valukas. "We asked the companies, 'What are your criteria? What is it that causes increased risk and therefore justifies higher premiums or other action?' They could give us nothing. All we got was, 'We know this is a bad neighborhood' or 'We've read about that neighborhood.' " In other words, it was not the structure itself or the owner that was a risk, but the neighborhood.

Yet in investigating the home insurance industry, Valukas got some strange responses from agents in the field, considering that the insurance industry prides itself on hard data. Typical comments were: "Frame buildings are not good risks." "Building is in good shape, but the area is bad." "I don't know who will take it. Big problem with the area." "Most companies don't want to write [policies] in Chicago." "Forbidden area." "Will not write an old house in that area."

The industry says that it is doing nothing wrong. "The whole idea of underwriting is to discriminate—that is, to make price distinctions among insurance risks," says Donald W. Seagraves, vice-president of the Alliance of American Insurers, a trade association located in Chicago. "It would clearly not be fair to charge all purchasers of insurance the same price, because loss frequency and severity vary greatly from one area to another and among individual risks within each area."

No one would dispute Seagraves on that point. The real point is that home insurers have been completely arbitrary in their underwriting practices for city neighborhoods. "Many of these practices are unsupported by credible data and companies sometimes act non-rationally in the face of contrary data," says the Michigan report.

Clearly, something has to be done to prevent insurance companies from redlining neighborhoods and whole cities. The FAIR plans set up in twenty-seven states aren't filling the gap. (FAIR, which stands for Fair Access to Insurance Requirements, was established to provide insurance for property owners in riot-torn neighborhoods.) Except in Illinois, Massachusetts, and Rhode Island, they cost more than regular insurance for fire coverage only—no theft, liability, or replacement coverage. The plans have been so poorly administered that they lost more than $50 million in 1976. The General Accounting Office, the Congressional watchdog agency, has accused the FAIR system of failure to check applications carefully, the result being a high incidence of fires and possibly arson in FAIR-insured structures.

Some states are taking action against insurance redlining. Illinois, for example, passed a law in 1977 prohibiting discrimination on the basis of the building's location or age or the age, sex, race, color, ancestry, or occupation of the applicant. Like most such laws, however, its effectiveness will depend on the enforcement mechanism. Unless something is done, more neighborhoods will be threatened with decline. "If neighborhoods . . . are to remain viable," concluded Anton Valukas in his report, "homeowners in these areas must be able to obtain insurance coverage at reasonable rates."

Another source of discrimination against city homeowners and city neighborhoods is the appraisal process. The appraisal is an important step in buying a home, because it determines not only the market value of the house but, indirectly, the size of the down payment. Say a potential buyer wishes to buy a house for which the current owner is asking $30,000. If the house is appraised at $30,000 and the buyer is able to get an 80 percent mortgage, his down payment is 20 percent, or $6,000. If the house is appraised at only $25,000 however, the bank will finance only $20,000 of the $30,000 sales price, meaning that the down payment increases to $10,000—a 67 percent increase.

Such discrepancies in appraisals are not uncommon in older neighborhoods, because the appraisers' own guidelines seek "conformity" in neighborhoods. "Maximum property values are realized when a reasonable degree of sociological, economic, and physical homogeneity is present," states the 1975 training manual of the Society of Real Estate Appraisers. Homogeneity is measured by such factors as similarity of ethnic, cultural, educational, and social backgrounds; similarity of income; and similarity of land uses. Thus, city neighborhoods, which have a higher incidence of racial, cultural, and land-use mixture than do homogeneous suburbs, will be affected adversely when it comes to appraisals.

The appraisers also discriminate against city neighborhoods on the basis of age. According to the "life-cycle theory" expounded by their manuals, neighborhoods experience an initial state of growth and development lasting about ten years, then go into a peak period of some thirty more years. After the fortieth year, property values in the neighborhood are expected to drop off "because of infiltration of lower use groups, inharmonious land uses, and/or greater appeal of newer and more attractive houses elsewhere," according to the American Institute of Real Estate Appraisers of the National Association of Realtors (known as AIREA). This criterion alone would make two-thirds of the housing in Chicago suspect.

Appraisal bias may be nearing an end, at least on paper. In 1977, the AIREA, the Society of Real Estate Appraisers, the U.S. League of Savings Associations, and the Mortgage Bankers Association of America entered into a voluntary agreement with the federal Departments of Justice and of Housing and Urban Development to develop an affirmative action program on appraisal practices. The new edition of the AIREA handbook, released in 1978, contains such statements as "The notion that racial or ethnic homogeneity is a requirement for maximum value is without empirical support" and "Neighborhood trends do not necessarily depend upon the age of the neighborhood or the income of the neighborhood residents." While such reforms are to be applauded, the appraisers' actions will have to be monitored closely by neighborhood groups to see if they are lapsing back into the kinds of discriminatory practices that have hurt neighborhoods in the past.

Although the picture I have painted so far is grim indeed, my intention has not been to launch a unilateral attack on the politicians, bureaucrats, and businessmen who have borne the brunt of criticism in this chapter. I sincerely believe there are *many* well-meaning public officials, corporation executives, and private businessmen who are seeking desperately to do something about the problems of our cities. Why, then, has the solution not come more swiftly? The answer to that question, I believe, goes back to the theme stated at the beginning of this chapter: the immense complexity of the problems confronting our cities. The temptation is to conceive grandiose schemes that appear to be able to solve the problems—but then the problem changes, and a new scheme is needed. Solving urban problems is not impossible, but a great deal of energy, commitment, and patience is essential. As John Gardner, the founder of Common Cause, once said, "There are no easy victories." We just have to keep on trying.

2

SOCIAL FACTORS IN
NEIGHBORHOOD DECLINE

Federal tax and spending policies, lender disinvestment, and other large-scale forces all figure in the rise and fall of neighborhoods. But people rarely decide whether to move into a particular neighborhood on the basis of a well-considered analysis of taxation and investment trends. They are more likely to judge a neighborhood by their everyday experiences with matters of poverty, race, crime, and the quality of the public schools. If people see a neighborhood attracting a poorer, predominantly nonwhite population, with an accompanying increase in crime or decline in the quality of the schools, those families who can move out of that neighborhood will do so, leaving behind the worst cases—unless, of course, there is an organized effort to face these problems. In this chapter we shall look at the various pathological conditions, such as poverty, race, crime, and declining schools, that adversely affect neighborhoods, before offering suggestions for combating these problems later in the book.

It is no revelation that poverty and race are closely associated. While the percentage of families below the poverty line has decreased in recent years—from 22 percent in 1959 to 12 percent in 1977—the relative proportion of poverty among blacks and other minorities remains high. Of the $11.4 billion in total welfare funds distributed in 1976, for example, 37 percent went to nonwhites. In the Aid to Families with Dependent Children program, 44.3 percent of the $10.3 billion total went to some 1.5 million black families. One-third of all black families live in poverty (defined as $5,500 income or less for an urban family of four), versus one-ninth of all white families. Unemployment figures parallel those for poverty: roughly 13 percent of blacks were out of work in 1977, versus 6 percent of whites. The statistics for teenagers showed even greater disparity: 39 percent unemployment for black youths compared to 14 percent for whites.

When people make a decision about where to live, one of their principal evaluations is the racial and economic composition of the neighborhood. Despite the evidence to the contrary—that numerous middle-class areas are predominantly nonwhite, or that many white neighborhoods are miserably poor—most people, white and nonwhite, associate poverty with race, and vice-versa. Such "prejudice" is a fact of life, one that cannot easily be wiped out by wishful thinking by well-meaning civil-rights activists and social-worker types. If a neighborhood is changing from predominantly white to nonwhite, people *perceive* that neighborhood to be changing from "middle-class" (whatever that means) to "poor." If they believe that the change can be "controlled," so that the shift from middle-class and white to poor and black is gradual, they may decide to stay in the area and invest in it, a point we shall return to in Chapter 7. If the change happens too fast—more accurately, if people *see* it as happening too fast—they will bail out.

In fact, that is the way unscrupulous real estate operators "bust" a block. The blockbusters "steer" a nonwhite family (or several such families) into a white neighborhood and then start rumors that the neighborhood is "changing." Once a few white homeowners start to panic, selling their homes for less than they hoped to get (but glad to get anything), the real estate operators feed on this fear and spread the word: "The Hart family down the block just sold, and I hear that the Clarks across the street are moving out. You don't want to be the last white family on the block, do you?" Such practices are against the law and professionally unethical, but unless there is some mechanism to control them, they continue unabated in older, slightly deteriorating sections of cities.

One of the early signals of neighborhood change occurs in the schools. Schools are crucial to the life of city neighborhoods because they determine whether young, relatively affluent families who already have children or plan to have children will move into and stay in the neighborhood. Here, again, the average person associates good schools with racial composition and social class (income plus professional status). Parents want their children to go to school with other children who share a similar background. For the white majority, that means sending their children to schools that are mostly middle-class and mostly white. If the schools show signs of "tilting" toward having a large number of poor, nonwhite children, those families with options will take action.

In most cities with an appreciable nonwhite population, the percentage of nonwhite students in the public schools is generally higher than the percentage of nonwhites in the population. In St. Louis, for example, nonwhites comprised 56 percent of the grade-school population in 1970, even though nonwhites were only 41 percent of the city's population. In Wilmington, Delaware, the grade-school population was 65 percent nonwhite in 1970, whereas the city's was only 44 percent nonwhite. In Newark, New Jersey, a similar pattern—75 percent nonwhite enrollment in the grade schools, 56 percent nonwhite population in the city. In Washington, D.C., the schools were more than 90 percent nonwhite, even though the city was about 73 percent nonwhite. (Nor do these figures show the effect of school-boundary gerrymandering, which exaggerates racial segregation even more.)

What these figures indisputably prove is that white families with children avoid the urban public schools at all costs, particularly if the schools are populated by poorer, minority-group students. Few will try to reform the system, because they can't risk their children's education while the schools are being improved— if they are *ever* improved. Instead, they'll put the children in a private or parochial school, or they'll try to get their children placed in "special" public schools where the quality of education—and the background of the students—is more middle-class. They may even move to a suburb or another city neighborhood with "good schools." Nick Carbone, a city councilman in Hartford, Connecticut, underscored this point when he told a House committee in 1977 that "the critical thing about [housing] choice in Hartford was the school system." A survey in Hartford of families from 1965 to 1970 showed roughly that families with children who had an income of less than $5,000 moved into the city; so did childless couples making more than $15,000. But families with children and who made more than $10,000 chose the suburbs.

This pattern is particularly noticeable among white, middle-class families in which the children are about to enter junior-high school. The fear of racial fights, drug use, and sexual assault is often enough to persuade even the most liberal parents to seek an alternative to the public schools. One young mother who was one of the original "pioneers" in the Park Slope section of Brooklyn said that her decision to move out of the neighborhood came when her daughter asked her not to give her juice for breakfast. When she asked why, the daughter replied, "Because I don't want to use the bathroom at school. You don't know what it's like in there." Thus, the schools were a factor in pushing another well-meaning family out of the city, an event that is repeated all too frequently in neighborhoods across the land.

Compounding the problems of race, poverty, unfit housing, inadequate health care, and inferior schools is that of crime. While it is true that the poor and racial minorities account for a higher percentage of criminal arrests, they are also the more frequent victim of crime. While blacks account for less than 20 percent of the population, nearly half of all murder victims are black. Blacks are four times as likely as whites to be assaulted, mugged, or raped. People whose family income falls below $7,500 a year suffer forty-five crimes for every one thousand persons; those with incomes over $25,000 a year suffer only twenty-five crimes for every thousand persons.

The correlation between crime and these other social indicators seems well-established; since there is more poverty and destitution in the cities, it is not surprising then that cities are the locus of the crime problem. Indeed crime—or, more accurately, the fear of crime—is often the primary concern of people in cities of over fifty thousand population, as a 1977 Gallup Poll demonstrated. Another Gallup Poll in 1975 disclosed that one in four respondents reported having been touched by crime in some way during the previous twelve months. (These figures are probably low, as studies show that only about one-third to one-fifth of all crimes against people and property get reported at all.)

As is true for so many of these negative indicators, it is people's *perceptions* that count. A decade ago, for example, a Harris Survey of Baltimore residents showed their fear of crime to be much higher than the objective risk. The respondents were thirty-eight times more fearful of assault than the known assault rate would justify; six hundred times more fearful of rape; and a thousand times more fearful of homicide.

Fear of crime can have a debilitating effect on city dwellers. It forces them to distrust others and behave in ways they normally would not. Even the most well-meaning and enlightened can succumb to this irrational reaction. Under such circumstances, it is not surprising that families that have any choice about where they can live will move from what they perceive to be an unsafe neighborhood into a safe one. Why, they ask, should they place themselves in any greater danger than necessary? As these more stable families move out of a declining neighborhood, they leave behind two groups: the predators—the gangs, the street toughs, the junkies, and other elements of the criminal sector—and the prey—welfare families, public-housing tenants, female-headed households, and the elderly. It is no longer a neighborhood. It is a jungle.

In the jungle, youths account for an inordinately high percentage of crime. Two-thirds of all people arrested for major crimes are twenty-one or younger. In the cities, many of these crime-prone youths are organized into street gangs. In the South Bronx alone, according to police, there are nearly ten thousand of these self-styled vigilantes, ages thirteen to thirty, who have formed into hundreds of "cliques," or gangs, supposedly to protect their turf. That they also steal cars, rob and burglarize stores, and victimize innocent people in the course of these selfless activities is not the kind of image the gangs like to project. "We're a group of guys working together to help out people," says Ace, seventeen-year-old leader of the Cypress Bachelors, a Puerto Rican gang in the South Bronx. But Dr. Harold Wise, the founder of the Martin Luther King, Jr., Health Center, says that the gangs have helped make the South Bronx a "necropolis—a city of death." Their very presence drives stable families out of the neighborhoods.

Unfortunately, street gangs are only one part of what might be called a subculture of crime that feeds on a neighborhood, often devouring it in the process. This local underworld might include such relatively innocuous members as bookies and numbers runners or it may also contain hardened criminals—organized racketeers, extortionists shaking down the local merchants for protection, and others who think nothing of using violence to get their way. By creating an atmosphere of fear and intimidation, this small subclass can impose its will on respectable elements of the community to the extent that normal societal relations are turned upside-down. Instead of the criminals being regulated by the majority, it is they who establish and control the community's standard of behavior.

Let me give an example from personal experience. Most people consider parks and playgrounds to be desirable elements of any well-planned, livable neighborhood. Yet I've lost count of the number of parks and playgrounds I've seen go unused or underused because they had become home base for gangs, winos, or street toughs. I recall one such "tot lot" in Arlington, Virginia, where I used to work as a planner. I cannot ever remember having passed that place and seeing a child flying high on the swings or climbing the monkey bars. It had been taken over by the local drug merchants, its small pavilion—theoretically a place for families to hold cookouts and picnics—turned into a drop for the junkies and dealers. Once it became known that this tot lot was a drug drop, concerned parents naturally ruled this playground out of bounds for their children. A few misfits had been allowed to dictate conditions for the majority. So notorious was this case, in fact, that whenever county planners hinted at building a tot lot or playground in another neighborhood, a hue and cry would be raised by local residents who feared that the proposed facility would become a drug drop, too. And so, facilities that should enjoy heavy use are shunned.

I came across a similar pattern in Pilsen, a predominantly Mexican-American neighborhood of Chicago where I used to live. In Pilsen, as in many inner-city neighborhoods, the schools are the center of drug activity. Up to a few years ago, dealers could walk in the front door of the high school, make their sales in the washroom, and walk out again without so much as being questioned about their activities. Besides the drug dealers, members of rival gangs of Mexicans and non-Mexicans would enter the building and instigate fights. The upshot of this situation was that many students were terrorized at the thought of having to go to school. Their parents and community leaders demanded action. In 1977, when the city opened a new high school to serve the neighborhood, the local community council convinced school authorities to make the building a "closed campus." Today, every student entering Benito Juarez High School must wear an identification badge or risk being thrown out of the building. At a certain hour the doors are closed and no one, identification badge notwithstanding, may enter. While this system has been reasonably successful in cutting down the number of fights and other incidents of violence in the school, it is yet another indication of how a small subculture can infringe on the freedom of the large majority.

Fear of crime has also made the elderly population of our cities prisoners in their own homes. Due to the widespread publicity given to specific instances of violent crime against the elderly, it is popularly believed that they suffer a higher rate of crime than the rest of the population. Actually, this is not the case. According to a 1974 study by the Census Bureau, the general population suffered thirty-two crimes of violence for every thousand persons; young people (aged sixteen to nineteen) experienced ninety-three crimes for every thousand persons; and the elderly, by comparison, suffered only twelve crimes for every thousand persons. Yet millions of old people are so frightened of what might happen to them should they venture out into the streets of the city that they lock themselves in their apartments. This self-imposed imprisonment is a sad commentary on how our oldest citizens live out their lives.

To get a glimpse of conditions in the nation's most crime-ridden neighborhoods, it is only necessary to take the examples described above and magnify their impact tenfold. Imagine a neighborhood where the local economy revolves around crime, where numbers-running, racketeering, robbery, burglary, theft, extortion, drug-pushing, gambling, and prostitution are so common that they are an accepted part of life—accepted, that is, because the climate of fear is so pervasive that law-abiding people are afraid to speak up for fear of retaliation by the criminals in their midst. In such a subculture, the pimp drives the flashy car, while the self-respecting working man takes the bus to work. Given such a contrast in role models, it is not surprising that the underworld claims the allegiance of those sufficiently young and impressionable not to know better. Instead of revering conventional authority figures, such as policemen and teachers, adolescent boys emulate the local hoods and throw rocks at the police. Young girls look up to the prostitutes, not the school nurse. Values are turned topsy-turvy.

It is no simple task for a neighborhood besieged by crime to overcome it. Such an effort takes first-rate organization, unalloyed support from the police and other agencies of government, and, most of all, courage on the part of local residents. Most people prefer to run away from the problem. For those who cannot or will not run away, the fight against crime in the neighborhood is an uphill struggle, and I would be remiss to give the impression that it is anything less. It *can* be done, as we shall see in Chapter 7 with the case of Mount Auburn, a predominantly black section of Cincinnati. But it is not an enviable task. In fact, it may be the toughest assignment any neighborhood will have to take on.

Yet while reducing crime in city neighborhoods would seem to be an issue that should enjoy popular support, there has been little in the way of actual reduction of crime. The reasons are complicated and various, depending upon which expert is consulted. Some say it is the leniency of the courts, others, the inadequate rehabilitation programs in the prisons; some say the root is poverty and related social causes, others that certain individuals possess criminal tendencies. The experts are equally at odds when it comes to solutions. More police? Better equipment? Longer sentences? Improved rehabilitation programs? The opinions are as numerous as the number of experts.

There are some who say the answer is to bring back the foot patrolman. "In the 1940s, when you had your policeman on the beat, you had your man on the street," notes Ira Lipman, the president of Guardsmark, Inc., a private security company with offices in Memphis and New York. "The police don't walk the beat any more. The police are like SWAT teams—they're there for the crisis, not everyday crimes." Yet even the beat-cop solution comes in for criticism. A year-long study of neighborhood patrols in Kansas City, Missouri, by the Police Foundation found that they don't necessarily deter criminals nor do they necessarily make residents feel safer. The Kansas City police decided to go back to deploying police by type of duty, rather than by geographical area.

Technology alone won't make cities safer, either. In the aftermath of the 1968 riots, Congress established a new Justice Department agency, the Law Enforcement Assistance Administration (LEAA) to provide technical assistance and special funding to local police. From 1969 to 1977, the LEAA distributed $6 billion in grants to local police departments. A good portion of the money went into hardware—armored vehicles to control rioters, helicopters, fancy new patrol cars. (Some of these patrol cars cost $49,000 each.) Not only was the program rife with fraud and misuse of public monies, it also didn't do much to stop crime. A 1977 report to the Attorney General by a special investigating committee found that, in the first eight years of the program, the crime problem hadn't disappeared and there was no real indication of a dramatic change.

It should be clear from even this brief survey that crime, like other problems affecting neighborhoods, is a complex issue that defies simple solutions. Before leaving the subject, however, one form of crime deserves special consideration, because its effect on neighborhoods can be devastating. That crime is arson.

Arson has been called "the fastest-growing crime in America." In the last ten years arson has increased 325 percent every year. One-third of all fires are believed to be the result of arson; there is an arson fire every minute in the United States.

One of the myths about arson is that it is merely a crime against property. It does destroy property—$1.4 billion worth in 1975—inflicting more damage than any other major property crime, according to a government-commissioned report. An official of State Farm Insurance Company has estimated that arson accounts for 25 to 30 percent of the average property owner's insurance bill. But arson also kills. A thousand people died in arson fires in 1975, including forty-five firemen, according to the government study; another ten thousand were injured. It is estimated that within four years arson will account for more murders than any other cause. Yet less than 2 percent of all arson cases result in the arrest and conviction of the arsonist.

Wherever there are large numbers of deteriorating or abandoned buildings, those buildings become the targets of vandals, junkies, pranksters, and others who either purposely or accidentally set fire to them. Even when the buildings are occupied, they represent a target. In some cities, for example, the only way people on welfare can get out of their lease is if they're burned out. As a result, there are numerous cases of arson by welfare recipients. So, too, the many buildings insured under the FAIR plans the states set up after the 1968 riots have shown a disproportionately high incidence of fires. In Boston, for instance, four in ten arson fires occur in FAIR-insured buildings. In Illinois, the Legislative Investigating Commission reported the fire rate in FAIR-insured buildings to be about double that of those in the voluntary insurance market—some 140 fires totaling $2.9 million in damage for the FAIR buildings during an eight-month period of 1977, compared to 79 fires and $1.1 million damage for the "voluntary" buildings. A report by the General Accounting Office, the Congressional watchdog agency, found that many FAIR plans actually encourage arson by insuring buildings for more than they are worth.

Insurance fraud is not supposed to be a primary motive for arson. According to the government-sponsored study, *Arson and Arson Investigation*, insurance fraud has been the motive for only 5 percent of all arsonists (although the latter accounted for 17 percent of all arson fires). But even this report admits that the big fish often manage to slip through the net, so the amount of arson-for-profit in this country undoubtedly is much higher than estimated.

It is certainly so in Boston, where in 1977 thirty-three alleged conspirators were indicted for torching buildings for profit. The ring included six lawyers, four public insurance adjusters, two former fire captains, a city electrical inspector, four finance-company and credit-union officials, several contractors, an assortment of property owners and street hoodlums, and, most notably, a detective lieutenant in the state fire marshal's office. They were indicted on arson and bribery charges involving fires in thirty-five buildings, in which $6 million in damages was claimed and at least three people lost their lives.

The case was broken through the efforts of an enterprising reporter, Mark Zanger, and a group of citizens called the Symphony Tenants Organizing Project, or STOP. Over a four-year period, more than twenty buildings were set on fire in a small section of the Fenway area, near Symphony Hall. Several people were killed, hundreds of others were driven from their homes in fear. At first, the group could not say for sure that the buildings were being torched. After a while, however, they were able to *predict* with uncanny accuracy which buildings would go next. They did this by examining real estate records and noticing that a small group of investors were selling old apartment buildings back and forth to one another, giving the structures an inflated market value. They would then insure the buildings at those high prices, move everyone out, and have the buildings torched. One group of buildings was sold back and forth six times over a four-year period, its value going from $230,000 to $540,000 before it was burned. Various inspectors, public officials, and insurance company figures who were allegedly part of the deal covered the tracks of the "torches," the paid arsonists.

The Boston case is just one example of a problem that neighborhood groups are going to have to contend with more and more frequently, now that underworld figures can see the profits to be made in the arson business. As one of the indicted landlords told a Boston arson-squad member, "You have to understand—this is the modern way to refinance."

By now it should be evident that numerous factors determine whether a neighborhood is declining, stable, or on the upswing. Social, economic, political, even cultural factors all become part of the maze of considerations that influence the actions of public officials, legislators, bankers, real estate operators, property owners, and tenants. Each response in turn activates responses from the other actors, as when a homeowner's decision to make a substantial investment in his property encourages a lender to make additional home improvement loans on that block—or, more likely, a lender's decision to redline a neighborhood prompts the homeowner to let his property decline.

The problem of trying to describe the process of neighborhood decline involves the ancient chicken-and-egg dilemma. For example, which comes first—the lender's decision to redline, or the homeowner's decision to let a property decline? The lender might say that his wariness about putting money in a certain neighborhood comes from his perception that property owners are not keeping their buildings in good condition. The property owner, on the other hand, says that if the lender had more confidence in the neighborhood and made loans, he would be able to maintain his building properly. And while these seemingly simple decisions are being contemplated, a dozen other variables are flying in simultaneously to confuse and complicate the situation: Is crime (or the fear of crime) going up, stabilizing, or going down? Is the city making any substantial investment in the area, or is it withdrawing public services and improvements? How is the racial, social, and economic profile of the families moving into the neighborhood (and who provide a forecast of what the social composition of the neighborhood will be) changing? Each of these factors alters people's perceptions about all the other factors, making it that much more difficult for the actors to make a "simple" decision. Taken together, these "market factors" influence the decisions that lenders, public officials, property owners, and tenants make about a neighborhood. But remember: these are not simple decisions, and each decision changes the overall picture, so that the next decision has to be made on the basis of an entirely new situation. That's why the process of neighborhood decline seems to be—and is—so complex.

Rolf Goetze, a planner with the Boston Redevelopment Authority, offers one method of neighborhood evaluation. Goetze assesses neighborhoods from both the *actual* condition of the housing and the *perceived* value. Take a neighborhood where the housing is in good shape, but where the city decides to locate a trash landfill. It would be rated as having "good housing conditions" but might be considered "declining" or perhaps "rapidly declining" as far as "market perception" goes. Such an appraisal emphasizes the fact that market perception, a product of social and economic indicators, weighs heavily in determining neighborhood quality. It also implies that what might be a good strategy for revitalizing a neighborhood with fair-quality housing and a stable market might not work for a neighborhood with poor housing and a declining real estate market—or for a neighborhood with good housing and a rising market.

Another description of neighborhood decline has been presented by a San Francisco consulting firm, Public Affairs Counseling, in a 1975 HUD report entitled *The Dynamics of Neighborhood Change.* This report outlines five stages of neighborhood decline: Stage One, "Healthy"; Stage Two, "Incipient Decline"; Stage Three, "Clearly Declining"; Stage Four, "Accelerating Decline"; and Stage Five, "Abandoned." It also describes the physical, social, and economic conditions in each stage, as well as estimating the probable level of public services.

In "healthy" neighborhoods, the houses are structurally sound and well-maintained. The residents are in middle-to-high income and social-status positions, mostly white-collar professionals or skilled blue-collar workers. They are ethnically homogeneous, educated (high school or above), and family-oriented (or childless couples). They take pride in their neighborhood and perceive it as a safe, reputable, socially cohesive place. They put a lot of money into their homes—regular financing and home insurance are available to them—and they get back a good return on property value and market confidence. The public services in their neighborhood are efficient.

In "incipient-decline" neighborhoods, the houses begin to show the first signs of neglect. The housing stock in such neighborhoods is getting old, and some nonresidential uses are infringing on the residential areas. The residents have a lower social status and income level than in Stage One neighborhoods, with a decline in the level of education and job status. Such neighborhoods may experience an influx of pioneering minority families, leading to a fear of possible racial change. There is a decline in the neighborhood's reputation, with the result that property owners begin to cut back on maintenance. Property values are steady, but not inspiring. The property-tax burden increases, especially for the elderly homeowners. There are more renters.

In "clearly declining" neighborhoods, conditions are quickly becoming critical. There is visible deterioration in both public areas and in private residences. Homes are being subdivided to make way for renters, and the increased density is taking its toll on the buildings. The buildings need major repairs, but property owners are reluctant to make the investment, cutting back even further on maintenance. There is a major decline in social status, with more welfare families (many of them headed by single mothers) and poor families. There is an increase in the number of unskilled workers and unemployed. The schools have more and more minority-group children, and there is an increasing fear for personal safety throughout the neighborhood. Property values are falling, insurance and financing are hard to come by, and investor confidence is declining rapidly. More houses are being rented, but escalating operating costs are putting the small investor-owners in a budget bind. Residents perceive a decline in the responsiveness of public services, at the same time that there is an increasing dependence on such public and social services.

"Accelerating decline" neighborhoods are one step away from disaster. The old buildings in the neighborhood are deteriorating almost beyond repair, and many of them are being abandoned, only to be vandalized and perhaps torched. Socially, the residents are at a low point—poverty, unemployment, and other social problems dominate their lives. There is an increasing number of minority families, the only whites being the elderly or the poor who have no choice. Crime and fires, including arson, are on the rise, and people fear for their lives. The real estate market is practically nonexistent—no buyers, no home insurance, no conventional mortgage financing (only government-backed loans). Many of the buildings are owned by absentee owners, who, feeling the crunch of decreasing rents and accelerating costs, opt to milk the buildings. Public services are at the absolute minimum.

An "abandoned" neighborhood is in the final stage of decay. The buildings are severely dilapidated, many of them abandoned or demolished. The empty lots are littered with trash, not to mention abandoned cars. The neighborhood is noisy, and the area reeks of garbage. The families who remain are at the lowest levels of social status, income, and opportunity. Crime and arson are commonplace. Fear and apathy are written on the faces of those unfortunate enough to have to live under such conditions.

For each state, the report also describes the likely actions of families, investors, and public and private decision makers. In "healthy" neighborhoods, all actors are making positive contributions to the area. In "incipient decline" neighborhoods, there begins to be a change in the kinds of families moving in. Public services start to lag, some businesses relocate, insurance companies increase their rates, banks get tougher on housing loans, and some real estate operators engage in the first efforts of blockbusting. In "clearly declining" neighborhoods, absentee ownership increases and more affluent white families start to move out. Landlords may convert their buildings to rooming houses or denser apartment buildings, maintenance is curtailed, and "milking" may start. Redlining by insurers and lenders begins, and public agencies may encourage actions that bring more low-income and welfare families into the neighborhood. For neighborhoods in "accelerating decline," the scenario is one in which families who have a choice move. There is little new investment in the neighborhood. Landlords start to be late in mortgage payments. Tax delinquencies are common. The final state, "abandonment," is one where even the poorest tenants engage in rent strikes, because property maintenance has fallen to practically nothing. Building owners get whatever they can out of the building and run. The banks foreclose on properties, while the city tries to recoup its taxes. Public agencies consider the area a slum ready for clearance.

The thing to keep in mind when considering these descriptions of neighborhood decline is that they are *not* predictions. One of the unusual characteristics of neighborhoods is their ability on occasion to defy the seemingly normal process of aging. Neighborhoods have "the power of regeneration," according to the authors of *The Dynamics of Neighborhood Change*. Stage Two need not automatically lead to Stage Three: it is possible to intervene in that process and turn a so-called Stage Two neighborhood into a healthy, Stage One neighborhood. Decline, even in the very worst neighborhoods, is not inevitable.

What is needed to reverse decline, of course, is intelligent, aggressive action on the part of the federal government, city hall, financial institutions, the real estate industry, private homeowners, and tenants. The first step in solving complex urban problems is to dispel certain popular misconceptions about cities and urban problem-solving. One of the false beliefs that Americans have succumbed to is that if we put enough money and manpower into a task, we can lick any problem. Such an attitude probably had its origins in our frontier experience; today, the space program has perpetuated such a myth—indeed, Daniel Patrick Moynihan calls it the "man-on-the-moon syndrome." Once Neil Armstrong took that giant leap for mankind, it became common practice for public officials and policy makers, as well as the man on the street, to say, "If we can put a man on the moon, why can't we solve the housing crisis?" Or the welfare crisis, or whatever crisis was on the cover of that week's *Time*.

But propelling a man to the moon and returning him to Earth is a straightforward technical problem. Could we build a sufficiently powerful ship, stock it with oxygen and supplies, and devise the right guidance systems? On space flights, there are none of the complications that arise when humans are forced to interact with one another: any problems that do occur on the space missions are technical matters that can be solved by adjustments to the hardware.

People, unfortunately, do not adjust so easily. "As long as city planners, and the businessmen, lenders, and legislators who have learned from planners, cling to the unexamined assumptions that they are dealing with a problem in the physical sciences, city planning cannot possibly progress," wrote Jane Jacobs. If we fall back on space-age technology to save the cities, we will find ourselves stuck with a portfolio of failures like Operation Breakthrough.

No, advanced technology and hardware programs alone won't reverse urban decay. Houses, stores, schools—all are vital, of course. But buildings are only part of an equation that includes health care, jobs, transportation, and numerous other variables that affect the quality of life in our cities. How often have we heard, for example, about millions being spent to build housing, only to have it turn into a slum in a few years? New buildings mean nothing by themselves without revitalization of the social and economic fabric of the neighborhood.

Nor can money alone solve urban problems, as the sorry record of too many federal programs shows. Unless the groundwork for a program is laid properly—establishment of strong community support, involvement of all necessary participants, consideration of the political, social, and economic aspects—the structure will fall, and no amount of money will shore it up. That was a vital lesson of the Great Society. "Despite the sound and fury of the federal programs," writes William C. Baer, "they have signified nothing; Watts [fill in your city's worst neighborhood] remains largely as it was before the riots. Deterioration, disinvestment, and abandonment are still there for all to see, and they will remain. . . . " Like love, the factors necessary to revitalize neighborhoods—effective leadership, community backing, political savvy, expertise, imagination, and determination—cannot be bought.

This is not to imply, of course, that our cities are flooded with money and programs for rebuilding neighborhoods. Quite the contrary. To give just one indication of the shortfall, in some countries, 40 percent of the families receive housing aid; in the United States, less than 2 percent of the population is subsidized. More to the point, the subsidies reach at best only 15 or 20 percent of those in need.

At times it seems that, just when we think we have solved a problem, another pops up in its place. Building lots of cheap housing in the city, for example, solves the immediate problem of sheltering the needy. But the very existence of cheap housing may also attract poor migrants from outside the city, who will themselves have to be housed. In *Urban Dynamics*, Jay W. Forrester, a professor at the Massachusetts Institute of Technology, describes computer models that purport to show the probable "negative" effects of various "positive" public actions. While the validity of Forrester's models is open to debate, the general premise rings true: simple solutions to complex problems just don't work.

I like to compare the process of reversing neighborhood decline to squeezing a balloon. Push down on one end, and the balloon simply bulges at the other end; but poke it from several sides at once, and you can pop it. Similarly, in fighting neighborhood decay, a *comprehensive* approach is crucial.

Not only must a community organization approach the problem from different angles, but no single program can be expected to "solve the urban crisis." If a program works well in one context, there's no guarantee it will work well somewhere else. A revitalization plan devised for a neighborhood showing the first signs of decline might fail miserably in a truly blighted area. Surely the worst cases of urban decay—Watts, the South Bronx, and on through the list of "necropolises"—will require more money, time, and effort than less blighted neighborhoods. Yet even in those neighborhoods where success seems highly likely, there are so many unknowns that nothing can be guaranteed. In any neighborhood renewal effort, the level of support in the community, the cooperation between public- and private-sector leadership, the quality of the professional staff—all these will vary from program to program and from neighborhood to neighborhood. All the pertinent factors have to be accounted for; the principal actors must be induced to have a role in the solution.

It is also important to realize from the beginning that instant cures are hard to come by. Without a sustained effort, many new social programs announced with brass bands and hoopla ultimately fail. "It's not a two-year process," says William Plechaty, a Chicago bank official. "It's a ten-, or fifteen-, or twenty-year process." After all, that's how long it probably took for the neighborhood to decline. And in any public effort, a great deal of inertia must initially be overcome—from the bureaucracy, the labor unions, the political forces, the special interests. Instantaneous solutions to long-standing problems just don't happen in real life.

To be successful, a revitalization effort must change people's *attitudes*. Citizens have to believe that the neighborhood can be saved. Lenders have to feel secure in their investments. City officials have to have some assurance that they are expending public money and manpower wisely by supporting the neighborhood's revitalization. We "have to be very careful not to overpromise and then under-deliver," notes Robert MacGregor, executive director of Chicago United, a group representing major Chicago corporations and minority-owned businesses. It all gets back to this matter of restoring *confidence* in the future of the neighborhood.

Finally, the initiative must come from the *grass roots*. If local people are not involved in the solution of neighborhood problems, the effort is almost sure to fail.

The most effective way I know of for people to get the clout that is needed to succeed in the world of city politics is through the establishment of a strong, unified community organization. It is to that matter that we now turn.

PART TWO

Organizing the Community

Don't ask f'r rights. Take thim. An' don't let anny wan give thim to ye. A right that is handed to ye fer nawthin has somethin the matter with it. It's more thin likely it's only a wrong turned inside out.

—MR. DOOLEY
(Finley Peter Dunne)

3

FROM THE
GRASS ROOTS UP

A community organization is essential to any neighborhood that hopes to win the battle against decline. Too many forces and institutions stand poised to destroy your neighborhood—greedy slumlords, insensitive government bureaucrats, uncompromising financial institutions, power-hungry legislators. A neighborhood without an organization to fight for itself will surely be overrun by one or more of these forces.

In this chapter, we'll seek answers to such questions as: How do you start an organization? What problems can you anticipate in organizing from the grass roots up? How have other community groups overcome these problems? By drawing on the experiences of others, it should be possible to fit the concepts and suggestions discussed below to your unique situation.

Don't be surprised if the toughest opposition initially comes from your neighbors themselves. They may be suspicious of anyone who wants to butt into their affairs. Some may deny that the neighborhood has any problems at all. A few will object to forming a community organization because they don't want to "get involved" in politics, or because they are fearful of confrontation. "That's not what good, hard-working Americans do," they'll say. Or they may simply be lazy or uninformed. Others have already given up without trying, having adopted the attitude that you can't fight city hall. Overcoming inertia of this kind is difficult. So are your other responsibilities: raising money, hiring a staff, keeping people interested in what you're doing, and building the organization. None of these tasks is very rewarding in itself. And the worst part of all is that the problems never end. The price of organizing a community, experienced activists say, is eternal vigilance.

But you *do* have a few things going for you. You have numbers: votes, people, bodies, workers—a strength no bureaucracy or corporation can hope to match. More important, you know that what you're doing is right. After all, who knows better than you and your neighbors what the future of your neighborhood should be? In short, you have the force of democracy behind you, and that, as Mr. Dooley would say, is somethin' they can't take away.

The rewards are often pitifully small. "If I knew then what it was going to be like, I'd have given up years ago," says my friend Herman Jensen, a retired Air Force sergeant who is well into his second decade of community activism in Arlington, Virginia. Yet I don't think Herman would be happy if he didn't have a meeting to go to, or a new report to study, or a rezoning proposal to battle. Like marriage, community activism requires a commitment that defies rational analysis.

Getting Started

Most community organizations get started because a problem or crisis moves people to action. The issue need not be a federal case. As one activist put it, "At the local level, you organize around dog shit, stop signs, whatever people are talking about." Since most neighborhoods are plagued with problems, the most difficult task is likely to be the choice of the right issue with which to begin. It must be pervasive, concrete, and highly visible. Only then will it attract people's attention and keep them motivated.

The issues confronting city neighborhoods are many and varied. For Birmingham, a Hungarian section of Toledo, the issue was the "battle of the books." In 1974, library officials threatened to close the Birmingham branch because not enough books were being circulated to justify keeping it open. In protest, 150 women and schoolchildren descended upon the library one morning, swamping the staff with requests for library cards, causing huge backups at the checkout counter, and practically burying the clerks under stacks of books. Library officials reconsidered, and the branch was kept open.

Quite a different issue faced the people of Northside, a section of Brooklyn. In 1969, a cardboard-box manufacturing company threatened to move its five hundred jobs out of the city if it couldn't find room to expand. The city started condemning land for the expansion, even though it would have meant the removal of ninety-four families. "This neighborhood was programmed for death," said Jan Peterson, a local resident and organizer. After a protracted struggle, the Northside residents won a compromise. Some of the homes were indeed bulldozed for plant expansion, but others were saved, and replacement housing was built for forty families.

In Chicago's Pilsen, the target was the Metropolitan Sanitary District. In putting in a sewer main, the MSD damaged a number of homes and a church, but refused to pay for repairs. So Pilsen Neighbors, a local community group, organized a series of protests against the MSD and eventually won a $50,000 settlement for seventeen property owners whose buildings had been damaged.

In the Morris Heights section of the Bronx, the target was one landlord who was systematically milking fifteen buildings. "We had rent strikes, we picketed his office, and we had him investigated at the state level," said Jim Mitchell, a young organizer. "He's now selling used cars in Yonkers, and the tenants have a new management."

I could go on listing examples of neighborhood issues, but these cases, though widely varied in their specifics, sufficiently illustrate the need to find a "hot" issue that will spark people's interest and get them involved. The issue must be clearly identifiable to the man on the street, and it must move him to action. If it fails to meet these criteria, the problem is not a real issue, only an imagined one.

But finding an issue is only the first step in an organizing effort. How do you bring about a successful resolution of the problem?

First, assemble a small group of people—a steering committee, if you will—who want to do something about the problem to get the organization rolling. The steering committee should begin by developing an agenda for the first organizational meeting; since at least one issue has already been identified, it should be at the top of the agenda. The committee must also immediately raise enough money to keep the organization going until more stable financing can be arranged, and it should publicize the meeting to attract as many people as possible. (See Chapter 4.) Finally, the committee should make overtures to the existing community institutions and power bases—the churches, settlement houses, block groups, social-action groups (Junior League, League of Women Voters)—to determine their interest and support. The existing power structure, if sympathetic to your cause, can prove extremely helpful to any fledgling community organization, and you need as many allies as you can get. Be aware, though, that the existing power structure may be totally unsympathetic and may, in fact, be in league with your enemy.

The first organizational meeting should be held at a convenient time and place, so that the largest number of people can attend. Make sure it doesn't conflict with another important meeting. Provide child-care services so that parents can come. The agenda for this first meeting will be heavy, so start on time and keep to a schedule. After the call to order, state briefly the purpose of the meeting, which, of course, is to see what the community plans to do about a problem that has been identified by a number of local residents.

The next order of business is the election of a temporary chairman to run the meeting until the permanent officers can be picked. Ask for nominations from the floor; write the names on a blackboard; call for a close to nominations; then take a vote, preferably by secret ballot. A volunteer should take minutes of the proceedings.

At this point, the temporary chairman will most likely want to open the floor to a discussion of the items on the agenda, beginning with the previously identified neighborhood issue. Those in attendance should be encouraged to participate in the discussion of this issue and to identify other problems that might be addressed at this or future meetings. Much of this first meeting will be taken up with the airing of grievances, since the people who take the time to attend probably have complaints or problems they want made known. The temporary chairman should get these grievances out before the whole group, so that the overall goals and objectives of this fledgling organization can begin to take shape. For example, if a number of residents complain about vacant buildings being vandalized and others express concern about certain property owners not maintaining their buildings, it is clear that "housing" is a major area of concern for many residents. As the discussion continues, other goals and objectives will begin to emerge; by the end of the meeting, it should be possible to list a number of general reasons for establishing a community organization—"to enhance the environment of the community," "to improve housing conditions for all residents," "to improve the quality of life for this and future generations of local residents." These will become the founding principles upon which your organization will be built, just as the prefatory remarks of the Constitution ("to form a more perfect union . . .") give the reasons for the founding of the United States of America.

Certain other business matters should also be attended to at this first meeting. The temporary chairman should ask for volunteers to serve on a number of general-purpose committees, which have responsibility for maintaining the organizational structure of the group. The *finance committee* studies the organization's financial needs and resources, develops a budget, and recommends ways to raise money. The *publicity committee* establishes a link with the press and finds ways to increase the public's awareness of the organization. The *membership committee* works to attract new members. The *election committee* arranges for the nomination and election of permanent officers or a board of directors and verifies election results. The *bylaws committee* drafts a set of bylaws or a constitution by which the organization will be run. (Someone familiar with *Robert's Rules of Order* should be appointed parliamentarian to decide procedural and constitutional matters.) In addition, the temporary chairman should ask for volunteers to serve on issue-related committees, which deal with the major problem areas identified during the group's discussion—housing, schools, streets and sanitation, zoning, and so on. In the future, new business will be referred to the respective committee for review; the committee will study the matter and issue a report to the general membership, which retains the power of decision over all major areas of concern.

Finally, steps should be taken to create a group identity. The most obvious way to do that is to give your organization a name, something that identifies your purpose, your geographical area, or some historical point about the neighborhood. A name that can be condensed into an acronym works especially well—for example, "SCAR," the Southeast Council Against the Road. Hold a contest for the best name. Do the same to create a logo, or symbol, for the organization. Use the logo on your stationery and other identifying items. For example, the Adams-Morgan Organization emblazoned its logo on a homemade banner and hung the flag on a pole in the middle of one of the busiest traffic circles in Washington—a clear symbol that this was "AMO territory."

As your organization becomes established, you'll want to open an office. The very existence of an office lends credibility to the organization. A basement or garage will do for starters, but later you can move into a storefront or a small office building, depending on your budget. The office should be clean and pleasant, but not fancy: You don't want potential contributors to get the idea that your group is rich.

As this first meeting draws to a close, the temporary chairman should summarize the results and set a date for the next meeting. Make sure to collect the names and addresses of everyone at the meeting. Give everyone a job for the next meeting, so that they all feel involved in the organization. And don't be afraid to pass the hat: you need money to keep going. Finally, allow time for dessert and nonalcoholic beverages to be served, so that people have the opportunity to meet informally after the business part of the meeting is over.

Holding that first meeting is just the start of your work, of course. Having established your organization and formed your committees, you are ready to research the issues your group has identified as the worst problems. Dig out the facts from newspaper clippings, magazine articles, books, reports, studies. If public money is being spent on the problem, find out who is spending it, how, and where. Such information should be contained in public files. (Although, to be frank, many public expenditures are hidden by shrewd bookkeeping.) Most important, find out who is directly responsible for remedying the problem—the mayor, the board of sanitation commissioners, the city council, or perhaps the president of a bank. The person or persons with the power are your target.

Get your own experts to help you analyze the information you've gathered. Call upon lawyers, accountants, students, professors, and others with special skills to help you. Make your group as familiar with the details as the enemy is. Then put all the information together in a form that is easily understood and will make the greatest impact. Summarize your results clearly, give the background information needed to explain your conclusions, and describe how or why the problem must be rectified. Keep it short. Trim the fat. The study must be authoritative, but not necessarily long and complicated. Get to the point fast and stick to it.

Tactics

For your first venture into confrontation politics, try to pick a problem that holds a high probability of being successfully resolved. Gaining that first victory, no matter how small, inspires confidence in the organization and in its leaders. People begin to say, "Hey, this new group is really doing something. They're not just all talk." Especially in the early stages, don't joust with windmills. In that way, your members won't be discouraged.

Wishing for victory is one thing; actually winning it is another. While no single organizing tactic can be guaranteed to produce results, certain principles of strategy making have proven their worth to community groups over the years. In *Rules for Radicals,* the late Saul D. Alinsky outlined some of the major concepts he found productive in a lifetime of community organizing work. These principles, which have been used—and refined—by present-day activists, can provide the basic strategy for your organization. The first rule is: *Power is not what you have but what the enemy thinks you have.* Or, as Betty Hyatt would say, "Give the appearance of strength, even if you don't have it." Hyatt, one of the early leaders in the fight to prevent a road from being built through Southeast Baltimore, said that at first the road opponents numbered only eight. But whenever they attended public hearings or wrote letters of protest, each of the eight opponents spoke for a separate "organization"—a one-member organization, to be sure, but public officials were never the wiser. They thought they were dealing with hordes of indignant taxpayers. Later, when the antihighway group's membership swelled, this tactic was no longer needed. In the beginning, though, it was absolutely crucial to create the impression of power.

Rule Two: *Stay within the experience of your people.* In other words, take actions that your members—and the public—comprehend and appreciate. Marie Nahikian of the Adams-Morgan Organization in Washington, D.C., remembers how she and her neighbors dealt with the redlining issue: "We went to the rich areas where people could get loans, and we painted a red line around their For Sale signs." The symbolism of the rich being "redlined" had a very powerful effect on the AMO protesters, who were themselves victims of real-life redlining.

Conversely, *whenever possible, go outside the experience of your enemy.* Make the enemy uncomfortable; put him off balance. Shel Trapp, a Chicago organizer, recalls how a Spanish coalition from the Northwest Community Organization used this tactic against former Chicago School Superintendent James Redmond. "They wanted a bilingual program for the schools, but Redmond wouldn't give in," says Trapp. "So they arranged a meeting with him at his office, but instead of speaking English, they spoke Spanish. Redmond had to call all over the building to get an interpreter. The group went off into a corner and started talking in Spanish, and then they all laughed! Redmond kept getting angrier and angrier because he thought they were laughing at him. He got so angry he just gave them the program." This story illustrates another maxim: *Ridicule is a most potent weapon.*

The logical extension of the principles of staying within the experience of your sympathizers and going outside the experience of your enemy is to *capitalize on your unique assets.* The simplest example would be the neighborhood threatened by the construction of a new federal highway that capitalized on its historic character to get itself declared a historic district. Once officially declared historic, the neighborhood is protected by federal laws from undue encroachment by federal projects, particularly interstate highways. As we have seen, this technique saved Southeast Baltimore from ruin by the highway barons, and it got a highway rerouted around the Lafayette Square neighborhood of St. Louis. Not every neighborhood is a historic district, of course, but it's hard to imagine a city neighborhood without its own special qualities and assets. Use these attributes to benefit the neighborhood.

One special attribute of many inner-city neighborhoods has until recently been ignored. Today, however, from New York's Puerto Rican barrios to Chicago's Polish "Stanislowowo" to Oakland's Chinatown, there is a growing interest in and awareness of ethnic heritage. For years the "ethnics" were made to feel ashamed of their background, as if they were not first-class citizens; in response, many members of minority groups went overboard to assimilate into the majority culture, changing their names to "American" names and making other efforts to hide their heritage. In recent years, however, perhaps spurred by the example of the blacks with their "Black is beautiful" motto, the so-called white ethnics have begun to dig back into their "roots" to find the strengths and qualities that constitute the basis of national pride.

Today, white ethnic neighborhoods are capitalizing on their heritage instead of trying to hide it. As a result they are finding a new source of community identity and solidarity. When the Birmingham neighborhood of Toledo found that the city planned to cut a swath through the neighborhood to widen a road, for example, the community organization turned the issue into a matter of ethnic pride: *Hungarian* homes would be destroyed, and with them an irreplaceable asset would be lost. "The street widening would have been a disaster to a unique community where people believe that life is more important than money," said Rev. Martin Hernady, the local priest. In protesting the street widening before the city council, the neighborhood group reinforced the importance of the ethnic factor by having everyone wear buttons that said "Hungary Power." Said Joe Szegedi, a local grocery owner, "The whole point of our effort was to keep our neighborhood and preserve our ethnic way of life." Apparently this outpouring of ethnic pride worked: the city council voted down the road widening.

A similar revelation occurred to the people of St. Louis's Hill. Faced with a series of onslaughts from outside that threatened to destroy the neighborhood, the community hired a couple of students from Washington University to make a detailed survey of the neighborhood. The results were surprising. Three-quarters of the people surveyed wanted the Hill to stay an Italian community. "They told us to stop being 'Americans' and start being Italo-Americans," said Rev. Salvatore Polizzi. "We had taken so much for granted. I don't think we were ever ashamed of our heritage, but we had failed to see the value of it." Instead of feeling inferior about their heritage, the community now takes pride in the values and traditions of being Italian—love of family, strong neighborhood ties, religious and moral dedication, neighborly compassion for those less fortunate, even a sense of closeness to the soil, as exemplified by the many grape arbors and garden plots in the neighborhood. They even have a motto for it—"Pride builds."

In a later chapter, we'll look at how white ethnic neighborhoods can work cooperatively with racial minorities and nonethnic, majority-culture groups to achieve common goals. For now, it is important to remember that ethnicism—or what some call cultural pluralism—is a valuable organizing tool, particularly in city neighborhoods where ethnic groups historically have congregated.

To return to our list of organizing principles, however, *a good tactic is one that your people enjoy*, so figure out ways for your people to have fun when confronting the enemy. A corollary is that *a tactic that drags on too long becomes a drag*. Your people get bored doing the same thing over and over, and the target learns to adapt to the technique.

Here's an example of how to put fun in your fight. "When we first started the antiredlining battle, the local bank president told us that the bank didn't make loans in our area because it was a slum," recalls Shel Trapp. "Needless to say, people got mad about that. But what could they do? We had only $36,000 in deposits in that bank, so it wasn't worth it to pull our money out. We tried picketing. Nothing. We kept picketing. No results. They just ignored us and went on with business.

"Then one of our ladies said, 'Let's have a bank-in!' We said, 'Great idea!' Then we asked, 'What the hell's a bank-in?'

"The next day, we had our bank-in. We put five of our people at each of their windows. They would each withdraw a dollar. Then they'd deposit a dollar. Then they'd ask for change. We even tied up the drive-in windows. And we sent a racially mixed couple to get a loan.

"Then Josephine, the lady who thought this all up, dropped two dollars in pennies on the floor. All the guards came rushing over to pick the money up. She thanked them, and dropped the coins again. Finally, the bank president came running out of his office, asking what we wanted. We told him we wanted a meeting with the bank's board of directors that afternoon at two o'clock. 'But all the directors live in the suburbs!' he bellowed. Right, we said, that's the problem—they live in the suburbs and won't make loans in the city.

"Well, we got our meeting, and we got a $4 million loan commitment, a review of all previously turned-down loans, *and* a $1,000 contribution to the community organization."

Another rule: *The threat is usually more terrifying than the thing itself.* "We have problems with outside people parking their cars on our streets," says AMO's Marie Nahikian. "We put wheat-pasted signs over their windshields saying, 'We cannot guarantee the safety of vehicles parked in this neighborhood.' They usually don't park there again."

While your tactics should not be allowed to become tedious, it is nevertheless essential *to keep the pressure on.* Marie Nahikian explains: "We were trying to get a piece of land for a neighborhood park, but the mayor just wasn't listening. We did all the usual things, picketing, protest, and so on. But for the final tactic, we called the mayor's office *all day,* for three days straight. Finally, the mayor told the budget officer, 'Get AMO that land, and tell them to get off my back.' "

Attack the enemy at his weakest point is yet another good tactic to keep in mind. "We had one slumlord who didn't care about being picketed at his office or at his club," recalls Shel Trapp. "He would laugh about it. But we found out that he had a girlfriend he would see every Tuesday afternoon. We followed him to her apartment, waited a while, then knocked on the door. We confronted him right there. He agreed to fix up the building, but only after we caught him with his pants down."

Let me interject a brief aside about picketing and demonstrations. These two workhorses of organizing can be used quite effectively by community groups, particularly to force a direct confrontation with the target, such as through the occupation of his office. But they must be carefully planned and orchestrated to work right. In organizing such an activity, therefore, be prepared: know where to go, how long your group will demonstrate, the identity of the target, his exact office number, and so on. All this should be worked out *before* your people march off, and all the other preliminary work, such as making of the placards and banners, should also be carefully planned beforehand. Before the actual demonstration begins, when your people are gathered to make the "march," give them a pep talk that reinforces why you are holding the demonstration, what your precise goal is (to confront the enemy), and how it will be carried out—how many hours you'll picket, which office will be occupied, what to say to the press, and so on. If you plan to occupy someone's office, advises Ed Shurna of the National Training and Information Center, sneak a couple of your people in ahead of the demonstration, on the pretext of doing business with the target. Then they'll be able to open the door or provide other help once the main body of demonstrators arrives. Finally, know the law, and obey it. The Constitution guarantees the right of peaceable assembly, but the laws of trespassing sometimes make picketing and demonstrations illegal. Don't provoke a confrontation with the police (unless they are your target): if they tell you to keep moving or to provide access on a sidewalk, do so. In some cities you cannot picket a person's home, although you *can* distribute leaflets to his neighbors. Follow the law.

Another organizing tactic: *Demythologize the enemy.* Planners, engineers, bankers, lawyers, architects, sociologists, and other so-called experts like to wrap themselves in a protective layer of jargon, highfalutin language, and technical showmanship—charts, drawings, scale models. They believe that because they have received advanced training in a speciality, they have the right to decide the public policy issues that fall into their area of expertise.

Suddenly, architects become "experts" not only on whether a proposed building will stand up, but whether it is "good" for the public. Moreover, these experts think so little of the public that they won't even attempt to "translate" their complex ideas into language that the layman can understand. Usually that's a sign the expert is either lying, doesn't understand the problem, or is being paid to say what the enemy wants him to say.

A few years ago, for example, a lead company in St. Louis asked the city for the license to pump waste water from its industrial operations into the abandoned mines that lay under the Hill neighborhood. (The area had once been a source of clay to make bricks.) The lead company's engineers kept assuring everyone that the water would not cause any damage, but they could offer no proof that the flooding would not cause the delicate underground structure to collapse, destroying the homes above. The city was ready to take the company's word and grant the license, until the leader of the Hill 2000 community organization, Father Polizzi, produced some surprising evidence: photographs of a school that had collapsed under similar circumstances. These photos, coupled with the expert testimony of an engineering professor from a local university, totally deflated the lead company's arguments. The license was denied.

Community activists should also *beware of constructive alternatives.* Sometimes, the enemy, seeing he is about to be defeated, tries to turn the tables on you and says, "All right, if you're so smart, tell us what to do." Be careful how you handle this situation. It's not your role to tell the sanitation department how to pick up the garbage: all you care about is that they pick it up regularly. Don't fall into the trap of trying to do the enemy's job. Let the enemy solve his own problems. Concentrate instead on making sure he meets your demands.

Finally, *the confrontation must appear logical in its progression.* Start small, and work up to more drastic measures. Otherwise the enemy can gain sympathy by claiming that your group overreacted to the alleged abuse. Also, *the enemy's response should determine the level of confrontation.* If he agrees right away to negotiate with you, it's not fair or wise to keep harassing him. If he is recalcitrant, *then* dig in for the long fight.

In short, to use Alinsky's phrase: *Pick the target, freeze it, per-*

sonalize it, and polarize it. The ordinary person can't get excited about fighting for vague generalizations such as "good housing" or "safe streets." But anyone can be turned into an activist if children are being bitten by rats, or if people have to live in unsafe housing because the landlord won't make the required repairs.

Let me add one last word about tactics. These organizing principles have a proven record of achievement. But like all "rules," they were made to be broken. Use them to fit your needs, not to dictate iron-clad strategies for your organization's campaign.

Negotiating the Settlement

Eventually, if your organizing strategy works, your group is going to have to confront the mayor, or the planning director, or the local HUD officer, or whoever the target might be, at the bargaining table. The moment when the target agrees to negotiate is a crucial one for your organization. How you handle this final negotiating session may determine whether your group survives.

The final process has three parts: preparation for the negotiation, the actual session, and the follow-up.

In *preparation* for the negotiating session, several key decisions must be made. Who in your organization will attend? (Usually, it's best to have as many people as possible, as a show of strength.) Who will speak? Where will it be held—your turf or the enemy's? What are the terms of the negotiation session? For example, will the target be allowed to send a representative, or must he appear in person? These matters must be anticipated, worked out at a meeting of the leadership, and then, if time allows, approved by the members.

The list of demands must be specific: "The Department of Sewers will repair all broken sewer mains in the 1400 block of Lexington and the 1500 block of California." Put a specific time frame on performance: "Work will begin within five working days and will be completed within thirty working days from the start of work." Finally, demand a follow-up meeting to make sure that the target has complied. "The director of the Department of Sewers will meet with the community on (date, time) at (location) to determine if his department has complied with this settlement."

Demands like these place specific burdens upon your target. They are not wishy-washy generalities, subject to "interpretation" by "experts." Don't talk about "developing a commitment to improve the environment of our neighborhood" or other such nonaccountable phrases. Once again, don't fall into the trap of becoming an "adviser" to the enemy. Tell him what he's doing that is wrong and what you want him to do to improve performance, but let him figure out how to do it.

Of course, you have to come to the table prepared to bargain. It's morally uplifting to take the self-righteous stand that your demands are nonnegotiable, but will it win the point? Probably not. Instead, be prepared to give up some things to achieve the items you really want. Include some demands that you're ready to waive as your part of the compromise. You might be willing to give on certain specifics—forty working days for completion of the project instead of thirty, for example. But you'll also want to set an absolute minimum below which you refuse to go.

Before the actual session, try some role playing to see whether you've got your arguments down pat. Appoint someone to be the enemy and have him give all the counterarguments he can think of to frustrate you. Anticipate the alternatives the target might offer instead of agreeing to your demands, and prepare your reaction to these alternatives. Work out all the snags *before* you go into the final session. And have all the latest facts and information available, too. You don't want to be surprised by a last-minute revelation.

The *actual negotiating session* will be only as fruitful as the preparation that preceded it. The culmination of the session should be the signing of the demands by the target and by the appropriate representatives of your community organization. This should be carefully orchestrated by the chairman of the meeting. He should list each demand individually, then ask for support from the floor on that issue: "Do we agree that all sewer mains in the 1400 block of Lexington Street should be repaired?" The "audience"—your members—will of course support him. Rob Schachter, an organizer for Chicago's Metropolitan Area Housing Alliance, recommends that you then dramatize the issue by having one or more persons tell a horror story about just how bad the sewer problem on Lexington Street is. Then close in for the kill: make your target sign the demand, point by point. After the meeting, send a copy of the signed agreement and a confirming letter to the target.

But what if the target fails to show up, or sends a representative who pleads that he doesn't have the authority to agree to your demands? Or that someone else is actually responsible for the sewer problem? Or that it's not a sewer problem at all, but something else? Or that your group is really the problem, not the sewers?—all familiar ruses used by persons in authority to avoid responsibility. Then you're right back where you started, and the whole process of confrontation must begin anew.

Even if you get a signed agreement, the job is not over. You still have an "accountability" session. The target must be brought back to the community for it to be determined whether he has complied in full with the signed agreement. Until such an accounting has been made, the victory is not complete. As Shel Trapp puts it, "Paper victories are great if you're collecting toilet paper." When you get full compliance, *then* you can really celebrate your victory.

Of course, one battle does not win the war. Victories should be used to continually build the organization—to increase the public's awareness of the organization, to attract new members, and to increase the loyalty and hard work of the present members. Take pleasure in the victory, yes, but then move on to new issues.

Organizing Tenants

This is a good point to pause and consider the special concerns of tenants, because organizing renters poses a couple of major problems. For one thing, they don't have as much vested interest in their buildings nor in the value of surrounding property as homeowners, so they often feel less of a commitment to the neighborhood. It is therefore vital to impress upon them that the apartments they live in are their homes: they have an obligation to safeguard them, and, in any case, they will not likely solve their problems by trying to move away from them, since conditions for tenants are roughly the same throughout a given housing market. The second problem is that a tenant can be thrown out of his apartment by the landlord, particularly if the tenant has gained a reputation as a complainer or organizer, even though the tenant may well be within his rights. This is called a retaliatory eviction.

The first order of business in organizing tenants, aside from familiarizing yourself with the general principles expounded in this chapter, is to study your state law on evictions. More than twenty states forbid retaliatory evictions, according to Michael McKee of the People's Housing Network. In Massachusetts, for example, it is illegal for a landlord to evict a tenant for organizing a tenants' union. New Jersey law lists thirteen specific "just causes" for eviction, including nonpayment of rent, destruction of property, and engaging in illegal activities; if the cause of action is other than these, however, the landlord must prove that he is not retaliating against the tenant. New York State has a "rebuttable presumption" clause in its law, which means that, if a landlord tries to evict a tenant who has made a formal complaint to a housing agency, the burden of proof is on the landlord to show that his action is not in retaliation. Even where such laws are on the books, however, it is possible for a landlord to get even with a tenant by locking him out of his apartment or throwing his furniture out on the street and then waiting for the wheels of justice to grind to a slow resolution of the case. At the start of your organizing effort, therefore, you must warn tenants of the danger of retaliatory eviction, so that they can decide whether or not to participate.

The three major issues of particular concern for tenants are rent-related matters, condominium conversions, and building maintenance.

Rent issues include such matters as security deposits, advance payment of rent, and rent increases. Many states and cities have laws, such as rent-control statutes, to deal with these problems, but again their enforcement varies widely. Some jurisdictions have set up landlord-tenant mediation boards to settle minor disputes, but their rulings often are not legally binding and therefore are difficult to enforce. Experience has shown, however, that just bringing the two parties together to discuss the matter can often lead to a resolution of the problem.

Condominium conversion is a growing phenomenon in many cities, particularly where the housing market is tight. In a condominium a person actually owns his apartment and shares the cost of maintaining the grounds, lobby, heating plant, elevator, and other semipublic areas. Condominium ownership offers many of the same income tax and equity benefits of owning a single-family home without the burden of having to mow the lawn. The major drawback is that converting an apartment building to condominium ownership invariably results in higher total housing costs for the occupants, plus the necessity of having to raise money for a down payment on the mortgage. (The primary reason landlords convert to condominiums is that their costs, especially for utilities and taxes, rise faster than income, so it is smarter to sell the building than to rent it.) Often in such cases some tenants, particularly the elderly or others living on fixed income (such as welfare recipients), can't afford to buy into the "condo." As a result, they get pushed out of their apartments.

If your state or city does not have a law to protect tenants involved in condominium conversion, get one enacted. Such a law should contain a clause stating that a minimum percentage of tenants must agree in writing to the change—35 to 50 percent is the usual number. Current tenants should be given the right to purchase their own apartments first or that of another tenant, should one become available. Special provisions should be made for the elderly and other hardship cases; for example, a requirement to allow them to live in the building as tenants for a stipulated period. All tenants should have the right to remain in their apartments for a reasonable period (six to twelve months), to afford sufficient time to find another place to live. Finally, such a law should emulate that in effect in the District of Columbia, which prohibits condominium conversion in apartment buildings occupied by low- and moderate-income families when the vacancy rate for similarly priced apartments in the city falls below a certain percentage.

When confronted with inadequate building maintenance, one avenue of pursuit for tenants is the use of a receiver. Under receivership the court appoints a person or agency to take control of the building, collect the rent, and make all repairs necessary to bring the building up to code, in addition to paying the mortgage, taxes, and utilities. Once all code violations have been erased and the building is on time with its other payments, the receiver is relieved of his duties. While that procedure sounds simple enough, receivership is really a last-ditch effort. It may work for a while, but the situation often reverts to previous conditions, especially if the landlord is milking the building. Considering the time and legal costs, receivership probably should be considered only when the landlord has abandoned the property.

For these and other problems where a reasonable agreement cannot be made between landlord and tenants, the most effective route for tenants is the confrontation tactics described earlier in this chapter, with one notable addition: tenants can withhold rent as a weapon to use against the landlord. Hence, the rent strike.

As with all organizing tactics, a rent strike should have a clear purpose: to bring the landlord to the bargaining table, make him agree to a list of demands, and build the tenants' organization in case a further confrontation becomes necessary. But a rent strike is also a unique tactic, requiring special knowledge. Again, know the law. Are rent strikes legal in your state? If so, under what conditions? You might want to get the advice of a lawyer, but don't rush out to hire one: lawyers, like other professionals, have a habit of taking over organizations they're supposed to be advising. (See p. 92, "Working with Professionals.") The same goes for hiring a professional tenant organizer.

Know your target, too. If the landlord in question has only a few properties, a rent strike could bring him to his knees, whereas a major slumlord might not be affected by a rent strike in only one or even in a few of his buildings. And of course know your own strength. Those experienced in organizing tenants say that you should have at least half the tenants committed to striking before even considering a rent strike.

Controlling the rent money is a key element of a rent strike. The tenants should set up a rent collection committee of trusted leaders to whom striking tenants *must* pay their rent. I underscore "must" because a rent strike is not a rent holiday. Your tenants' group must be able to prove to a court, as well as to the public, that the rent is being paid, albeit to a tenants' committee, not the landlord. Any tenant who fails to pay would be subject to eviction, and one eviction during a rent strike is enough to start a panic that could lead to the strike's collapse. It is incumbent upon the rent collection committee to collect the rent, keep accurate books, and thereby maintain the integrity of your organization and the righteousness of your goals.

The ultimate goal is, of course, to get the landlord to agree to your demands, whether through legal channels or through direct negotiations with the landlord. Any such agreement should contain a number of key provisions. First, the landlord should recognize the tenants' organization as the sole collective-bargaining agent and not discriminate against or threaten any tenant. Second, he should complete all repairs, improvements, and maintenance work necessary to bring the building up to an agreed-upon standard; these items should be spelled out in detail, with a date for completion. A portion of the rent roll should be kept in a separate account, under the watchful eye of the tenants' organization, to pay for this work.

The landlord should also make all emergency repairs during the rehabilitation period; should the landlord fail to do so, the tenant would have the right to deduct the cost of such repairs from his rent. All work should be overseen and approved by a committee of tenants, which should also hear grievances on such matters as the return of security deposits. All contested matters in the landlord's standard lease should be renegotiated, with particular attention given to rent increases. The standard lease should be rewritten to conform with the agreement. Finally, the tenants' group should have the option to renew the agreement before its expiration date. The agreement could conceivably go beyond these basics, to include rent control during the period of the agreement; the right of tenants to have access to the landlord's books (to see if he is gouging them on rent); the elimination or reduction of security deposits; tenant control of a portion of the rent roll to pay for maintenance, repair, and capital improvements; and veto power over structural or ownership changes in the building, such as conversion to condominium ownership.

Leadership

Eugene McCarthy, the former senator who challenged Lyndon Johnson on the Vietnam War, laid bare the paradox of leadership when he said, "Leaders must be good followers." Leaders must be dynamic, forceful, visionary, even charismatic (to use that worn-out phrase of the sixties), yet humble enough to realize that they do not have all the answers. Furthermore, says MAHA's Rob Schachter, a good leader must be "narrow on the issues, but flexible on the tactics." He must, in other words, have a clear vision of the organization's goals, yet he must be wise enough to seek counsel from the members in determining the ways to achieve these goals. But good leaders need not have all the virtues of Jesus or Gandhi. Ordinary people will do—provided they have an extraordinary commitment to their neighborhoods.

Good leaders just don't happen. They are made. Only the experience of taking up a challenge, confronting an enemy, and fighting through on an issue can test whether a person has leadership qualities. Naturally, there may be awkward moments: the first time a neophyte has to speak before a public group could prove embarrassing for both him and the organization. But such risks must be taken to create new leadership. Special training is available through such groups as the Midwest Academy, the National Training and Information Center, or the Industrial Areas Foundation. (See the List of Organizations and Institutions at the back of this book.) At a more advanced level, says Bill Ariano, executive director of Baltimore's Southeast Community Organization, leaders should be encouraged to attend seminars or take retreats where, isolated from their usual surroundings, they can talk to one another, work out problems of group interaction, and develop themselves more fully.

Recognize, too, that there are different kinds of leaders. The leader who is good at organizing a committee of businessmen to handle finances might not be the best person to face the mayor the next morning in a showdown over community development funds. Some leaders work well in small groups or among their own friends and neighbors; others are street fighters who thrive on toe-to-toe confrontations with an enemy. There are leaders who can tough it out in a public fight, and there are leaders who are expert negotiators behind closed doors. Your organization needs to nurture all kinds of leaders.

Finally, leaders burn out. After months or years of work, it is not uncommon for even the most dedicated leaders simply to give up, to demand time for their families or jobs or for health reasons. (That's one reason why you must keep developing new leaders.) But you can't just kick out leaders who have lost their effectiveness without so much as a thank you. It is important, both for their pride and for the organization's future, that old leaders be given jobs or honorific posts where their experience and skills can be put to good use, but where they will not be obliged to contribute as much time and effort as before. The benefit to the organization is that new leaders will see that there will be a place for them within the organization when the time comes for them to step aside. That sense of continuity is important to maintain.

Working with Professionals

There comes a time in the life of every organization when a special job requires the services of an outside expert, or the organization gets so big that it needs to hire professional staff. What should you be aware of in hiring a consultant, professional staff, or some other kind of expert?

Marie Nahikian, a past director of the Adams-Morgan Organization in Washington D.C., warns, "Watch out that they don't rip you off." She tells of one agency that came to AMO with a proposal to set up a "toy-lending library" in the neighborhood so that they could study how children play. Free toys for the kids— what a fine idea! But then the agency brought in children from outside the neighborhood to study "group interaction"; finally, the professionals just packed up their toys and left when they got sick of the study. "There was no way that the community could benefit from that experience," says Nahikian.

Not only can professionals *use* you, they can *usurp* you. The authors of *The People's Guide to Urban Renewal and Community Development Programs* show exactly how this applies to lawyers (although the criticism could be extended to architects, planners, or sociologists, as well):

> The greatest danger is that lawyers sometimes take over organizations—actively or by default—not because of their politics or leadership abilities but simply because they are lawyers. They have skills and knowledge not readily available to other people. The legal process cloaks itself in a peculiar jargon and complicated paperwork—

not because the law is so difficult to understand but in order to keep it mystified and inaccessible to the people. Many times people assume lawyers know all the answers; lawyers often assume this too. Actually, lawyers simply have certain skills as do organizers, housewives, and other workers. How these skills should be used and for what purposes can only be determined by the community groups lawyers are serving. Lawyers may understand the law—they do not necessarily know about a particular neighborhood, what its problems are, and how these problems should be solved. The community politics and objectives should determine the legal strategy, and not vice versa. The lawyer should not be left to decide "legal" questions which in fact are political issues.

Nonetheless, technical experts, including professional staff, may be essential to an organization's growth. Happily, many neighborhood groups around the country have found ways to get the services of professionals while maintaining political autonomy.

In Brooklyn, for example, the Pratt Institute Center for Community Economic Development (PICCED) offers technical services to community groups throughout New York City. "Our role is basically to come in and facilitate the work of the neighborhood organizers and community leaders," says Ron Shiffman, an assistant professor of architecture at Pratt and PICCED director. "We don't consider ourselves organizers. We work *with* organizers." Policy making always remains with the community groups. PICCED's overall goal, he says, is to "provide the community with the tools," not the decisions.

Some community groups choose to assemble an advisory team of experts to provide ongoing help. The Emergency Tenants Council, a largely Puerto Rican group, worked closely with an architect, a public-interest development corporation, and a law firm to redevelop twenty acres of slums in Boston's South End. "They have been more than paid consultants," says Luz Cuadrado, ETC's executive director. "Some of them have donated their own time. But they didn't make the decisions. The community did." The same applied for ETC's staff. "They helped a lot in the technical part," says Cuadrado. "But the community did the fighting, the organizing, getting people to picket."

One of the more formal technical-advisory approaches is that of the Professional Planning Group, which assists the Roxbury Action Program. "It's a mini-think tank," says former RAP director George Morrison. The planning group—which consists of architects, planners, landscape architects, lawyers, businessmen, and professors and students from Boston-area universities—meets weekly to discuss plans for the redevelopment of the Highland Park neighborhood of Boston. "It's understood that this is a place where the students can get some technical training and field experience, but we make the decisions," says Morrison. "They work for RAP." It was the Professional Planning Group which put together the package that helped RAP build its first "showcase" project, a 115-unit housing redevelopment—and they did it in nine months, something of a record for such a project. Says Morrison, "I don't know how we could have done it without their services."

In short, there are numerous examples of community groups working cooperatively with professionals, hired both as consultants and regular staff, to carry out neighborhood programs. (See the List of Organizations and Institutions at the end of this book.) What should you look for in such an arrangement?

First, consider the obvious expenses—salaries, overhead, materials. How will your group cover these costs? Nobody comes free, not even students—somebody has to supervise them. These costs should be included in your budget.

Then consider what *kind* of professional help you need. Do you want technicians who will supply the numbers and the drawings and then won't be heard from again? Or do you want people who are politically sympathetic to your cause and will become advocates as well? Do you want passive strategists or ideological zealots? Do you hire a fighter or a negotiator? Even the background and temperament of your professionals can have a tremendous bearing on your success. Jack Gleason, one of the antihighway battlers in Southeast Baltimore, says their choice of lawyer definitely affected the outcome of the case. "There was a lawyer who wanted to take it on for free as an advocacy thing, but he was known as a Don Quixote," he recalls. "We decided to go to a prestigious and competent law firm, Semmes, Bowen and Semmes. And we raised the money to pay them, rather than get free legal services." Did the tactic work? "I know that it affected the state highway people to have one of their own [a lawyer from Semmes, Bowen and Semmes] tell them that his clients had a good case against the road and were prepared to take it all the way to the United States Supreme Court. From that point, the highway people started looking for ways to build the road around Fell's Point."

Furthermore, you must decide if your professionals should be local people or outsiders. The professional with a local base is "accepted, credible—he doesn't have to establish himself," says Maureen Hellwig, herself an indigenous planner for Community 21/Northwest Community Organization, in Chicago. "The neighborhood people respect him, because he's chosen to stay. He also shares a common area of knowledge. He has a basic familiarity with the neighborhood." On the other hand, Hellwig notes, "You can be so close to the local situation that it hurts your judgment." That can sometimes be the advantage of calling in an outsider, who is unencumbered by local traditions. Such was the case when Community 21 hired an outsider to supervise the neighborhood's planning effort. "She came in very naïve about the local politics," says Hellwig. "She didn't expect much from the city, but she got a lot."

In the case of paid consultants, advises C. Scott Clark, past president of the Mount Auburn Housing Foundation in Cincinnati, "Retain part of the fee until the job is completely done." Taking this precaution gives you some leverage in case the consultant, in your opinion, fails to live up to his end of the contract.

The most important thing to remember in dealing with professionals, staff members, and consultants alike is that there should be a clear understanding of the services they will perform *and* the areas where they will be ruled out of bounds. The latter most definitely includes final decision making on policies and programs. The membership must retain control of those matters. The professional's duties should be spelled out in writing, in the form of a letter of agreement or a contract, with a clear stipulation of the reasons for which he can be fired and the procedure governing such a situation. Failure to exercise iron-clad control over your professionals, however well-meaning they may be, could result in your organization losing control over its own destiny.

Building Coalitions and Networks

Some issues transcend neighborhood boundaries. Insurance redlining, for instance, often blankets a whole city, not just one neighborhood. In such a case, it is wise for neighborhood groups to work together toward a common goal. That is the basis of a coalition.

It may at first seem unprofitable for one neighborhood group to spend precious time and effort on issues affecting some other neighborhood. But the basis of coalition is that all member organizations ultimately will benefit. "People in neighborhoods realize that, for them to survive, they are going to have to form coalitions with their adjoining communities, so that they can all get a piece of the pie," says Ron Shiffman, of Brooklyn's Pratt Institute. "Through the coalition process they are able to negotiate more for their own neighborhoods than if two neighborhoods fight each other and neither of them gets anything. Coalitions can expand the pie, rather than having neighborhoods fighting for a restricted pie."

Chicago's Metropolitan Area Housing Alliance got started in just such a way. Eight neighborhood organizations found that they were getting a runaround every time they went to housing court. Instead of fighting the issue singly, they held a joint meeting, confronted the housing court officials, and won a monthly day in court for the member organizations.

One of the most experienced coalition-builders in the country is Shel Trapp, a former turf organizer on the West Side of Chicago, now staff director at the National Training and Information Center. "There are some dangers in forming a coalition," he warns. "The local group is going to have to give up some of its identity to the larger group. But there are ways to deal with that. You can have all your press releases list each member group. At meetings, put the leaders of each group at the front table, with signs identifying their organizations. Encourage groups to bring banners and signs or badges to coalition meetings, so that they can hold on to their local identity.

"Coalitions are built on power, not paper," Trapp continues. "The only way coalitions will work is if they have strong local power bases. The local groups must be able to deliver the people.

"Another danger is that coalitions can be split by victory—one group gets greedy and wants more than its share of the spoils. To avoid this, agree beforehand how you will negotiate with the enemy and how you will split the pie when you win.

"Finally, recognize that there are some issues around which neighborhood groups may not be able to coalesce. You're not going to get a coalition of black and white groups to promote busing on the South Side."

Despite these dangers, coalitions have many benefits. "They give you more *power*," says Trapp, clenching a fist. "And, if you have strong power bases within the coalition, you can share actions and spread your manpower." Trapp gives the example of three neighborhood groups which were all having trouble with the same slumlord. They agreed that each group would picket his home once during the week, and then all come together on Friday night. The slumlord eventually signed the agreement. Another advantage of coalitions is that they turn neighborhood leaders into "city leaders." Says Trapp, "It charges them up."

But coalitions can survive only if the member organizations see results. "There should be a payoff for every group in the coalition," says Trapp. "Otherwise, there's no reason for them to participate, and they won't come back."

When an issue extends beyond city and even regional boundaries, however, there may be a need to establish a statewide or national *network*. A network, for lack of a better definition, is a loose, wide-scale coalition of coalitions. The People's Housing Network, for example, pulls together housing groups from all over New York State to lobby for tenants' rights.

The workings of a network can be grasped by briefly examining a case involving National People's Action, a national network of antiredlining groups, based in Chicago. In October 1975, NPA learned that a federal report condemning two notorious mortgage banking houses was being withheld from the public by the then Secretary of Housing and Urban Development, Carla Hills. NPA invited leaders from a dozen cities around the country to meet in Chicago, where they pondered how to get Hills to act on the report and suspend the two firms. One option was for all the groups to go to Washington to demonstrate at Hills's office, but that would have been too costly. Instead, it was decided that each group would hold demonstrations at HUD offices in their areas to complain about local issues, and to send a delegation to Washington to emphasize the national issue. Thus, instead of getting coverage only in the Washington papers, the network's demands were spread over a dozen cities. Eventually, Hills was pushed into meeting with NPA to discuss mortgage banking practices.

Community Organization vs. Community Development

Much of this chapter has focused on the confrontation side of organizing—stopping the city from ruining the neighborhood, preventing highway officials from building a road, picketing a slumlord. As a community organization begins to grow and mature, however, it reaches a point where a crucial decision must be made: shall the organization go on confronting "the enemy"? Or shall the organization negotiate with the enemy and ultimately enter into partnership with him? And if the latter, under what terms and for what purpose?

"We knew we could stop the city from doing things, through the usual confrontation tactics," says Jack Gleason, the first president of the Southeast Community Organization. "But if we were going to achieve the revitalization of Southeast Baltimore, there were things *we* had to do, from the positive standpoint—housing, school reform, and so on. That's when we went into the neighborhood economic development stage."

It is a bold step to go from telling someone in authority what he is doing wrong to deciding for yourself what must be done and how it shall be done. This is not to say that beating the enemy over the head is not hard work, or that it does not require imagination, determination, and all the other fine qualities demanded of good leaders. But to take a neighborhood, erase the slate, and say "Here is what *we* want and how *we* propose to get it" requires a different, if not greater, commitment. Mayor Daley of Chicago always hit his critics with one question when they charged him with not doing enough. He would ask, "How many trees did *you* plant today?" Daley knew that it takes one kind of talent to be able to complain and criticize and quite another to plan and build.

Nor is the move from community organizing and confrontation politics to community development and negotiation politics without risk. There is the real and present danger that your group may be co-opted by the enemy. SECO itself was split over this very issue, when one faction wanted to stay with confrontation politics, while another wanted to move on to a development strategy that would have involved forming partnerships with former enemies. Those who favored confrontation were motivated by the fear that SECO would lose its credibility with the people by "going establishment." It might accomplish a great many paper goals, they implied, but at the cost of the community losing control over its own destiny.

The last temptation is the greatest treason:
To do the right deed for the wrong reason.

"You ask yourself, by making partnerships with the city or with business interests, can you maintain your autonomy, your clout?" notes SECO's Jack Gleason. "We came up with the strong conviction that the difference between success and failure in a community development effort was the existence of a strong community organization. You can't do community development without having strong roots in the community."

Gleason has put his finger on what may be the answer. Organizing and development are not separate issues. Organizing cannot proceed if there are no goals, no targets to shoot for. Likewise, development has no worthwhile purpose if the people are not behind it. In my opinion, it is the litmus test of an organization's maturity when it can use both organizing/confrontation tactics *and* development/partnership strategies. Neighborhoods have to know how to defend themselves, but they must also know what they're defending themselves for. In Part Three, we'll examine ways to develop long-range goals and plans for your community. But first, we must not forget two key ingredients for every community organization, money and publicity.

4

MONEY AND
PUBLICITY

No organization can survive without money. Even the smallest group has to pay for the phone, stamps, and stationery. How much money do you need, and where do you get it?

Before turning to these matters, let me issue a couple of warnings. First, any money-raising campaign should fit into your organization's overall program for development. Avoid financial ventures that fail to promote the organization's goals. "Don't raise money just to raise money," says MAHA's Gale Cincotta. "While you're fund-raising, you're also organizing, informing the business community, the churches, and so on, trying to get them involved in the issues, not just in giving money." As a corollary, since one of your goals should be to maintain an open, democratic structure, don't charge membership dues. It's a sure-fire way to raise money, but it may also exclude people. Encourage *donations* from your members, but don't disenfranchise those who can't (or won't) pay dues.

The second point is that new organizations too often make the mistake of looking for a handout from outside the community before tapping local resources. The catch phrase is, "Let's apply for a grant." Seeking grants is fine. (See p. 106, "Grantsmanship.") But not before you have dipped into the local well for support. It's amazing how much wealth neighborhoods have. "We make three or four thousand dollars in a day or two just selling used books," says Rachele Wall, of the West Village Committee, in New York City. "We also have an auction where we make five thousand dollars in one day. We say to people, 'Look, if you've got something you're going to throw out, give it to us instead.' " In the early stages especially, fund-raising should be an integral part of organizing. Getting a grant from some far-off foundation may bring in a windfall, but not necessarily many new, enthusiastic members. With those caveats clearly in mind, you're ready to start raising money.

The Basics of Fund-Raising

The first step in initiating a fund-raising campaign is to pull together a mix of people to form a finance committee. Look for people who have something to give—*time* (ministers, old folks), *expertise* (accountants, lawyers), *facilities or services* (ministers again—get their basements for meetings; school teachers with access to duplicating machines), *prestige* (doctors, athletes, public officials), and—lest we forget—*money* (local businessmen, bankers, etc.). They should immediately begin the process of establishing a nonprofit corporation and getting tax-exempt status for your organization under either Section 501(c)(3) (for a "charitable, religious ... education" organization) or 501(c)(4) (for a "civic league or social welfare organization"). Contact the local IRS office for a copy of *How to Apply for Recognition of Exemption for an Organization*, Publication 557, which explains the process; and *Income Tax Deduction for Contributions*, Publication 526, which describes which kinds of organizations are exempt. It's imperative to have tax-exempt status, not only to save you money, of course, but also so that your donors can write off their contributions to you. A storefront lawyer may be able to help you, or get advice from a friendly nonprofit group that has gone through the process. It takes a while to get the applications approved; in the meantime, you might be able to have donations funneled through another tax-exempt organization.

The committee's next responsibility is to develop the budget. Here is where you will cash in on the experience of your bankers, accountants, and other businessmen. Form a subcommittee to work up a proposed budget. The final budget will, of course, have to be approved by the general membership.

Finally, the committee should conduct research to see who in the neighborhood has money to give. If the committee has been well selected, they should have no trouble identifying money sources. Start with the committee members themselves. After all, that's why you asked some of them to join, isn't it? Then expand the scope to local businesses, institutions, churches, unions, and wealthy residents.

Certain tricks of fund-raising can be learned only from experience. Gale Cincotta, that wily ex-housewife who through numerous battles has earned the reputation of "Mrs. Neighborhoods, U.S.A.," and Ed Shurna, a staff member at Chicago's National Training and Information Center, regularly give groups of organizing trainees some tips that you can't learn from books alone. Here are some of their thoughts about getting money from potential donors:

Keep your contributors informed. Put them on steering committees, call them, send them reports. Give them a package of "accomplishments"—press releases, news clippings, written material on each victory.

Find a "friend" who will crack the door: "Mr. X of Downtown Bank gave $100 this year, and he said you might be interested in helping us." Or find one key person in each company who will put you in contact with his colleagues. Then ask each new donor to sponsor a luncheon of other businessmen so that your community group can deliver its spiel.

At these luncheons, put pledge cards on the tables and have shills planted in the audience to write a check on the spot. If you can't get them to pledge, have them put down a time when they're available for appointments.

If you get a hard-line businessman who wants to know what the *community* is contributing, you should have figures ready on how much time your volunteers spend on the organization. Businessmen appreciate that time is money.

Rehearse your speech. Try role-playing, too. There's nothing worse than to get an appointment with a big spender and then to forget what you wanted to say.

Tell businessmen about the practical benefits of community development: "Creating a better neighborhood will help your sales, because people will be out shopping if they're not afraid to walk the streets." Or, "Your insurance rates may go down if the neighborhood improves."

Keep plugging away, even if you don't get any money at first. Businessmen respect salesmanship. At some point, even out of sheer frustration, they're going to give you some money.

If it's impossible to get money, get in-kind help—professional services, auditing, products. "Xerox wouldn't give us any money, but they gave us $1,000 worth of copying paper," said Shurna. Ask to use their building for meetings or for office space.

If they make a pledge, don't bill them annually. Send them monthly bills. It seems like less of a bite.

Be innovative. "We had a luncheon for funeral directors and florists," said Cincotta. "They all knew each other, of course, and they had a great time."

The funeral director/florist luncheon illustrates an important point: with so many groups looking for money, you've got to be clever, inventive, and ready to capitalize on your assets. "We have a lot of famous artists in our neighborhood, so we had a big art show," says Rachele Wall of New York's West Village. "We threw a big cocktail party, very chic, with champagne and hors d'oeuvres. We had a couple of hundred paintings, and we sold them as a gallery does, on a percentage basis. We made $9,000." Many historic neighborhoods sponsor house tours for which they get both excellent publicity and revenue from the sale of refreshments, tickets, pamphlets, guidebooks, and souvenirs. There are lots of ways to raise money (see the list on p. 105) but it's usually a lot more fun and more profitable if your fund-raiser somehow fits in with your overall neighborhood image.

My favorite fund-raiser is the annual Hill Day Festival in St. Louis's Italian neighborhood. Preparations for the "Festa Italiana" start the day after the *last* Hill Day. "All year long, our women work three nights a week in the school cafeteria making things for the festival," says Mary Ronzio, a volunteer for the Hill 2000 community group. They make artificial flowers, red-white-and-green hats, Italian recipe books, stuffed animals, purses, candles shaped like frogs or Volkswagen automobiles, embroidery, pillowcases, quilts, scarves, crochet work, dolls, and other handicrafts. One year, Mrs. Carolyn De Mattei alone made a thousand hats. Everything is stamped "Made on the Hill." Throughout the year, as many as two hundred people work steadily toward the big day. On Hill Day, five hundred people are on the job to greet crowds that have numbered as high as 150,000.

Hill Day may be the grandest ethnic festival in this country. In St. Louis, it's the oldest, and still the best, of a dozen such fests. The day starts with a High Mass at noon, usually celebrated by the archbishop. When the ceremony is over, the fun begins. There's Italian singing and folk-dancing. A parade of floats depicting scenes of Italian-American history. A display of Italian-made automobiles. The traditional grape-stomping contest. Bocce games. Eating contests. A flea market. A concert in the park. Many times, Joe Garagiola, a native son who went on to the big leagues with the St. Louis Cardinals baseball team and NBC Sports, has been the host for a kind of homespun vaudeville show. And everyone, no matter what his or her nationality, wears a button that pleads, "Kiss me, I'm Italian."

But what makes a festa a festa is food. In the weeks before Hill Day, the women work twelve hours a day, cooking and freezing Italian delicacies in incredible quantities: sixty thousand meatballs for hero sandwiches, eight thousand pizzas, a ton of salsiccia (sausage) and mortadella (a kind of bologna), a thousand pounds of mastaccioli (a pasta), and even more lasagne—enough to make seven thousand servings of each. Not to mention some of the real specialties: gnocchi, risotto, eggplant parmigiana, spiedini, and bracinolone. And the pastries! Pinolata, cialde, sfingi. To top off the meal, there's gelati and granita. And to top off the day, there's a gigantic fireworks display.

Hill Day is a success not only because of the publicity it creates and the money it brings in (enough to finance the Hill 2000 Corporation's programs for a whole year), but because it reinforces the community's goals: identification of the residents' Italian-American heritage; neighborhood self-help (all services and supplies are donated); and commonality of purpose. Besides which, the people have a helluva good time doing it—and having fun is a vital ingredient in any money-raising enterprise. After all, it's hard to get people enthusiastic about a project that's going to be sheer drudgery.

The following list provides additional suggestions for more than fifty fund-raising projects that have proved successful in other communities. There's no guarantee that any of them will work for your group, and merely copying someone else's idea could lead to disaster, particularly if poorly executed. Another St. Louis neighborhood tried to run an ethnic fair, but neglected to buy enough weather insurance (you really *can* buy it!), and took a beating when it rained the day of their event. Use these suggestions to stimulate even better ideas that will really work for your neighborhood. Many of them are described in full in Joan Flanagan's excellent *Grass Roots Fundraising Book* (see Bibliography).

ad books	door-to-door sales
antique fairs	(cards, cookies, etc.)
art sale	fair
auction	food sale
bazaar	garage sale
Bingo or Lotto*	house tour
block party	"Las Vegas Night"*
book sale	lawn and garden work
bottle returns	marathon
carnival	market day
caroling	movie premiere
carwash	movies
celebrity lecture	"Night at the Races"*
cocktail party	outing, excursion
coffee/at home party	party
concert	plant sale
cookbook	potluck dinner
craft festival	radio or television marathon
dance	raffle (prizes donated by
dinner, dinner dance	merchants)*
direct mail	recycling program

*Check to see whether this event is legal in your community.

rent-a-kid program
rummage sale
speaker's bureau
sports benefit
tag sale
talent show

telephone solicitation
theater benefit
tournament (tennis, squash)
tour
trick-or-treating
white-elephant sale

In conclusion, remember these points about raising money:

1.) *Keep accurate accounts.* Baltimore's Bill Ariano recommends that you have a fiscal officer—a finance committee member or a staff member with accounting skills, or a qualified bookkeeper—whose reports you can understand. Have an auditor in several times a year, just to keep on the safe side. Put a strong check on office supplies, photocopying, and other routine expenditures: they can eat your budget up if someone isn't watching them carefully. Require your fiscal officer to report regularly to the finance committee. Don't jeopardize the good work your organization is doing by keeping bad books and thus opening the door to scandal.

2.) *Develop diversified money sources.* Don't keep going to the same donor. Don't rely on the government to bail you out. Don't be so reliant on one source that you lose your autonomy.

3.) *Integrate your money-making campaign with your organizing program.* Make sure both fit into the goals and policies of your organization.

4.) *Have fun making money.* Use your fund-raisers, particularly the parties and events, to celebrate your victories. Let your members get some enjoyment out of their hard work.

Grantsmanship

There's a wonderful cartoon by the *New Yorker* artist Robert Day, depicting a young man throwing handfuls of money out the window of an office building, as his boss rushes in. "Just a minute, young man," says the boss. "That's not quite the way we do things here at the Ford Foundation."

Getting a grant these days *is* hard work: no one is throwing money out windows. The demand from well-meaning groups like yours simply outstrips the supply. You may devote tremendous amounts of time and effort—a year is not uncommon—to writing grant proposals, only to come up dry. That's why your members should debate whether to get into the grantsmanship game at all. Certainly you don't want to do so before having exhausted your local financial resources.

Some major sources of grants are businesses, churches, unions, and government. Most large corporations, as well as the big churches and unions, have separate philanthropic foundations. (See the List of Organizations and Institutions.) Remember, if you can't get cash from these sources, get something else—office space, services, or supplies.

The most comprehensive listing of federal programs is the *Catalog of Federal Domestic Assistance*, put out by the Office of Management and Budget. It describes the programs, the purpose of each, who can apply, the application procedure, and where you can get more information. Many federal grants are made through "requests for proposals" in the *Commerce Business Daily*, a Department of Commerce publication. It's a smart idea, when applying for a federal grant for the first time, to get help from an experienced grantsman.

The best resources for private philanthropy are the Foundation Center and the Grantsmanship Center. Write them for their most recent publication lists. In particular, you will want to become familiar with *The Foundation Directory* (seventh edition, published by the Foundation Center, 1979), which lists more than 2,500 foundations with assets of $1 million or more. Once you've gone through this impressive document, you must narrow your choice to a few hot prospects. Again, the odds improve if you stay local, so apply to the many small foundations where the competition is usually less keen. Do extensive research on the target foundations. Read their annual reports. See what kinds of activities they have supported recently. Don't be afraid to ask what they're looking for. Make sure, too, that the foundation makes grants for the kinds of things you are requesting. Some foundations don't give money for brick-and-mortar projects, even though they may be interested in housing or community development. Don't waste your time applying for something that you can't get. Contact someone at the foundation and ask, "What does your foundation want to do with its money?" This can save you untold amounts of time. My wife literally spent months working on a proposal to a major federal foundation, but not until she picked up the phone and talked to some of the funding officers did she learn that her proposal did not contain the right "buzz words."

The grant application itself is made in the form of a proposal, a written statement of why you need the grant, how much you want, and what you'll do with the money. Two former foundation offiers, F. Lee Jacquette and Barbara I. Jacquette, have some good advice for proposal writers: "Keep the written proposal short and clear. State at the outset what is to be accomplished, who expects to accomplish it, how much it will cost, and how long it will take. Avoid broad, sweeping generalizations. . . . Test the proposition on others before submitting it. Be prepared to rethink and to rewrite."

An excellent booklet, *A Guide to Fundraising and Proposal Writing*, gives a useful ten-step approach to proposal writing. Here is an abbreviated version:

1.) *Introduction.* Tell who you are, what you want to do, how much money you need, who will conduct the project, and where.

2.) *Information on your group.* Explain your organization's history, accomplishments, structure, the size of its membership, its philosophy, mission, purpose, and future plans.

3.) *The problem.* Describe the identifiable, measurable social condition—for example: "The Uptown neighborhood has the worst housing in the city." Show that the condition is unacceptable to you or someone else. Analyze the causes of the condition.

4.) *The goal.* The goal must be related to the problem and must be measurable in terms of numbers of people affected ("150 families will be rehoused"); quantitative improvements ("150 houses to be rehabilitated"); and time ("within a two-year period").

5.) *The objectives.* Spell out the major checkpoints needed to ensure that you fulfill your goals: "By the end of the sixth month, twenty-five families will be rehoused."

6.) *Activities.* List the steps that will be taken to achieve each of the objectives: First month: "Occupy office and hire staff."

7.) *Resources.* Describe the people, money, supplies and equipment, and technical assistance needed to carry out each of the activities: "Registered architect: $1,000 fee for blueprints and drawings to redesign structures."

8.) *The evaluation.* Tell how you will determine whether the project accomplished its goals.

9.) *The budget.* Justify all projected costs and show the expected sources of income, particularly if you are applying to more than one source for grants. Be sure to tell how much your organization will contribute, either in money or in-kind payments (services, office space, volunteer time). The budget must be professional-looking.

10.) *The appendix.* Include all the backup material that will reinforce your proposal—health statistics, housing data, census information, news clippings, studies, annual reports—plus your articles of incorporation (assuming your group is incorporated), bylaws, personnel policies, résumés of staff members, IRS documents, and related information.

In addition, some foundations require grant applicants to get recommendations from authorities in the field. Find out from your sources at the foundation which authorities have the most clout and what they should say.

Finally, meet the deadline for applications. Foundations are very strict about deadlines. Allow plenty of time to revise your application.

The following checklist, adapted from *A Guide to Funding Sources Research*, should help you avoid the worst mistakes. In addition, consult the books suggested in the Bibliography of Reference Materials for more detailed information on writing proposals.

CHECKLIST FOR YOUR FOUNDATION PROPOSAL

1. Is the proposal *appropriate* to the funding source?
2. Is the *purpose* of the proposal clearly stated in the introduction?
3. Is the *program plan* logical, flexible, and related to the problem you have defined?
4. Are the *objectives* measurable and clear? Are they realistic?
5. Have you described the *local resources* you have put together

(voluntary contributions of manpower, donations of computer time or office space) to aid your organization on the project?

6. Have you provided for an *evaluation* of the project?
7. Have you described the *new or unique aspects* of the project?
8. Have you *coordinated* the project with similar ones being done by other groups?
9. Have you described how the *results* of the program can apply to the work of other groups?
10. If you are unknown to the funding source, have you included a *history* of your group?
11. Have you explained why the organization is well-suited to carry out this project?
12. Is the description of the *project personnel* detailed, but not boring?
13. Is the *budget* explained in detail?
14. Is the budget projected over the total time of the project?
15. Have you detailed the *donations* your organization will make to the budget?
16. Is the *narrative description* of the proposed program concise (four to six pages, not including appendix)? Is it typed, double-spaced?
17. Is there material in the narrative that belongs in the appendix?
18. Is there material in the *appendix* that could be omitted?
19. Has an experienced person read and criticized your proposal?
20. Have you included the *Articles of Incorporation* (if your group is incorporated) and the *notice of tax exemption* from the IRS?

Don't be disappointed if you don't get your grant. There are always more applicants than available dollars. And don't expect to keep coming back to the same foundation. "Most foundations don't want to fund you for more than two years," says Maureen Hellwig, a planner with Community 21/Northwest Community Organization, in Chicago. After two or three years, the foundation expects you to be on your own. As Robert A. Mayer puts it, foundations "do not like to breed albatrosses."

Going Public

With the possible exception of the CIA, every organization needs to publicize its efforts—to attract new members, to gather support on a specific issue, to raise money, to influence public officials, to keep the troops loyal and interested. A publicity campaign is designed to achieve that kind of recognition. First, however, your organization must decide the purpose behind its publicity efforts. The organization should have a clear concept of the reasons for gaining publicity and a policy for carrying out these goals. In contrast, when is publicity to be avoided? Obviously, you want to minimize bad publicity. You also need to consider how much the publicity should be focused on individual leaders or staff members. Who shall speak for the organization? These issues must be thrashed out by the membership, and a policy defined.

The next step is to appoint a chairman to head the publicity committee. The publicity chairman should be someone with imagination, good stage presence and speaking ability, and familiarity with the local press. His efforts and those of paid staff charged with publicity work should be overseen by the publicity committee, which should make regular reports to the general membership.

A number of publicity techniques, each with advantages and disadvantages, have proven useful to community groups. A *direct telephone campaign* has the advantage of neighbor-to-neighbor contact at moderate cost, but requires an army of volunteers and, unless there is some kind of written follow-up, may not be effective. The same applies to *door-to-door solicitation*, which has more personal appeal than telephoning and allows simultaneous distribution of written material, but which requires even more volunteers. *Bumper stickers* and *posters* are useful in announcing a single event—"Come to the Belden Neighborhood Fair, September 13–14"—but cost money and lose their news value fast. *Leaflets, flyers*, or *handbills* are often cheaper to print than posters, but are hard to distribute. *Exhibits* at public buildings or gathering places can help show off the neighborhood, but their construction requires people with artistic talent and the immediate effect on the public is probably not great.

Setting up a *speaker's bureau* brings the personal element into play and is especially useful when your organization is trying to influence a small group, such as potential donors. I've seen some masters at this game, people like Arthur Ziegler of the Pittsburgh History and Landmarks Foundation, who can give such a spellbinding talk on why such-and-such building should be saved that the audience not only wants to make donations, they also want to join the cause. To be effective, however, a speech requires the talents of a uniquely gifted and knowledgeable person; otherwise it can turn into a fiasco, and your group can actually lose points with the public.

One way to get around this problem is to use a prerecorded, synchronized *slide presentation*. Take lots of good color photographs of your neighborhood, mount them on slides, and arrange them in proper order in a carousel. Write a script describing the slides, get your best public speaker to record it on tape, or ask a professional announcer from the local radio station to volunteer his services. (Put a "beep" or tone in whenever the slide is supposed to be changed.) You might also get the audiovisual or speech class of the local college to put the slide show together for you. Presenting such a "speech" can be a very effective technique, as I've seen demonstrated by members of the Hyde Park Restoration Effort, a community group in St. Louis. They trot their slide show around to conferences and public events, winning audiences to their side, especially when one or two Hyde Parkers round out the presentation with a description of their own experiences of life in the neighborhood, followed by a question-and-answer period. Obviously, there is some expense in this—less than there would be to produce a 16 mm film, but still high. Yet, if you get volunteer services—coupled perhaps with a donation of equipment from a local camera shop—you can keep the cost of your permanent "road show" to a minimum.

The final option is *paid advertising*. Most struggling organizations can't afford to pay for publicity, but there may be occasions when it is absolutely imperative, as might be the case if your side of a controversy has been shut out of the media and you feel you must make a statement. If you must deplete your precious coffers by paying for ads, get the most for your advertising dollar. Try to share the cost of the ad with other groups who sympathize with you. The authors of *The Grassroots Primer* advise, "Always ask people to do something (write a letter, send a coupon, attend a hearing, vote for your side, etc.), and always tell them where to contact you to join or send money." In general, though, paid advertising should be a last resort.

Perhaps the fastest and cheapest way to get publicity is through the media. What's the best way to get the word out to the newspapers, television, and radio? My advice is to put yourself in a reporter's shoes. A reporter needs at least one fresh story every working day. If your group can supply him timely, interesting ideas for stories, you'll be helping him, while gaining valuable free publicity for your organization.

As a journalist myself, I've found that the most important quality a reporter looks for in any source is reliability. The reporter must trust the source to give him accurate, complete, newsworthy information. A reporter hates to be chewed out by his editor or news director for having submitted an inaccurate story, but his embarrassment will be compounded if the error is attributable to a once-trusted source. "They get screwed over once, and they drop that issue the next time," says Chicago's Gale Cincotta.

The first rule in dealing with the press, then, is *be reliable, consistent, and honest.* As Gale Cincotta puts it, "Make sure it happened like you say it happened, and that you're not 'media-freaking' someone."

Second, learn to *cultivate the press.* Get to know which reporters cover your beat. Spend time with them, even when there's little prospect of an immediate payoff in terms of a story. "You must have great patience with the press," says Rachele Wall, a leader of the West Village Committee. "You don't always go to them to get a story put in. Sometimes you just talk to them, and say, 'I didn't come here to get a story put in, but I want you to know what we're doing about such and such.' Very often, they *will* put a story in." Make reporters identify with your organization. Invite the press to community functions—not just the newsworthy ones, but social functions as well. In a sense, you are trying to get on the reporter's good side as well as giving him background material for future stories, without corrupting his integrity or your organization's.

The third point is to *meet the media's technical needs.* Deadlines are crucial to reporters, therefore, give them plenty of notice about upcoming events. (See p. 115 for information on press releases.) Don't schedule a press conference for five o'clock if you hope to have it covered by the six o'clock news program—television people need more time than that to set up their equipment and edit the film or tape. The new mini-cams are also making live television coverage of events more feasible; but it is still advisable to give the press, especially the electronic media, as much notice as possible so that they can meet their deadlines. Radio news is more flexible, since reporters can phone in stories.

How else can you help the media do their job? If a new reporter comes on your beat, fill him in on your organization's background. Give reporters material to use for the days when they're frantic for a story—weekends, the "dog days" of August when everyone is on vacation, or other slack periods. Grant reporters exclusive interviews whenever possible. After all, every reporter wants to beat the competition.

Finally, be creative in dealing with the press. Figure new ways to get your message out. Mary Perot Nichols, a former editor with the *Village Voice* and one of the leaders of the antihighway fight in Greenwich Village in the sixties, recalls how her group "had an art show to raise money, and the *Times* covered it from that angle, so we got a story on the arts pages." Or try for coverage on the op-ed page by writing a letter to the editor. (A tip from a former editor: if your letter gets published, have someone else write the next one. Editors like variety, too.) Reply to television and radio editorials. Get your announcements read on the "community bulletin board" segments carried by many radio and television stations. Do the same on the "calendar" pages of your local newspapers. Suggest ideas to the producers of radio and television talk shows—"The Crosstown Expressway: Pro and Con"—and mention competent spokesmen from your neighborhood as possible guests for such shows. Some cities have community newspapers that carry free classified advertisements: put your notice in that space. In short, become familiar with your local news media and use all their services to help you get your message out.

Some words of warning about the press. Don't expect reporters to give only your side of the story. They have to be objective, which means that they must present all responsible viewpoints in a story. Of course, objectivity can be turned to your advantage. "I had a television group contact me, and they were a hundred percent against us," recalls Rachele Wall. "But after I talked to them, I convinced them that our program had merit. They polled both sides, but at least we got our side in." Also, don't blame the press for bad publicity your organization might suffer. Their job is to report the news, not cover it up. Finally, don't count on the press to be friendly forever. Reporters tend to favor underdogs, because they make "good copy"—David and Goliath and all that. But, notes Mary Nichols, "As you begin winning, sometimes the press turns on you." The press may suspect you of selling out to the establishment, or worse. In that situation, you have to convince the reporters and editors that your ideals are still high, your struggle remains valid, and the press should continue to cover you.

Periodically, your group will want to notify the media of important meetings, fund-raising functions, press conferences, and similar events. The time-honored and still most effective way to reach them is the press release. But to get reporters to take an interest in your activity, you have to write a good press release.

The form of the press release is nearly as rigid as the Spenserian stanza. It contains several elements placed in specific positions on your organization's stationery, as the following sample release illustrates.

Sample Press Release

Citizens for Better Housing
21 Center Street
Newtonville, Minnesota
833-5555

FOR IMMEDIATE RELEASE   Contact: William Exter
                                          833-5555 (office)
                                          555-8383 (home)

CITY NEIGHBORHOODS REDLINED
BY BANKS, NEW STUDY SHOWS

Lending institutions systematically refuse to make mortgage and home improvement loans in older neighborhoods of the city, according to a report issued today (April 5) by Citizens for Better Housing.

"The banks and savings institutions are redlining the older areas, and nothing is being done about it," said Edna Falls, president of CBH.

Falls called upon Mayor York and Governor Abrams to appoint a blue-ribbon commission to investigate the charges made in the citizens' group's 92-page report, "Starve the City, Feed the Suburbs." (A copy of the full report is attached.)

The report states that eight of the city's ten major lending institutions devote less than 10 percent of total assets to inner-city mortgage lending. An average of 70 percent of all mortgage loans are made in the suburbs.

Citizens for Better Housing is a nonprofit coalition of nineteen neighborhood organizations and block clubs devoted to improving housing conditions in the city.

At the left side of the page is the release date, usually "For Immediate Release," but sometimes for release at a specific time and date to coordinate with your scheduled activity. On the right-hand side is the "contact," the person or persons responsible for answering reporters' questions, granting interviews, and giving out more information. Below the "release date" in the center of the page (or, sometimes on the left side), is the "slug," or headline, in capital letters and never more than three lines long. Then comes the body of the release, beginning with the "lead," or the newsy first sentence of the story. The lead should tell the press what is newsworthy about the item you're describing in the release. It should answer the standard journalistic questions—who, what, when, where, why, and how. The rest of the story can be fleshed out in subsequent paragraphs. If you go on to a new page, put the word "-MORE-" at the bottom right side. To end the release, center the journalist's final symbol, "-30-," below the last sentence.

Some tips from a former reporter who has read all too many

press releases: First, keep them short—one page, if possible, two pages at the most. Editors get piles of releases dumped on their desks every day. Rarely do they read more than the first page. If the story is worth covering, they will assign a reporter to ferret out the facts. (That's where your "contact" comes in: he must be able to work closely with the press and answer their questions.) To avoid writing more than two pages, try to put the extra information into some kind of "backup" report—an added item that can be clipped to the press release—and say, "See attached report" or "Full schedule of events attached." Don't burden editors or reporters with too much material in the release itself.

The more the release looks like real news copy, the greater its chances of being used. Therefore, use white paper (8½ by 11 inches) and a standard typewriter head. *Never* use a script font to type your release. If possible, do not hyphenate at the end of lines, and keep paragraphs whole as you go from one page to another.

In the body of the release, double-space the copy, particularly the lead. This is especially true for straightforward announcements of upcoming events, which very often will be used verbatim by the editor. To make your release seem more like a news story, you might also want to include quotations from key individuals or a document you are citing. It's also more dramatic to cite specific actions your group undertook: "Citizens in the Belden area today called upon State Asemblyman Egan to introduce a bill . . ."

I always like to see a press release end with a brief description of the organization, just so that the reporter knows exactly who you are: "BCO is a nonprofit development corporation, founded in 1972, to promote better housing conditions for the Belden community."

Including black-and-white photographs with the release improves your chances of being publicized, especially in the newspapers. The photos should be clear "glossies" (not matte finish), preferably 8 by 10 inches. Each photo should have a caption telling who is in the picture and what they're doing: "Left to right, Congressman William Jones, BCO President Merrill Smith, and Rev. Arthur Herndon, attending the BCO swearing-in ceremony for new officers." This should be typed on a separate piece of paper and taped or glued to the back of the photo. Well-composed, "active" photographs have the greatest chance of being used.

Finally, make sure the press release gets to the right people. Your publicity chairman should have a list of the reporters and editors who cover your beat. The release should be addressed to them personally. Better yet, hand-deliver them. A release mailed simply to "The Editor" or "News Director" will get lost at a busy newspaper or broadcast station. Don't hesitate to send more than one copy of the release to a newspaper or station; doing so only enhances your chance of being covered. Your publicity committee should follow up on the release by calling the appropriate editor or reporter and asking if he received the notice and whether he needs more information.

Another traditional way to tell your story is the press conference. A good press conference is not easy to pull off. Your publicity committee may put in hours of work, only to find that no one picked up the story. How do you avoid such a catastrophe? First, you must get the press to show up. Then you must give them a story that is worth running.

Do your homework, and follow the steps outlined above. Give the press plenty of notice. Feed them press releases and backup material. At the press conference itself, give reporters a "press kit" with the release, pertinent reports, a brochure about your organization, and reprints of any relevant news stories. Follow up with phone calls to reporters and editors. Schedule the event so that the television crews can get their film or videotape back to the station in time for the evening news show.

The choice of place is also crucial. Holding the press conference in your neighborhood has the advantage of creating "local color," as newsmen like to call such a setting, and makes it easier for your people to get there. But if your neighborhood is far from the media center of the city, it may be inconvenient for reporters and broadcasting crews, who often have to cover several stories a day. Sometimes, therefore, it is worth holding a press conference downtown. No matter where you hold it, always remember to pick a room smaller than you need, to give the appearance of a crowd of great numbers.

You also should decide beforehand exactly who will speak. The most effective format is for one person from the community to orchestrate the press conference, describing the major issues and then passing the microphone over to others for further elaboration. It is useful for each spokesman to identify himself and his organization, creating an impression of widespread support for your cause.

At the press conference itself, don't be surprised if you wind up holding two separate sessions, one for the print media, one for the broadcasters. The demands of television are such that each station may want to get its own "shot" of your key leaders giving their speeches. They may even ask you to rehearse your lines!

Any mistakes will be quickly forgiven if you deliver a good story. And here is your greatest risk: call too many press conferences that fizzle out and you're asking the press to write your group off as a bunch of deadbeats.

This is all the more true for television, which requires not only a good story, but "good film," as the people in the business say. It is a somewhat sad commentary on the medium that many television executives worry more about the image than the substance of the news. You may be compelled, therefore, to create a "media event" to get your story on the air. In other words, you need a gimmick, and a good one. Television is getting sophisticated. No longer will camera crews rush over to cover ten people holding signs up in a "protest march." But remember: if you hope to avoid seeming to pander to the media, you've got to come up with ideas that don't diminish your organization's integrity.

Bill Kelch, a leader of the West Canton community in Baltimore, found his group being ignored by the media in their fight to prevent the state from mooring a six-hundred-inmate prison ship near their community. In desperation, he entered a hog-calling contest in the knowledge that the media would cover such an unusual event. He didn't win the contest, but he did get his picture in the newspapers and on television, wearing a T-shirt with the words "No Prison Ship" on it. From then on, the media were able to identify Kelch as an anti-prison-ship spokesman. His original technique was certainly a gimmick, but it gave him the opportunity to tell West Canton's story. Thus, the gimmick was justifiable.

To reiterate, your group has to be innovative to get the media's attention these days. Keep the gimmicks within the bounds of good taste and, most important, make sure they fit into an overall publicity policy that preserves the integrity of your organization.

The Neighborhood Newsletter

Once your organization is founded, you'll want to keep your members regularly informed about upcoming meetings, rallies, reports, activities, and numerous other items. Probably the best way to reach a large number of people is through a neighborhood newsletter. Newsletters fulfill a variety of purposes. "We send out a newsletter once a month," says Rachele Wall, of the West Village Committee in New York. "Any form of communication with people who are your allies is very important." Newsletters are a good way to keep reporters apprised of what's happening in your community, but their main purpose is to keep your own membership informed, especially about events not covered by the regular press. Not only can newsletters be a unifying device, they also serve an educational purpose, carrying information on homemaking, the schools, new residents, neighborhood history, and perhaps reminiscences by old-timers who recall the early days of the community.

Putting out a newsletter on a regular basis is a challenge. You'll want to appoint one member of your publicity committee to take charge, preferably someone with publication experience. He should have volunteers or even staff members to help. To get started, I recommend pulling in the services of the local high-school or college journalism department. Get one of the teachers or a qualified editor on the school paper to help you with the mechanics. It's not as hard as it seems: if high-school students can put out a newspaper, your organization can publish a newsletter.

The task will be made much easier if you get a copy of the booklet *How to Do Leaflets, Newsletters, and Newspapers*. The author, Nancy Brigham, designed it precisely to help community groups get started with basic publications. Brigham covers every area: finding stories; writing and editing; printing techniques; layout and design; paste-up (getting the pages ready so that they can be photographed and turned into printing plates); and costs.

One other publication that your group should put together is a pamphlet or brochure describing the group, listing its major activities and accomplishments, and offering other necessary information (addresses, phone numbers, and names of officers or honorary members). It should be four to eight pages long and professional-looking. (But not too "slick"; otherwise, potential donors may look at it and say, "If they can afford to print up such a fancy brochure, they don't need my money.") You may want to gather your favorable press clippings and reprint them in the brochure.

At this stage your community is organized, funded, and ready for action. But what are your plans? Are your goals still tentatively or incompletely sketched out? Without long-range planning and precise objectives, your organization will flounder. So now let us turn to the task of completing your plan.

PART THREE

The Basics of Neighborhood Revitalization

5

HOW TO COMPLETE
A NEIGHBORHOOD
PLAN

The task of completing a neighborhood plan is complicated and difficult, and no community organization should approach it haphazardly. Be prepared for at least six months' work gathering the necessary information and another six months' effort to decide how to use that information in devising your plan. Over that one-year period, there will be many meetings, trips to city hall, late runs to the post office, and occasions when you'll say, "Why did I ever get into this?"

There are several valuable secondary benefits derived in completing a neighborhood plan. First, the process of preparing the document is in itself an extremely effective community-organizing device. Nothing brings people together more than tackling a difficult project that holds the promise of yielding positive results. Once the plan is completed, it provides a rallying point for neighbors to gather round. Then, putting the plan into action sustains the interest of those who have been working hard all along and encourages new recruits to join the organization, should the old horses tire.

Second, a completed plan provides a concrete statement of the hopes and aspirations of the neighborhood, as expressed by the people who live there and know it best.

Third, a neighborhood plan can be a proclamation to decision makers—the mayor, the city council, the bureaucrats. It serves as a guide for those decision makers sympathetic to the neighborhood, a clear statement upon which to act on the neighborhood's behalf. (It also is a notification to those who would oppose the neighborhood's desires, letting them know what they are up against should they try to challenge the neighborhood on any matter contained in the plan.)

Finally, such a plan is a caution sign to "outsiders"—real estate developers, highway engineers, urban renewers, and other "agents of change." It says that *this* neighborhood has taken account of itself and knows where it wants to go: anyone else's scheme will be scrutinized by the community organization.

In short, completing a neighborhood plan is one of the best ways for a community group to end the futile struggle of fighting *against* things and to take up the much more positive role of working *for* the neighborhood's betterment.

This chapter traces the basic outline of a neighborhood plan. In the next chapter, we'll look at three specific problems of neighborhood planning—zoning, code enforcement, and the automobile nuisance. These three nemeses of planning might be said to have particular application to less deteriorated neighborhoods, although they occur in all neighborhoods. In subsequent chapters, we'll look at suggestions for tackling the problems of the worst neighborhoods, particularly housing rehabilitation programs and programs to solve the race/crime puzzle. By putting this information together with the material on special areas—commercial revitalization or historic preservation, for example—the community organization should be able to package a comprehensive program for future development.

Before going any further, let me interject one note of caution: As with much of the material in this part of the book, the following suggestions of what a neighborhood plan should contain should be looked upon as a guide, not dogma. No one can describe the single best way to develop a neighborhood plan (or, for that matter, a comprehensive program of development); nor can anyone say with absolute certainty that every neighborhood needs such a plan or program. But experience and common sense show that a neighborhood plan is advisable and that it should contain the following elements or parts.

1.) *Description of existing conditions.* This is the raw data necessary to develop the rest of the plan.

2.) *Analysis of existing conditions.* This part of the plan interprets the information accumulated in the first part. Here, citizen planners begin to look more closely at existing conditions: Why are buildings being abandoned? Why is traffic cutting through the neighborhood? What can be done to remedy these situations?

3.) *Statement of goals, policies, and recommendations.* Goals are the broad objectives of the neighborhood. Policies are the general courses of action that lead to the goal. Recommendations are the specific programs, procedures, and actions that carry out policy.

4.) *Priorities.* This is a list of the things that should be done first. It is a statement of what is most important to the neighborhood.

5.) *Implementation Program.* This says how the plan will be put into action. Responsibility will be placed on specific parties (the city government, the state legislature, the neighborhood group itself) to carry out the recommendations.

Taking Stock of the Neighborhood

There are many good reasons for gathering information about your neighborhood. Obviously, it is necessary to know the current situation in order to plan for the future and propose solutions to neighborhood problems. If, for example, your community organization believes that abandoned buildings are a threat, it is vitally important to know exactly how many such buildings there are in your neighborhood—and then to find out who owns them, how badly the buildings are damaged, and how old they are. Moreover, this information can be used to compare your neighborhood with another one. You might, for example, compare the amount of park acreage per person in your neighborhood to the comparable acreage in several other neighborhoods in your city to show how your area has been shortchanged. Or you might compare your neighborhood to the "ideal." Take the example of parks: The American Public Health Association recommends that neighborhoods of two thousand persons housed mostly in apartment buildings have a minimum of 3.0 acres of park land. By knowing the total amount of park land in your neighborhood, you can tell whether your area measures up to the ideal. If your data show that you have less park land than the "ideal" neighborhood or other similar neighborhoods in your city, your community organization will probably want to recommend action in its plan, such as "Acquire 1.3 acres of park land."

To take stock of your neighborhood, your community group will need to do research in the following areas: the history of the neighborhood; the status of its citizens (income, age, race, employment, and so on); the condition of the neighborhood in relation to important social factors (crime rate and health indicators, for example); and the availability of public and quasi-public services (health care, transit, welfare, and so on).

There are several ways to go about your research: a small committee can do all the work; several committees can be set up to handle specific tasks; or you can use committees but have some of the work done by people not on the committee, such as block captains. Having a small committee do everything requires less recruiting and ensures that the results will be fairly uniform; the disadvantage is that fewer citizens will be involved in the project. Breaking the work down by committee means that you will have to recruit, train, and coordinate more people; on the other hand, more people will be actively involved. Using committees and block captains complicates the logistics problem even more, but increases the amount of participation. My experience has been that a few generals always rise to the top, but if they cannot mobilize a staff of sergeants and privates, they won't have the support they'll need to get the whole job done. In other words, a community group that can't get volunteers ought to consider backing up one step and organizing more effectively.

From my own experience, I've found that the process of gathering information, while tedious at first, is crucial to the success of any neighborhood planning effort. Until you force yourself to acquire the facts, you will continue to be guided by false impressions and inaccurate information. In one neighborhood, I remember, we assumed from the beginning that the citizens would want more mini-parks. When we gathered all the information, we found that the neighborhood had more than enough parks. So much for our brilliant assumptions!

It is particularly worthwhile to have some perspective on your neighborhood's history and background, if only to avoid repeating the mistakes of history. When was the area first settled? Was there anything distinctive about the early settlers? How did the neighborhood figure in the history of the city or the region? What are the notable benchmarks in the area's history? Were there any famous residents? In what ways has the neighborhood changed from its founding to the present?

The answers to these questions may be buried deep in the sands of time, but with perseverance, you can dig them up. Go to the obvious sources first—the local library, the state or local historical society, the city or state historian. Then try the local newspaper office. Most newspapers keep a file of clippings. Another source of information is the old people in the neighborhood. Interview them about the old days. (It's a good way to bring the old folks into the planning process.) Better yet, encourage a journalism or history class at the local high school or college to conduct an "oral history" program, using your neighborhood as a laboratory.

The history section of your neighborhood plan need not be elaborate (unless, of course, you are seeking designation as a historic district; see Chapter 11). A paragraph or two may do the job; two pages should be more than enough.

As for the current situation, the first place to look is the U.S. Census. The census was created, of course, to determine representation in the House of Representatives. Since the original census in 1790, its scope has been expanded to take in statistics on the age, sex, race, marital status, and relationship to head of household, plus the condition of housing, for virtually 100 percent of the population. (I say "virtually" because even the Census Bureau misses a few million Americans.) All this information is broken down by state, then into small units called "SMSAs" (Standard Metropolitan Statistical Area—in layman's terms, a county or contiguous counties containing a major city), and finally down to the census tract, an area of several hundred households. The census reports can be found in most public libraries.

The U.S. Department of Commerce field offices in each state and the Census Bureau headquarters in Washington, D.C., are extremely courteous and helpful to the public.

But unless the boundaries of your neighborhood match those of the census tract, you will probably not be able to rely only on census information for your neighborhood. The census data are often out of date, especially toward the latter part of each decade.* Moreover, as a matter of privacy, the census takers are not allowed to ask certain questions, and sometimes the questions they do ask don't make sense. One of the worst cases is the attempt to measure housing quality by asking people if they have indoor plumbing. Housing experts know that the existence of plumbing is a poor measure of housing quality, but the census takers are reluctant to make subjective judgments about housing, even though they would probably be more accurate than the "objective" notation about sinks and toilets.

In all likelihood, then, you'll have to go beyond the census and gather your information from local sources. After you've scoured the public library and any special local libraries, check the following sources:

Municipal agencies. Trek down to city hall for information from its agencies, all of which publish some sort of annual report, budget statement, or program brochure. The school board will have information on school buildings, enrollments, reading scores, testing levels, extracurricular programs, and facilities and services. The health department or environmental-control department will have data on births, deaths, diseases, pollution, and other indicators of pathology. The building or housing department will have data on the number of deteriorated, dilapidated, or abandoned houses. The real estate or real property tax department will have books filled with maps (known as "plat books") showing the ownership of each parcel of land and buildings on it. The planning department or plan commission will have information on current zoning and future land-use plans for the whole city and its subsections. The traffic or transportation department will have figures on how many cars use a particular street during

---

*Beginning in 1985, the Census Bureau will be updating certain information every five years instead of every ten.

the day, what is being planned as far as street improvements, and how the roads are being maintained. (For bus and subway plans, check with the transit authority.) The budget office will have reports showing how your tax dollars were spent. The police and fire departments also compile statistics. By combing city hall, you'll come up with a wealth of information about your city and your neighborhood.

Business and industry. Certain businesses and industries also publish reports that can be of use to community groups. The local utility company may have statistics on energy use, future housing demand, and automobile use. The chamber of commerce probably publishes regular reports on the state of the local economy. So, too, do industry groups, such as the local homebuilders' association. Market analysis firms often release reports showing economic conditions in specific areas of the city.

Private noncommercial agencies. Groups like the local Community Chest and United Way have information about public programs, budgets, charities, and foundation funding. The League of Women Voters is always a fount of information on public matters. In some cases, activist groups such as the American Friends Service Committee, local housing or tenants'-rights groups, and holdover agencies from the War on Poverty may have conducted research useful to your community organization.

As you can see, there is no shortage of information about your city. Even so, you will probably find that certain critical information is missing. In that case, you will want to go directly to the people for the information.

One sure way to get the most up-to-date information about your neighborhood is to perform a survey of the households, usually by way of a questionnaire. A questionnaire has several advantages. It gives you the opportunity to ask questions that might not be answered anywhere else, and it permits you to ask people's opinions. If your neighborhood boundaries do not fall precisely within a census tract, rendering census information useless, it can fill the information gap. Finally, a questionnaire can be a useful organizing device, since it can reach all the families in your neighborhood.

But don't think you can just type out a bunch of questions, run off copies, mail them out—and Boom! there's your questionnaire. It's not that easy. A good questionnaire requires careful planning. In fact, I recommend that you *think backwards*. Figure out what information you want, then go back step by step and determine the best way to get it. If you think the questionnaire through from the start, you'll save in the long run and come up with better results.

For example, is it necessary to question every person (or every family) in the neighborhood? If you survey *everyone*, that's called a census. But you'll never get everyone—even the U.S. Bureau of the Census is less than perfect in that respect. But you can get what numbers experts call "statistically significant" results by polling a percentage of the neighborhood selected at random. (See the notes to this chapter for suggestions on how to get a random sample.) Sometimes a random sample of only a few percent of the total can still yield statistically significant results. (The Nielsen ratings, which determine what you'll see on the tube, are based on the viewing habits of less than *one thousand* of the *eighty million* families with television.) The sampling technique obviously requires less work and money to gather reasonably useful information, but unlike the census, it is not perfectly accurate. So, applying the principle of thinking backwards: If your purpose is to gather a certain amount of information at the lowest cost, use a sample. If you want to use the questionnaire as an organizing device or as a way to make sure that every family in your neighborhood has an opportunity to participate in the planning process, then the census is your choice.

Another choice you will have to make: Do you mail the questionnaires out and have your neighbors mail them back, or do you have volunteers conduct personal interviews using the questionnaires? The mailout costs money for postage, and unless you pay for return postage, people are less likely to return the completed questionnaire—if they even bother to look at it. The mailout is relatively simple, however, and could easily reach every one of your neighbors. On the other hand, using volunteers is time-consuming and requires a great deal of organizing, but it has the advantage of being extremely personal and it assures more accurate results. Again, the choice of method depends on your purpose in using the questionnaire: To gather information?

To test public opinion? To involve people in the community organization?

With your purpose clearly in mind, you are ready to design the questionnaire. Don't be afraid to ask for help. Go to the social sciences department or data-processing center of the local college and ask one of the professors to request volunteers from among students to help you design your questionnaire. You may even have a statistician living in your own neighborhood. If the information is going to be tabulated by computer, find out if the local bank, university, or business will donate computer time. If you hope to computerize the results, you will have to write a computer program, arrange to have the responses key-punched on computer cards, and then process the results.

You'll want to ask three different kinds of questions:

1.) *Basic demographic data.* These include such matters as the number of people in the family, their ages, how long they have lived in the house, whether they own or rent, their occupations, and so on. The answers to these questions will provide an accurate demographic profile of your neighborhood.

2.) *Opinion questions.* Here, you are trying to get an idea of your neighbors' concerns and, by extension, what the community organization can do about these concerns. One technique is to ask people to agree or disagree with a statement:

Dog litter is a serious problem in the Belden neighborhood:

_____ Agree   _____ Disagree   _____ No opinion

You can even allow for gradations of responses, from "strongly agree" to "strongly disagree," each of them coded by number for the computerization.

Or you can ask people to rank problems:

Below are listed ten issues facing the Belden community. Place a "1" next to the problem you think is the most serious. Place a "2" next to the second most serious problem and a "3" next to the third most serious problem:

_____ Dog litter	_____ Abandoned houses
_____ Trash collection	_____ Lack of open space
_____ Crime	_____ Vacant lots
_____ Traffic	_____ Schools
_____ Lack of parking	_____ Potholes

3.) *Open-ended questions.* Here, your neighbors can talk about anything that comes to mind. For example, you may ask, "What is the most serious problem facing the Belden neighborhood?" and follow with, "What should the Belden Community Organization do about the problem?" Obviously, open-ended questions do not lend themselves to computerization, but they often provide the kind of information that cannot be obtained by other means anywhere else. They also give people the opportunity to say what's on their minds—an important point in organizing the community.

Next, test the questionnaire. Try it out on a few people. Do they understand the questions? Are the questions too hard to fill out? Is the questionnaire too long? Is there enough room on the form? If you're using a computer, will it be able to process the responses? Work out the bugs on a small sample so you don't waste time and money.

Then, train the volunteers who are going to work on the survey. If you're doing a mailout, there will be fewer people involved, but they should be trained in recording the results, determining which answers to discard, and so on, in order to make the results uniform. If you are doing personal interviews, you'll have to spend more time training your interviewers. I recommend using man-and-woman teams. It takes twice as many volunteers, but people are less suspicious if a couple comes to their door than if a single man or woman knocks. Make sure they are familiar with the questionnaire. Let them try it out on one another.

You'll have to decide how to conduct the survey, too. Should the volunteers make appointments with the interviewees, or just appear at the door? Should the interviews be scheduled during the day or at night? How about doing the interview by phone? (If you have enough volunteers, a personal visit should be no more inconvenient than an interview over the phone—and it should yield better results.) Who should be interviewed—the man, the woman, or both? What about the kids or old people in the house? How personal should the questions be? For example, should you ask the family's income? Should you ask about race or ethnic origin, or should you let the volunteers record this from observation? Do you want the volunteers to make notes about the physical condition of the house? All these matters touch on the issue of privacy, and the community organization should have a clear idea of its own policy on these matters before sending volunteers into their neighbors' homes. Finally, there should be a publicity campaign announcing the survey, so that people know about it and will be less suspicious of the calls from volunteers. And all volunteers should be supplied with a letter of introduction or some other form of identification, signed by the president of the organization, so that people will know the survey is legitimate. Once the survey teams have built up a little experience, they should meet periodically with the person in charge and any expert advisers to iron out any problems.

The final step is to collate the responses. Make up a master sheet and record the total number of responses for each question and the percentage of the total for each response. Use this material as a data base to summarize the results. For example, the Arlington Ridge Civic Association of Arlington, Virginia, capsulized its income and population statistics this way:

Forty-five percent of the families in the area have incomes in excess of $15,000 annually; 28 percent from $15,000 to $25,000; 16 percent from $25,000 to $50,000; and 1 percent over $50,000. Approximately 35 percent of the employed persons work for the Federal Government. The population is predominantly white: less than 1 percent are black; less than 2 percent are of other races. In age breakdown, about 20 percent of the population are nineteen and under, 30 percent are twenty to thirty-five, 38 percent are between thirty-five and sixty, and 12 percent are over sixty.

Another Arlington group, the Ashton Heights Civic Association, distributed a questionnaire to 735 homes. Here is what they learned from the opinion questionnaire:

Results showed that 98 percent of the respondents were interested in maintaining Ashton Heights' single-family character. Major concerns included speculative land ownership and commercial encroachment, use of neighborhood streets for commuter traffic and parking, and lack of parks and open space within the community.

Visual aids also make a report more readable, especially when lots of numbers are being cited. If you draw up pie charts, graphs, bar charts, tables, and other graphic displays to represent the data collected, the reader will understand your results quickly and easily.

On the following pages is a sample questionnaire, a composite of actual questionnaires used by several community groups. It is meant to suggest but not prescribe the many kinds of questions that could be asked in such a survey and the various forms such questions could take. Adapt it to fit your particular needs.

Sample Questionnaire

Belden Community Organization

The Belden Community Organization is preparing a neighborhood plan for submission to the City Council. We seek your participation in this process. Completing this questionnaire will assist us greatly. All information will be kept confidential. No names will be used.

1. How many people live in your home? _____

2. What are their ages? (Give total number for each group)
   ____ Less than 6   ____ 20–34 years   ____ 50–65 years
   years old
   ____ 6–12 years   ____ 35–49 years   ____ over 65
   ____ 13–19 years

3. What type of housing unit is your home?
   ____ One-family   ____ Four to eight units
   ____ Two-family   ____ More than eight units
   ____ Three-family   ____ Other (specify) _____

4. When was this home built?

5. Do you own or rent?   ____ Own   ____Rent

6. How long have you lived in your present home? _____

7. How long have you lived in the Belden neighborhood?___

8. How long has your family lived in the city? _____

9.* Which letter, A, B, C, D, E, or F, best describes your total family income?
   A. ____ Less than $5,000   D. ____ $15,000–19,999
   B. ____ $5,000–9,999   E. ____ $20,000–24,999
   C. ____ $10,000–14,999   F. ____ Over $25,000

*(The question is worded this way so that the interviewee can simply name a letter, not family income. One suggestion might be to put this question on a small card and ask the interviewee to check the right letter. Don't force anyone to answer this question.)

10a. What is your occupation? _____
      Your spouse's? _____
10b. Number of years of school? _____
      Your spouse's? _____

Now we'd like to ask your opinion about a number of matters of concern to the Belden neighborhood.

11. In your opinion, what are the three most urgent problems facing the Belden neighborhood? (Indicate 1, 2, 3.)
     __ Traffic   __ Parking   __ Crime   __ Pollution
     __ Noise   __ Zoning   __ Schools __ Parks
     __ Recreation __ Services   __ Library   __ Senior citizen
                                                            problems

12. Think of two things you especially *like* about this neighborhood. What are they?
     (1) _____
     (2) _____

13. Think of two things you especially *dislike* about this neighborhood. What are they?
     (1) _____
     (2) _____

14. How would you classify the following facilities on your block?

	Good	Fair	Poor	Very Bad
Street paving	____	____	____	____
Curbs, gutters, and sidewalks	____	____	____	____
Storm drainage	____	____	____	____
Streetlights	____	____	____	____

15. How would you rate the following services and community facilities in the Belden neighborhood?
     (Good = 1; Fair = 2; Poor = 3; Very Bad = 4)

     ____ Public transit   ____ Police protection
     ____ Trash removal   ____ Fire protection
     ____ Water service   ____ Sewer service
     ____ Recreation programs   ____ Park maintenance
     ____ Street-sweeping   ____ Street repair
     ____ Snow removal   ____ Traffic control
     ____ Public schools   ____ Public library
     ____ Parks and recreation   ____ Health and hospital
                                                 facilities
     ____ Child-care facilities   ____ Parking
     ____ Welfare agencies   ____ Senior citizens' services

16. In your opinion, are any of the following of concern for the enjoyment of a safe and healthy environment in this neighborhood?

	Degree of your concern		
	Severe	Moderate	Slight
Auto traffic noise	_____	_____	___
Auto traffic hazards	_____	_____	___
House fires (arson)	_____	_____	___
Street crime	_____	_____	___
Property crime	_____	_____	___
Pollution (give source if possible: _____)	_____	_____	___

17. Here are some specific improvements for the Belden neighborhood that people have mentioned. How strongly do you agree or disagree that these changes should be made? (Strongly agree = 1; Agree = 2; Uncertain/no opinion = 3; Disagree = 4; Strongly disagree = 5)

_____ Reduce speeding
_____ Add more bike paths
_____ Enforce parking regulations more strictly
_____ Put traffic lights at bad intersections
_____ Redesign streets for more beauty and to slow cars
_____ Upgrade streets with paving and curbs
_____ Put in or improve sidewalks
_____ Install additional street lighting
_____ Build bus shelters
_____ Close streets for recreation purposes
_____ Start neighborhood recycling program
_____ Clean up alleys and public areas
_____ Control pollution (give source if possible:_____)
_____ Upgrade housing
_____ Regulate pets more closely

18. Do you agree or disagree with the following statement about this neighborhood? If you agree, please describe what you think should be done about it.
Statement: Streets are hazardous in this neighborhood.
_____ Disagree
_____ No opinion
_____ Widen or build sidewalks
_____ Change speed limit

_____ More police patrols
_____ More traffic signals or stop signs
_____ Other (specify: _____)

19. How often do you ride the bus?
_____ Less than once a week
_____ About once a week
_____ Several times a week
_____ Almost every weekday

20. Other neighbors we have talked to have given reasons why they like living in this neighborhood. How strongly do you agree with them that these are the advantages of living in Belden?

	Agree	Uncertain/ No opinion	Disagree
Nearness to downtown	_____	_____	_____
Nearness to shopping	_____	_____	_____
Quality of housing stock	_____	_____	_____
Friendly neighbors	_____	_____	_____
Quiet neighborhood	_____	_____	_____
Access to bus	_____	_____	_____

One other point about the questionnaire: use the survey as an organizing tool. Sometime during the survey, preferably right at the beginning, tell your neighbors *why* the survey is being conducted. Give a little spiel about your organization—its history, purpose, and record to date. Then hit them up for help with such questions as the following:

How much time would you be willing to give to the Belden Community Organization?_____hours a week
Do you have any special skills or training (e.g., typing, bookkeeping) that would be useful to the organization? If so, what are they?

_____

Would you care to contribute a tax-deductible donation to the organization? $_____enclosed.
Do you know the name, address, and phone number of other citizens in the neighborhood who might want to know more about the Belden Community Organization?

_____

_____

Will you attend our next meeting on (date, time, place)? _____
May we have someone contact you the day of the meeting to remind you? _____(phone number)

Don't lose a single opportunity to press your neighbors into action. Besides, they might feel insulted not to be asked.

No matter how well you think you know your neighborhood, you can probably learn a lot more about it by getting out and conducting a field inventory of its physical conditions in a close survey of every street. You'll be surprised at what you'll learn, and you may pick up some recruits as you get out into the neighborhood and talk to people about the project.

You'll need clipboards, pencils, colored pencils or felt pens, note cards, and a tape measure. If someone in the group is a photographer, have him bring film for both color slides and black-and-white prints. You'll need both kinds of pictures later. Each volunteer should also carry a letter of authorization signed by the organization's president, as well as publicity material to give to curious neighbors who might be enlisted in the cause.

Maps are critical. From your city's planning department or zoning office, get sufficient copies of:

Base maps. These maps show the outline of each parcel and the configuration of the streets and alleys. Use them to record information in the field. They come in various scales. For example, a base map on the scale of 1″ = 1200′ could be used to show conditions over a fairly large area. A base map on the scale of 1″ = 300′ (see Figure 1) would be used to "close in" on an area and show greater detail. Consult with the staff of the planning or zoning office for help in determining which base maps are available and most appropriate for your use.

Official zoning map. This map shows how each parcel in the city is zoned. The numbers and letters refer to the uses permitted by law in each district (zone) (see Figure 2).

Official general land-use map. This map shows the "highest and best use" of the land in your city, as approved by the city council, city planning commission, or other appropriate body. In layman's terms, it represents how the land *should* be used, not necessarily how it is being used today.

Figure 1

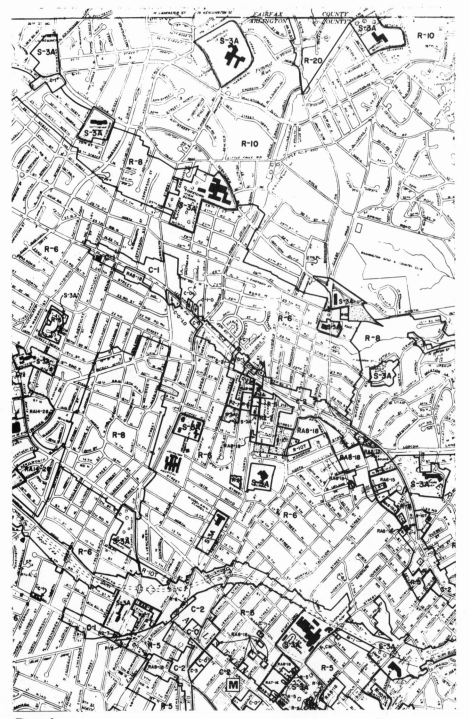

Figure 2

Real estate maps. These maps are so expensive to prepare that only a few copies may be available to the public. They are usually kept in the assessor's office and the public library. Real estate maps contain a wealth of useful information, including the name of the owner of each parcel, its dimensions, and its area in square feet or acres (an acre equals 43,560 square feet). By cross reference to the real-property-tax listings, you can determine the owner's address, the assessed valuation of the land and "improvements" (buildings), and the price at which it was last sold.*

While you're at city hall, it would be worthwhile to pick up a copy of the streets-and-thoroughfares plan from the city transportation department and a copy of the city housing ordinance from the housing office, health department, or code-enforcement office. The planning or zoning office will also have a copy of the official zoning ordinance text, which describes in legal terms the uses permitted in each zoning district. You'll also find that aerial photographs of your neighborhood (sometimes available from the planning or zoning office) can help you spot patterns that are hard to notice from the ground.

Before you set out to start the field survey, not only should you have prepared a good set of base maps for the surveyors, you should also have devised a systematic method to cover the neighborhood. Decide beforehand whether one team of surveyors will cover the whole neighborhood (starting in one corner and working toward the opposite end) or whether teams of surveyors will cover assigned sections of the community. If the latter is decided, map out the area each team will cover.

Ask the field workers to *key* their maps as they survey the area. A key is an agreed-upon code of symbols; for example, a color key can show the existing use of land—yellow for single-family houses, green for parks, and so on. A numerical system can be used to rate the condition of houses. A jagged line can indicate needed curb repairs. Make up a key that suits your needs—or use the one given below—then stick to it.

In conducting the survey, field workers are likely to observe many things that cannot be squeezed onto the maps, so room

*Some states allow "blind trusts," which can effectively disguise the ownership of a parcel.

should be allowed for other observations. Note cards can be used to take down details on these items, especially nuisances. For example, if a junk car is spotted, record the type and make of car, its location, the year of manufacture, and the license or registration number (if any). Later, this information can be turned over to the proper authorities so that the car can be removed. Anecdotes are also worth recording: "The new owner of the house at 1221 Campbell Street said he has just painted the trim." Details like these can help you get a better picture of what's happening in your neighborhood.

EXISTING USE OF LAND. On your lot-by-lot survey, determine how each parcel is actually being used—not what the parcel is zoned for, nor what the general land-use map says it should be, but what's actually there. If you use a color key, the conventional colors are:

Yellow: Single-family houses.
Orange: Two- or three-family houses.
Brown: Multifamily houses (apartment buildings).
Red: Commercial facilities. Sometimes red is used to indicate neighborhood shopping facilities, such as grocery stores, restaurants, and taverns, and pink or some other shade of red is used to indicate high-density commercial uses, such as office buildings or banks.
Purple: Industries, factories, terminals, warehouses.
Green: Public open space, parks, playgrounds.
Blue or
Gray: Public facilities (courthouse, city hall, jail, school, library, hospital).
White: Vacant land, unused land, undeveloped land.

Be sure to check houses carefully. What looks like a single-family home may be a "conversion," with two or more families living there. Two or more doorbells, electric meters, or entrances are a clue that the building has been converted.

· CONDITION OF HOUSING UNITS. Your community group will be most concerned with the exterior condition of the houses in your neighborhood. It is unlikely that you will want to inspect the interior, since that involves some touchy legal issues, such as trespassing. You should develop a scale of housing deterioration, with Class 1 houses being in virtually perfect condition or needing only minor repairs, down to Class 4, 5, or 6, depending on how refined you want to get. Refer to your city housing code to see what the city officials consider to be code violations. Be sure to take notes on the note cards so that you can turn over any information on possible code violations to the authorities. (See Chapter 6.)

Here is one rating system that might be appropriate for your neighborhood:

Class 1—Structure in sound condition. The building has few, if any, deficiencies. The roof may need a little patching, or the paint on the metal gutters may be peeling slightly.

Class 2—Structure in need of minor repairs. Paint is peeling or has chalked off to expose wood on gables, cornices, windows, doors, or other wooden parts of the basic structure. Minor cracks are apparent in wood or asbestos siding, but the sheathing is not exposed. Caulking has dried and is open wide enough to permit water to run through. The roof is in need of more than minor repairs. Some brick work, particularly the chimney or other nonstructural parts of the house, needs pointing (the mortar or cement between the bricks needs to be retouched). The porch, carport, or garage is in poor condition.

Class 3—Structure in need of major repairs. The building apparently needs new windows, siding, cornices, fascia material, or structural members. The masonry or foundation walls are cracked, or wood surfaces are rotten from lack of paint. In wood-frame houses, the walls or roof are sagging. The chimney is about to fall. The roof is leaking. While the building is in bad shape, it is still worth saving.

Class 4—Structure beyond repair. The building has so many things wrong with it that it is not economically feasible to bring it up to Class 1 standards.

Class 5—Transitional structure. The structure is not in keeping with its surrounding uses (a summer cottage among modern homes), is architecturally obsolete, or is otherwise potentially obsolete. This does not mean that the building is a candidate for demolition. It just seems out of place.

Also check these items:

1. The condition of the other buildings on the lot, including work sheds and separate garages.

2. The estimated year of construction, especially if the building has a lot of things wrong with it.

3. The type of structure, such as a wood frame or brick, especially if it is an anomaly.

4. Possible violations (such as construction work going on without a building permit) or uses not permitted by the zoning ordinance (such as a business in a residential district, or an enclosed porch too close to the lot line). These items will have to be reviewed in the "analysis" part of the neighborhood-plan preparation.

5. Abandonment or vacancy. Has the building been abandoned by its owner or left vacant for an unusual length of time?

YARD CONDITIONS. Unsightly yards can be as much of a neighborhood nuisance as bad housing. Check the following:

1. Weeds or other unsightly vegetation.

2. Broken, unpainted, or rickety fences.

3. Junk storage of old refrigerators or stoves.

4. Abandoned or junk cars or evidence that unsightly auto repair work is being conducted on the property.

5. Improper trash storage or trash cans not covered to keep out rodents.

6. Unsightly buildings, such as chicken coops, dog kennels, jerry-built work sheds, or pigeon hutches.

7. Insufficient on-site parking, lack of driveway space, or cars parked on the lawn or sidewalk.

8. Nonconforming lots, either too narrow or not permitting sufficient setback of the house from the street.

9. Improper grading or drainage, causing water to form pools or breeding areas for mosquitos.

STREET CONDITIONS. Examine the physical condition of the streets for the following:

1. Are curbs, gutters, and sidewalks in good condition? Are there spots where these items are missing? Is there evidence of cracking or heaving? Are the sidewalks wide enough?

2. What condition is the pavement in? Is it cracking or heaving? Is it properly crowned—humped slightly at the center line

and gradually sloped toward the curb for proper drainage? Are there potholes?

3. What is the width of the pavement from curb to curb? Can cars get by safely? Is there sufficient room for curbside parking?

4. Check drainage during and after a heavy rain to see if the storm-water drainage system, which should be separate from the sanitary sewer system, is carrying runoff water from the streets. Are the catch basins stopped up with leaves or debris? Are they in the right spot to catch the water?

5. Is the street's grade too steep?

6. Are there a sufficient number of street trees? What is their condition? Do they show any evidence of disease? Are the roots pushing up the sidewalk or pavement? Are the branches interfering with overhead wires? If they are in the public right-of-way, have the trees been planted according to city regulations? Some cities require a permit to plant a tree in the public right-of-way. (Some cities also have experts in the transportation or parks department who can advise you on what to look for concerning the condition of street trees.)

7. Are street lawns properly maintained? (The street lawn is the area between the sidewalk and the curb, or the area between the property line and the curb if there is no sidewalk. In most places, the public owns this land, but the adjacent property owner is expected to maintain it.) Are they cluttered with weeds or trash?

8. Is the street furniture attractive? (Street furniture is the name given to all the miscellaneous equipment along the street—benches, signs, bus shelters, lampposts, fire hydrants, emergency callboxes, telephone poles.) Is it located in the right places? Is there enough of it, or too much? In the case of callboxes and hydrants, are they visible? Are there unsightly billboards?

STREET LIGHTING. Check the streetlights at night, of course. The best time of year is during spring or summer, when the trees are full of leaves; then you can determine whether the light is being blocked. In technical terms, residential streets should be lighted to an average level of 0.6 foot-candles; but since it is impractical to measure the lighting intensity in foot-candles, use common sense to determine whether the street lighting is adequate. What kind of lamp is used—incandescent (which gives off a yellow-white light), mercury vapor (blue-white light), or sodium vapor (pinkish light)? Is the wiring overhead or underground? What kinds of standards (poles) are used? What kinds of fixtures? Do they enhance the streetscape or detract from it?

TRAFFIC. When surveying traffic conditions, look for hazards and danger spots. Certain questions are particularly important:

1. Are there dangerous intersections? Try to determine the reason why the intersection is a danger spot. Is the street too narrow? Is it poorly lighted? Is the stop sign obscured from the driver's view? Is there poor drainage at the corner, causing drivers to lose their brakes in puddles? Is the street too steep? Is there a blind corner? In some cities, it is forbidden to have a fence or shrubbery higher than three feet within twenty-five feet of the corner.

2. Are speed limits reasonable? Are they enforced?

3. Are school and pedestrian crossings safe? Are they guarded? During what hours?

4. Are there traffic obstructions? Railroad crossings, bus stops (where there is no lane for the bus to pull over), bridges, and other obstructions can bottle up traffic. Determine when these conditions are worst by talking to residents and others in the area who watch the site frequently.

5. Is on-street parking blocking traffic? What is the configuration: parallel, diagonal, straight-in? Are drivers from outside the neighborhood taking most of the spaces? (See Chapter 6.)

6. What are the traffic patterns? Are there one-way streets, reversible lanes, or other unusual configurations?

7. What is the traffic count? The city traffic department should have figures on both the average daily traffic and the peak-period traffic—the highest number of vehicles that pass a designated point during a set period, usually the rush hour. If you cannot get the figures from the city, count cars during the rush hour.

8. Are traffic signs and signals visible? Can drivers understand them? Are there places where signs or signals are needed?

9. Who is using your streets? Are local streets being used mostly by traffic that is serving the neighborhood? (See Chapter 6.) Or are "outsiders" cutting through the neighborhood instead of using the peripheral highways? Are heavy trucks, construction

equipment, and other vehicles not compatible with a residential neighborhood using your streets?

ALLEYS. Are your alleys being properly used? Are they dangerous? Are they well-maintained? Do they need paving?

PARKS AND OPEN SPACES. There are two kinds of park facilities, active and passive. Active facilities include baseball diamonds, playgrounds, and soccer fields. Passive areas include public gardens, beautification spots, sitting areas, and public lawns where ballplaying is prohibited. Of course, there is considerable overlap here, and many parks combine both active and passive areas. Determine which kinds of facilities you have and who is using them. Observe how each facility is being used, or ask someone who lives nearby (a shut-in or senior citizen, for example) to do so and make records on note cards.

You will also want to check the kinds of equipment at each facility—water fountains, play equipment, sports facilities, and so on—and see how well they are being maintained. Are public areas landscaped? Is the landscaping properly maintained? Are recreation areas lighted for night use? If there is a supervisory staff at recreation areas, get figures on the number of staff members, the hours during which they are available to the public, and the period during the year when they are staffing the facility (if the facility is seasonal).

Analyzing Existing Conditions

A stack of unprocessed questionnaires and sloppy maps is worthless. Before the information you have gathered can be used, it has to be put into intelligible form. The first step, then, after gathering the data is to collate the information. Here the computer really saves time. Charts, tables, bar graphs, and other visual aids help to display your results. For material that is best presented on maps, use colored pencils to draw the information you have culled on a base map. One map might show "Existing Use of Land," another "Condition of Housing Stock," for example. (The graphics section of your city's planning department might be able to help you with the maps.) Another technique is to place a sheet of tracing paper over the base map and color the information for each category on the tracing paper. These maps can then be used as "overlays." For example, the overlay showing "Existing Use of Land" could be placed over a base map showing "Existing Zoning." The places where the colors fail to match show clearly where the existing use of land does not conform to the permitted zoning. Such areas of discrepancy merit keen scrutiny. For even sharper results, use thin Mylar plastic instead of tracing paper and felt-tip markers instead of colored pencils.

Once the raw data you have collected has been organized and collated, I recommend setting up committees to study the major subject areas—housing, zoning and land use, transportation, and so on. Each committee should review the information in its special area of interest, paying particular attention to any alarming patterns that might indicate a problem.

INTERPRETING THE DATA. In order to see how the data you have accumulated can be translated into policies and goals, let's consider a few examples. Your questionnaire results show that the overwhelming majority of residents "strongly agree" with the statement, "The single-family quality of the Belden community should be preserved." Yet, from your field inventory, you note that, in one small pocket, a number of homes have been converted to two- and three-flat buildings; moreover, this area abuts a block that, while currently occupied by single-family homes, is zoned for apartment buildings. You have also learned from your search of real estate records and interviews with homeowners that a real estate developer has been buying selected properties on the block and has made overtures to a number of other owners. Upon further investigation, you learn that the developer also had a hand in converting the houses in your problem area. From this information, your committee should be able to discern a pattern of land packaging that eventually will lead to a proposal by the developer to replace the existing single-family homes with apartments or some other, more intense, use. That discovery could lead you to alert the neighborhood and to recommend in the final plan that the single-family character of the neighborhood be maintained.

Or suppose your traffic studies show a preponderance of accidents and near misses at a particular intersection. Do the traffic surveys show that the streets in this area are carrying more traffic than they were designed for? If so, does that mean that "commuters" are using these streets as shortcuts through your neighborhood? Or is a physical problem the cause of the accidents— poor visibility at the intersection, or an obstructed stop sign?

These matters should be thrashed out by the committees. Then each committee should prepare a report for submission to the community organization. The whole community should be given the opportunity to analyze the results of each committee's work, preferably at a series of neighborhood meetings. At this stage, the neighborhood knows its problems. Now it must look for ways to solve them.

Goals, Policies, Recommendations, and Priorities

You know what your problems are. Now you propose to do something about them. For each problem, you will want to state your *goals, policies,* and *recommendations.* A goal, wrote Charles Abrams, "is the end result or ultimate accomplishment toward which an effort is directed." A policy is the general course of action designed to achieve that goal. A recommendation is a specific program or idea to carry out the policy. Thus, the Goss-Grove neighborhood of Boulder, Colorado, has among its goals to "enhance the safety of the neighborhood." One policy designed to achieve this goal is to "eliminate hazardous turn movements at all locations of egress from the neighborhood to surrounding arterials [major roadways]." Or take the Mapleton Hill neighborhood, also in Boulder. The goal of that neighborhood is "to improve the quality of life for the residents." Among the policies designed to achieve that goal is to "maintain and improve the appearance . . . of the neighborhood." Its specific recommendation is to "put power lines underground." Goal, policy, recommendation—a logical progression from the general to the specific.

Another way to go about setting goals is to list your community's *strengths* and *weaknesses.* One section of Chicago's Community 21 neighborhood, for example, found its strengths included the availability of local shopping, the occupational homogeneity of its people, and the availability of public sewer, water, fire-protection, and transit facilities. Among its weaknesses were the lack of an elementary school and a park, incompatible land uses, high noise levels, and housing in need of major repairs. From such a list, it is easy to formulate goals: Your goals are to *preserve and enhance your positive characteristics* and to *reduce, mitigate, or eliminate your negative characteristics.* Thus, one goal might be, "Maintain present level of public transit," and another could be "Reduce noise levels."

Naturally, at each stage in the development of neighborhood goals, policies, and recommendations, you will want to open the process up to the entire community. As before, it is worthwhile to have the respective committees write draft reports, then submit them to the community organization for complete and open discussion. The community organization should recognize that these goals and policies constitute a fundamental statement of the organization's philosophy.

These debates will not always be cordial affairs. I remember one such clash in Lyon Park, a neighborhood in Arlington, Virginia. One faction wanted all the streets repaved and new sewers put in. The other group was afraid that the construction would mean that many old trees near the roadway would have to be cut down. I seem to recall that the streets faction won, with the other group getting a concession that as many trees as possible would be saved. The point is that controversy cannot and should not be avoided, but as many citizens should be brought into the planning process as possible to assure its fairness. It is surprising how many compromises neighbors can make, once everyone has been fully informed of the facts.

But it is not enough merely to have a collection of good ideas and suggested programs. Some sense of order has to be placed on them—demolishing the house at 909 Kensington, for example, is deemed more important to the community than having a new water fountain installed in the neighborhood tot lot. In other words, the community must establish its *priorities.* Why? For one thing, it alerts public officials to the true needs and desires of the community. If our hypothetical Belden Community Organization comes before the City Council with fifty recommendations, the council is free to approve them all without any determination as to which of the recommendations shall be carried out first. The bureaucrats can then implement the items in any order they choose—perhaps the easiest or least costly first, leaving the crucial items till last, or forgetting about them altogether. But when the Belden people declare that they want 909 Kensington demolished before anything else gets done, public officials have little leeway for discretion or whimsy. This process also makes the community organization think through one more time what *it* considers to be the gravest, and therefore the highest priority, problems before it. And frankly, in an age of limited resources, it makes the community organization say to its public officials, "Here's our laundry list. We must have Numbers 1 through 10, but we can live without Numbers 41 through 50."

Setting priorities should not be given short shrift. By establishing its priorities, the community organization is in effect laying bare its soul. An organization can mouth high-sounding goals— "a clean environment," "a decent home for every family"—but its statement of priorities gives notice as to its true intentions. The in-fighting that accompanies priority setting is also an essential step in the political growth of any community organization. Thus, priorities should be debated fiercely, battled over, and democratically voted upon, just as if each were a candidate for high office. The final plan should list the recommendations in order of priority.

Figure 3

20. Do you want to plant trees along **3rd Ave NW** from NW 46th St to NW 65th St?

Then place $50,000 in NIP bills below.

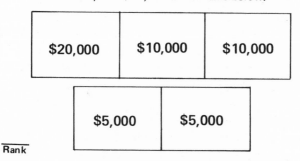

But suppose your recommendations will cost $1 million to implement, and you have a total of only $250,000 from your funding sources? Then, you might try an ingenious system developed by a citizen in Seattle. Make up a "ballot" describing each project and the money it will cost. Then make up play money (stickers in various denominations work best) adding up to your total allocation. Your neighbors can then vote their pocketbooks by using their money stickers to fund the projects they really want. (See Figure 3.)

With your priorities set, you are only a step away from completing the neighborhood plan.

Adoption and Implementation

The final challenge is to have your neighborhood plan adopted by the city. This is more than a formality: if you convince the city council to approve your plan, it then effectively becomes the planning document for your area. As such, it can be a powerful weapon for your community organization. Let me describe briefly how this worked in a community I happen to be familiar with.

Since 1964, Arlington, Virginia has encouraged citizens, property owners, and businessmen to develop neighborhood plans that indicate to the county board (the municipality's legislature) the wishes and desires of the local people on such matters as land use and zoning, transportation, parks and recreation, capital improvements, and beautification. By 1979, eleven community groups had had their neighborhood plans approved by the county board.

The program was started in the face of rampant development and real estate speculation that threatened the single-family character of many established neighborhoods. Developers were buying up blocks of houses, getting the land rezoned, and building office or apartment buildings. Two planning commissioners, Elizabeth Weihe and Hall Gibson, came up with the idea of a Neighborhood Conservation Program, which would work like this: A neighborhood (usually represented by a civic association) threatened by some sort of crisis—a zoning request for a high-rise building, for example—comes to the planning commission with its problem. A commissioner familiar with the Neighborhood Conservation Program outlines the requirements of the program to the civic association, after which the group decides whether or not to join the program. If it agrees, it must follow the procedures described previously in this chapter—survey the residents, inventory the existing conditions, and so on—and submit a draft plan within a year's time. This draft is then reviewed by the county planning staff and a subcommittee of the county planning commission made up of representatives of all the neighborhoods already in the program. This subcommittee makes whatever suggestions for improvement are necessary; then the plan goes to the planning commission and, finally, to the county board. If the county board approves the plan, it becomes recognized "in principle" as expressing the wishes and desires of the neighborhood on the issues and problems contained in the plan. The county board may agree to fund some or all of the capital improvements suggested by the neighborhood. Later, when hearings are held on any aspect of the county's master plan, the recommendations of the neighborhood are included; almost always, the master plan is changed to reflect these recommendations. Thus, while the neighborhood plan is only a set of recommendations, it usually gets translated into county board policy.

The results have been remarkable. Whole neighborhoods have been stabilized, because the real estate speculators know that if the county board has approved the neighborhood's plan, any change of zoning must be sanctioned by the community organization. "We have had no rezoning that was in opposition to an approved neighborhood plan," notes Elizabeth Weihe.

This brief outline makes it seem easier than it is to complete a plan. In fact, several neighborhoods gave up after years of trying. That's because the key to a successful neighborhood planning effort is citizen support, and that takes work—mobilizing people, drumming up volunteers for unglamorous jobs, making sure everyone has an opportunity to speak on the issues. In effect, the creation of a neighborhood plan becomes a political act. The community organization is saying to the legislature, "Here is our statement of how things should be. We have ironed out the details and inconsistencies with the municipal staff. We have sought the approval of our residents, businessmen, and property owners. This is what we propose for the future of our neighborhood. Do you support us?" The implicit threat is that the community will oppose any politician who votes against its plan. As a matter of fact, both political parties in Arlington have endorsed the Neighborhood Conservation Program in every election for over a decade.

Occasionally, there was opposition to a neighborhood's plan. In one instance, a property owner objected to a community's proposal to designate his land for future open space because he wanted to build a hotel on the land. The solution, albeit imperfect, was to designate his property as a "problem area," with the county board approving the rest of the neighborhood plan. This case shows that, unless there is virtual unanimity behind a neighborhood planning effort and all the compromises have been worked out beforehand, it will not have the necessary clout in the political arena.

This is especially important at the point where the community organization makes the presentation of its final draft to the city council. A strong show of support for the plan is imperative. First, the community leaders who are going to make the actual presentation should rehearse their statements, preferably before a citizens' group that has gone through the process before. The organization's president or the chairman of the planning committee should orchestrate the presentation, giving a brief introduction and then turning the podium over to the leaders of various interest groups within the community—business leaders, the elderly, civic activists, and so on. Each speaker should cover a specific area of importance—transportation, or senior citizens' housing, for example—and reiterate his support for the *entire* plan. To dress things up, use visual aids—maps and charts describing your recommendations, photographs of your neighborhood, even slides, if possible (that's why your photographer should shoot half his pictures in color). Finally, the person orchestrating the presentation should present the council with any letters of support, signed petitions, records of votes taken at community meetings in support of the plan, and any other evidence that shows your group has the community's backing on the plan. Of course, you'll want to pack the hearing room with your supporters as a visible show of support. The whole presentation should take no more than a half hour: public officials are busy, and going over your time allotment can work against you. Finally, the organization's president should ask the city council to approve your plan. If you've done your homework, the vote shouldn't even be close, and your plan will be approved. Congratulations!

A plan is just another piece of paper if it does not get implemented. Implementation of the plan should take in the following:

1.) *Budget.* How much money will you have to put your plan into action? From which sources—community-development block grants, foundation aid, loans, city bond referendums, special programs? How will the money be used? (Refer to your priorities.)

2.) *Timetable.* The schedule for carrying out your approved recommendations should also be stated clearly in the final document. Which actions must be done immediately? Which are long-range?

3.) *Responsibility.* Who is in charge of carrying out each of the approved recommendations—the city staff, the community organization, lending institutions, business groups? How will their actions be monitored to make sure they are doing the job properly? What sanctions will be imposed if they drag their feet? What kind of complaint mechanism is there in case you're not satisfied with the way the recommendation has been implemented?

4.) *Technical assistance.* If certain recommendations require further research or study, what kinds of technical assistance will you need? Will you be able to get this help from the city staff, or will you have to hire an outside professional (an architect, for example)? Who oversees this expert's work?

Planning the future of your neighborhood is an extraordinarily difficult assignment. It's hard to start with a blank slate, with barely a few notions of where you want to go, and to plod along trying to get a sense of the right direction for your community. It's much easier to react negatively to what others propose for your neighborhood than it is to anticipate problems and take positive actions. But numerous community organizations have gone through the process and have derived tremendous satisfaction from completing their plan. That document says, "Here is what *we*, the people of this neighborhood, want for our community. Here are the steps by which we hope to achieve those goals. Here is our future, as best we can determine it." And, of course, having a well-thought-out plan in hand makes implementing your neighborhood revitalization program all the more likely to succeed.

6

THREE NEIGHBORHOOD PLANNING PROBLEMS

In my work in neighborhood planning, I have come across three problems that afflict all neighborhoods, from the poorest ghetto to the richest suburb. They are zoning and land use, code enforcement, and automobile-related problems. These three are by no means the most serious problems facing city neighborhoods, but they are sufficiently bothersome to merit close attention and an analysis of various practical solutions.

Zoning and Land Use

To the average citizen, zoning and land use are foreign concepts. Even the terminology, mentioned in the last chapter, is a bit strange. How is the average citizen to sort these terms out?

To simplify things, recognize that we're talking about *control over how land may be used*. The first such land-use control was zoning, which made its debut in New York City in 1916. In 1924, the U.S. Department of Commerce designed a Standard Zoning Enabling Act to encourage the states to adopt zoning laws. In 1926, the Supreme Court declared zoning to be a valid exercise of the police power in the case of *Village of Euclid* v. *Ambler Realty Co.* (272 U.S. 365). Today, there is hardly a city in the United States without zoning regulations.

Zoning is based on the premise that the state may protect the health, safety, and general welfare of its people by *separating* incompatible land uses. The obvious example is that of the smelly factory in the middle of a clean, quiet, residential area. A zoning ordinance describes certain categories of uses, called "districts" or "zones," usually residential, commercial, and industrial. For each district the written ordinance (the "zoning text") makes certain restrictions on the following:

1.) *Use.* The ordinance tells which kinds of structures—houses, factories, apartment buildings, office towers—are permitted in each district. In a typical ordinance, for example, an "R-1" zone might allow only single-family, detached houses.

2.) *Lot size.* This part regulates the minimum amount of land needed for each use in the zone; for example, an R-1 zone might require a 10,000-square-foot lot for each house.

3.) *Height.* This section limits the maximum height of any building; for example, a house in an R-1 district may be no higher than three stories or thirty-five feet.

4.) *Setback.* The ordinance stipulates how close the structure may come to the edge of the property; that is, how wide the front, back, and side yards must be. A typical front setback in an R-1 district might be fifty feet from the street.

5.) *Bulk.* This is tricky. For residential districts, the ordinance most likely will stipulate the maximum portion of the lot that may be covered by buildings (or paved areas); thus, no building in an R-1 zone, for example, may cover more than 20 percent of the total site. For commercial and industrial areas, the bulk restrictions are often in the form of a "floor area ratio" (FAR). An FAR of 1.0 would permit a one-story building that covered the entire lot, or a two-story building that covered half the lot, or a four-story building that took up only one-quarter of the lot. (See Figure 4.)

In general, "higher" (low-density) uses are permitted in districts zoned for "lower" (high-density) uses, but not vice versa: thus, a single-family home would be permitted in a commercial district, but a gas station would not be allowed in a residential zone. Some ordinances say that only the uses described in the district regulations may be permitted in that district.

This information is used to make the zoning map, which shows the various zoning districts on a base map of the city (see Figure 2, p. 141).

But zoning maps don't materialize out of nowhere; if they did, every property owner would have the right to challenge the zoning on his land in court, on the basis of its being "arbitrary and capricious." To be valid, therefore, zoning must be a part of a wider planning effort. That effort is the city's master plan, or general plan for comprehensive development.

The general plan is a document that plots the long-range physical development of the city, particularly the major public systems and structures: the streets and transit systems, the utilities (notably storm-water drainage, fresh water, and sanitary sewers), and community facilities such as schools and parks. It also takes into account the interrelationships of land uses. The general land-use plan, for example, shows the *ideal* use of the land throughout the city—not the actual, present use (which may be charted on a map called "Existing Use of Land"), or what the land is zoned for, but what planners call the "highest and best" use of the land. By providing for these major elements on a long-range, comprehensive basis, guided always by a clear set of goals and policies designed to protect the health, safety, and general welfare of the public, the city should possess in its master plan a useful guide to its future development.

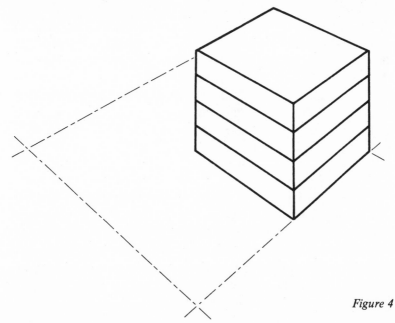

Figure 4

Ideally, the master plan should describe the future perfectly. Rarely does it achieve the ideal, nor should it be expected to do so. Someone always wants to change the master plan, either because he sincerely believes it to be wrong or because it interferes with his plans for developing his land as he sees fit. For example, a developer may own two or three acres of vacant land at the edge of your community, with an option to buy several adjacent lots currently occupied by older houses. The land is zoned for single-family use; the city's general plan and your community's neighborhood plan call for it to remain single-family; but the developer envisions an apartment-office-shopping complex on the site. To get it built, he has to have the zoning changed to a category permitting such uses. This is called rezoning. Let's use this example of a rezoning controversy to show how such matters are acted out in the typical situation. Later, we'll look at some ways to make zoning work for you.

First, *know the law*. Read your state's zoning and planning enabling legislation, as well as your city's zoning ordinance. If you don't understand them, get professional help. Don't get tripped up on a technicality, and don't let your opponent get away with technical mistakes.

Second, *know the procedures and where to intervene*. A rezoning matter must go through a stipulated process; at several points along the way, the public is invited to comment. The typical rezoning case requires the following steps:

1.) *Application or petition*. The property owner must submit a formal request for the rezoning and pay a fee. He may also be required to submit appropriate documents, such as a map of the land, a plan for the site and proposed buildings, and, in more and more cities, an environmental-impact report, showing the effect of his proposal on his own land and surrounding areas.

2.) *Public notice*. Part of the applicant's fee is used to notify the public about the rezoning request. Notices summarizing the proposed rezoning are usually posted on and around the property for a specified distance. The public is informed of the date of the first public hearing and is advised as to where and how it may comment on the rezoning application. All property owners within a certain radius are notified by registered or certified mail. Legal advertisements have to appear in the newspapers. Citizens who are on the planning commission's mailing list receive a summary of pending zoning cases. (Make sure your group is on that list.) Sometimes the city staff will notify interested citizens or community organizations. (Make sure they do this for every rezoning application in your area.)

3.) *Review by public agency.* The application and accompanying documents are then reviewed by the city staff to determine whether or not to recommend that the rezoning be approved by the appropriate officials. Each department of city government checks the application in its specific area of expertise—traffic, sewers, or land-use planning, following a procedure similar to the one outlined below. Then the chief executive officer of the city, either the mayor or the city manager or a duly appointed substitute, issues a staff report, allowing sufficient time before the first public hearing for the public to digest the report.

4.) *Public hearings.* At least one public hearing must be held on the rezoning. Many cities are now employing professional zoning "judges," called hearing examiners, to review certain kinds of cases. More often, the matter is heard before the city planning commission, an advisory body which makes recommendations on planning matters to the city council. Sometimes it is passed on to a specific committee of the planning commission or city council, such as the architectural review committee, for study.

At the public hearing, the procedure is usually for the applicant to state his case first; then the staff presents its report. Last, those members of the public who wish to speak *for* the rezoning are called to testify, followed by those who wish to speak *against* it. A time limit may be imposed on speakers. Sometimes it is necessary to fill out a card before the meeting, seeking permission to speak. A lot depends on local custom and law.

5.) *The decision.* Finally, the hearing examiner or the city council must decide to approve or deny the application. If the latter, the applicant must often wait for a specific period (six to eighteen months is not uncommon) before reapplying; this is to prevent frivolous rezoning requests. The application may also be denied "without prejudice," which means the applicant may reapply immediately.

The matter of what constitutes a majority may also be confusing. Some cities require only a simple majority of the voting members; a tie means denial. Others require a two-thirds or three-fourths majority. If more than a certain percentage of the property owners within a specific radius of the property sign a petition against the rezoning application, or if the planning commission recommends against it, the council vote may be upped to a two-thirds or three-quarters majority.

6.) *Appeal.* In some cases, an application that has been denied may be appealed administratively to a body called the "board of zoning appeals," which has the right to overrule the city council in certain instances. Or the property owner may choose to take the matter to court on appeal, in which case the burden of proof will be on him to show that the city council was in some way wrong, such as being arbitrary or capricious; otherwise, the courts, as they have since the *Euclid* case in 1926, will presume that the council acted properly. Moreover, the courts are also becoming much more lenient in granting "standing"—that is, the right to appear as an affected party—to persons who might not be affected directly by the rezoning (as would an adjacent property owner) but whose "environmental" rights may be violated. Thus, community organizations may—and I want to be cautious here—*may* in the future have greater standing in zoning appeals cases affecting their areas.

One technical point: to keep everything fair, "ex parte" communications are forbidden by law or ethical practice in many places. This means that the city council members and other decision makers may not get information "by and for one party only" during the proceedings. So don't take the president of the city council out to lunch to try to influence his vote.

Now that you are familiar with the procedure, your community organization will have to study the case carefully to see if it will support the rezoning or recommend denial. The following checklist covers the major points.

CHECKLIST FOR REZONING APPLICATIONS

The General Plan

1. Is the proposed use compatible with the general plan? With surrounding land uses?

2. If not, have conditions changed to warrant the change in zoning?
3. Is the proposed use *better* than that called for in the general plan?
4. Is the proposed use in conformance with the neighborhood plan?
5. If not, is it an improvement upon or compatible with the neighborhood plan?
6. Does it meet the neighborhood's needs?

The Zoning Map

1. How does the proposed use compare in terms of density (floor area ratio for commercial buildings; number of housing units per acre for residential areas) with what is currently on the land?
2. How does the proposed density compare to the maximum permitted under the current zoning? (This is the density that the developer is permitted "by right." He does not need city council approval to develop his land to this maximum.)
3. Does the proposal meet *all* zoning restrictions—height, density, setbacks, lot size, lot coverage?
4. Is there justification for the change in zoning, due to a change in the property or the surrounding area?
5. Is this a case of "spot zoning"? Spot zoning is a rezoning granted on a small property, making it vastly different from the zoning for all the properties around it, and thus making it incompatible with the surrounding land uses. Spot zoning is a complicated legal matter and could require the services of a good zoning lawyer to prove.

Administrative Details

Sometimes a rezoning application meets the test of compatibility with the general plan and the zoning district restrictions, but is inadequate in its specific details. The following problem areas are likely to be encountered:

1. *Parking.* Are there enough spaces for the anticipated use? Are the parking lots or garages well designed? Is there a land-

scaped buffer of trees or bushes, or a decorative screen of fences, between the parking area and the street? Do the parking lots have trees?

2. *Landscaping and buffers.* Is the site landscaped? Are surrounding areas buffered from any nuisances (noise, bright lights) on the site?

3. *Traffic and pedestrian circulation.* Is there proper ingress and egress for automobiles? Are the sidewalks wide enough for pedestrians? Have provisions been made for bicyclists? What about the handicapped and the elderly? Are there loading facilities for trucks (in commercial and industrial areas)?

4. *Utilities.* Are sanitary sewers, storm-water drains, water supplies, and other utilities sufficient to service the proposed development?

5. *Capital improvements.* Who will pay for street improvements, sidewalks, storm drains, street furniture—the city or the developer? Are they adequate to the task? Will the proposed development require the construction of more schools by attracting families with school-age children?

6. *Public safety.* Will the proposed use require special fire equipment (for example, equipment to fight a fire in a high-rise building)? Will it lead to increased crime in the area?

7. *Economic impact.* What will be the effect of the proposed development on surrounding businesses and industries? Will it bring in jobs and income to the area? Will it pay more in taxes than it costs the public to service? What effect will the proposed use have on the value of the surrounding property? What will happen to the people currently using the land? Will they be provided with housing or business space on the site? Will they be paid to relocate? (See Chapter 10.)

8. *Natural environment.* Will sensitive environmental areas— streams, hillsides, wooded areas—be protected? What will be done to save trees? Will the proposed use increase the amount of smoke, noise, dirt, or air pollution in the area? What about natural vistas—the view of the mountains or the lake or the ocean? Will these be protected? What about "solar rights"? Will adjacent property owners lose their view of the sun? (Given the energy situation, protecting solar rights is no longer a futuristic concern.)

9. *Man-made environment.* Will the proposed structure change the skyline of the neighborhood or the city? What will be done to protect historic structures? Will the project affect the area's "urban charm"? What will be done to protect the public's investment in the area?

If you lose a rezoning fight and appeal the decision in court, the burden of proof will be on you to show why the rezoning should not stand. Your only other option is to use confrontation tactics against the developer or to negotiate with him. Even if you favor the proposal, you might be able to bargain with the developer to include more public amenities, such as plazas, arcades, public areas, sitting areas, benches and street furniture, bike racks, bus shelters, skywalks or overhead pedestrian walks, open space, trees, landscaping and buffering, fountains, play areas and tot lots, land or buildings for schools, and entryways to bus or subway facilities. Get him to preserve any historic buildings on the site. In residential projects, do what they do in Montgomery County, Maryland: for projects of fifty or more units, the county requires developers to set aside 15 percent of the units (20 percent in "town sector" and "planned neighborhood" zones) for moderate-income families at moderate rentals. In return, the county grants developers up to a 20 percent "bonus" density: instead of being able to build fifty units, for example, the developer would be able to build a maximum of sixty units.

In conclusion, don't be afraid to put pressure on developers to make concessions to the community. After all, you're doing it for the public good.

The preceding description of the procedure for handling a rezoning application should give you a clearer idea of how to work your way through the zoning maze. There are, however, several other zoning-related cases that could come up in your neighborhood. I will mention them only briefly here, since the process for dealing with them is similar to a rezoning case, and you can consult the recommended books for further information.

VARIANCES. A variance is an exemption from the ordinance granted on the basis of hardship or unusual conditions. Suppose a house is built on a lot with a steeply sloping backyard; the owner wants to expand the house, but it would be physically impossible to build in back. So he asks for a variance to build in the front or side yard, even though he will not have enough setback. Variances should be granted only for real hardship, not just to save a property owner a few dollars; and the problem that leads to the request for the variance (a steep backyard, for example) should be specific to the property in question, not a general neighborhood condition.

SPECIAL EXCEPTION (CONDITIONAL USE). This is an exception provided for in the zoning ordinance, but usually requiring an application to the board of zoning appeals or city council before being granted. The nursery school is a common case. Almost all residential districts permit nursery schools, but the property owner must apply to the appeals board or city council for the right to operate. Sometimes a "use permit" is placed on the property, making the owner add parking spaces or landscaping. He may be required to renew his permit every twelve or eighteen months, so that the administering body can see if he has complied with any special restrictions deemed necessary.

NONCONFORMING USE. An example of nonconforming use would be a billboard, erected before the zoning ordinance was passed, in the middle of a residential area. Ordinarily, such a billboard would not "conform" to the zoning, but it is allowed to remain because it predated passage of the ordinance. In most cases, should the billboard be destroyed, it could not be rebuilt; if its ownership changes, it would have to be torn down. Sometimes nonconforming uses are "amortized" over a period of ten or twenty years, at which time they must be removed.

SUBDIVISION PLAN. When you subdivide land, you take a big chunk and cut it up into smaller lots. This must be done according to certain regulations and controls. Subdivision plans are more of a problem in suburban and rural areas and new cities, where there is more undeveloped land than in old cities.

PLANNED DEVELOPMENT. A planned development is usually a large-scale development in which the owner is required to submit a site plan showing exactly how he proposes to use the land; in most cases, if the site plan is approved, the developer is granted special concessions—higher density than would be permitted under ordinary zoning, or exemption from certain zoning or subdivision restrictions such as building height, for example. If the site plan is not approved, the developer is allowed to build on his land according to the regular zoning restrictions for that particular district. The idea behind planned developments is to foster original design concepts and encourage broad-scale development, instead of a piecemeal approach. The danger is that it is discretionary and therefore may become a political football. Community organizations faced with proposals for planned developments have their work cut out for them. For maximum influence, get involved in the negotiations early.

"NUISANCE" CASES. Three specific zoning-related "nuisances" seem to be popping up with greater and greater frequency: fast-food franchises, "adult" sex businesses, and group-care facilities.

Many communities are concerned about the "McDonaldification" of their neighborhoods. In Cambridge, Massachusetts, the Douglass Street Tenants Organization lost its fight to prevent McDonald's from tearing down one of the city's two pre–Civil War Greek Revival buildings. In Washington, the Ad Hoc Committee to Prevent Ginocide has been waging war against the Gino's burger chain. These groups are offended by the design of the buildings and the litter and traffic problems associated with them.

Some cities are taking action. Carmel, California, outlaws "formula restaurants." Palo Alto, California, requires all commercial uses to get the approval of an architectural review board. State College, Pennsylvania, puts strict regulations on screening for drive-in restaurants. Kansas City, Kansas, requires that all unpaved areas be landscaped. Detroit forbids drive-in restaurant patrons from eating on the premises. White Plains, New York, prohibits such establishments from locating less than three hundred feet from schools, churches, residential areas, hospitals, and other noncommercial uses.

Sex businesses—adult movie theaters, massage parlors, peepshows, and bookstores—pose a serious threat to neighborhoods. The Supreme Court has ruled that they cannot be banned outright, so communities must find ways to regulate them. There are two basic approaches. The "Detroit" system is to spread these sex businesses out by prohibiting them from locating too close to one another. The "Boston" approach is to cluster them in one area (which has since been dubbed "The Combat Zone") on the theory that the police and public officials can keep a better eye on them if they are concentrated in one district.

The third such nuisance, the group-care facility, refers to residential homes for the mentally retarded, juvenile delinquents, unwed mothers, and similar social-welfare cases. Many communities object to being flooded with "problem" members of society. For example, when the state of Illinois started releasing mental patients from state hospitals in an effort to "deinstitutionalize" their care, hundreds of these pathetic souls wound up in the Uptown neighborhood of Chicago, where they could be found roaming the streets at all hours, urinating on the sidewalks, and, in general, creating a public nuisance—through no fault of their own, of course. But when one neighborhood gets saddled with an undue share of these problem cases, there is good cause for public outcry.

Some states have passed laws in an attempt to handle the problem. The best law, according to Edith Netter, editor of *Land Use Law & Zoning Digest*, is Wisconsin's, which requires that such facilities be dispersed and that all communities take a "fair share" of them. In other words, the law implies that since society has deemed that special social-welfare cases be housed in group-care facilities, every community should bear a reasonable share of the burden.

These nuisance cases exemplify zoning used as a defensive measure to protect neighborhoods from objectionable land usage; but zoning can also be a positive tool for community organizations to use in preserving and enhancing their neighborhoods. We have already seen in the last chapter how neighborhoods in one community, Arlington, Virginia, have been able to intervene in the planning and zoning process. By making their wishes known to elected officials, these community organizations have used their political strength to get a say in future plans for their neighborhoods. The phenomenon of neighborhood groups having an advisory role in planning and zoning matters is spreading: among the cities with such a system are Birmingham, Alabama; Dayton, Ohio; the District of Columbia; Eugene, Oregon; Honolulu, Hawaii; Newton, Massachusetts; New York City; and Simi Valley, California.

Another way zoning can be used to protect your neighborhood is by *downzoning*, that is, rezoning to a less-dense use. Let's take a hypothetical example: Suppose that at one time a highway was planned to run through your section of the city. In determining the proper land use and zoning for the area near the highway, the city in the past assumed that the road would spur commercial and industrial development; therefore, it showed certain existing residential areas as future commercial and industrial areas, and zoned these areas accordingly. If for any reason the highway plans are put aside, there would be no need for all that commercial and industrial zoning. On the basis of that change in conditions, your community group could ask the city council to change the zoning to a lower-density category. That's downzoning.

The reason downzoning doesn't occur more often is that it is an invitation to a lawsuit. A property owner whose land is zoned for a shopping center believes it to be worth hundreds of thousands of dollars an acre; the same land zoned for single-family houses is probably worth much, much less. The land owner, therefore, sees downzoning as a confiscation of his property without just compensation. Under the Fifth Amendment, such a "taking," as it is called, would be illegal.

That, at least, is how the property owner sees it. As in most legal matters, of course, downzoning is much more complicated than that. The courts, you'll remember, presume that the legislature (in this case, the city council) has the right to regulate zoning. The burden in such a case, then, falls on the property owner to prove that the council: (1) failed to follow the required legal procedures (for example, failure to give notice); (2) acted arbitrarily or capriciously (for example, not basing the decision on detailed planning studies); (3) failed to act in the public interest or for the general welfare; or (4) deprived the owner of any reasonable use of his land (that is, confiscation). On this last point, it could be argued that being allowed to develop single-family houses is a reasonable use of land.

Because of the legal entanglements attached to it, downzoning is a device that community organizations should use cautiously. Try to get voluntary cooperation from the property owner first. Point out to him that the land may never be developed to the level it is zoned for, and thus he may be paying extra taxes for a dream. (This worked in High View Park, a middle-class black neighborhood in Arlington, Virginia.) If you are forced to take the matter to the city council for action, be prepared to show that the specific property or the surrounding area, or both, have changed to such a degree that the old general land-use plan is no longer valid; therefore, the zoning must be changed, too. But keep in mind that a forced downzoning stands a good chance of being challenged in court.

Despite the fact that zoning is one of the oldest methods urban planners have availed themselves of to regulate land use, it allows tremendous opportunities for novel thinking. Furthermore, one of the beauties of zoning is its adaptability to local conditions. For example, to protect the delicate environment of its hills and valleys, the city of Cincinnati passed a zoning ordinance setting up an "environmental quality district" to protect such natural phenomena as unique geologic strata, significant scenic views, and vegetation. Then Cincinnati carried the idea over to the man-made environment and set up special regulations for areas of heavy public and private investment, including business districts like the famous Findlay Market. In Boulder, Colorado, the Goss-Grove neighborhood has long been concerned about preserving its single-family character in the face of high-density zoning. "Rather than storming city hall with requests for downzoning," notes Dena Wild, a planner with the city, "the residents have developed the Pyramid Density Concept. There are three premises behind the concept: (1) new developments should not exceed twice the densities of the surrounding area; (2) new structures should reflect the traditional architectural detailing found throughout the neighborhood; and (3) the residents should be allowed to review and comment on both private and public projects affecting the neighborhood." At this writing, the Pyramid Density Concept is still under review in Boulder, but it and the Cincinnati example point to neighborhood initiative in the zoning process—another case of using the system to work *for* your community, instead of against it.

Code Enforcement

Almost every city and town in the United States has a housing code. The housing code is a local law or ordinance requiring property owners to keep their buildings and yards up to certain standards. (It is not to be confused with the building code, which covers *new* construction.) Code enforcement is a critical component in any neighborhood revitalization program. Since housing is a unique commodity—you can't move it, so one bad house affects every other house on the block—it is necessary to have certain minimal standards that every building must meet.

The authority to draw up housing codes derives from the states' power to pass laws to insure the health, safety, and general welfare of the public. Individual codes vary widely in terms of their requirements, enforcement procedures, and penalties for noncompliance. In general, however, they cover such matters as electrical wiring, plumbing, heating, and the basic structure of the house, as well as the cleanliness and upkeep of the yard. They are enforced by a housing inspection department, acting on the basis of complaints (usually by tenants or neighbors of problem properties) or as part of a systematic, house-by-house sweep through a section of the city. Violators are usually given a stated period of time to "bring the unit up to code," then are prosecuted in the municipal court or special housing court if the necessary repairs are not made. The penalty is usually a fine, although jail sentences may be imposed.

Because of its punitive nature, code enforcement has earned a bad reputation in housing circles. Here's what can happen. Some crusader decides that an area of the city is declining, as evidenced by the fact that the buildings aren't being kept up to code. Solution: Send in a team of inspectors to get tough on homeowners and landlords. Result: Resentment on the part of "good" homeowners and landlords, financial worries for homeowners who have to go into debt to clear up violations, and apathy on the part of slumlords, who are milking the buildings anyway and could hardly care less about the health and safety of their tenants. Thus, too much stick and not enough carrot gives code enforcement a bad name. Or, as Tom Ekvall, a planner in Lincoln, Nebraska, puts it, "You just can't go out and enforce the housing code without taking into account the needs of the neighborhood."

Used properly, code enforcement can be an effective tool for revitalization. But it cannot operate in a vacuum. Code enforcement must be part of an overall approach for saving a neighborhood. In *Flexible Code Enforcement*, Roger S. Ahlbrandt, Jr., lists a number of factors that are necessary for such a strategy, including:

1.) *City investment.* The city must do its share in providing public improvements and services to the area.

2.) *Lender commitment.* The money interests must be willing to make loans to property owners who are required to bring their buildings up to code.

3.) *Subsidized rehabilitation loans.* Hardship and high-risk cases must be given access to loan money.

4.) *Citizen participation.* The community must be involved in the process.

5.) *Targeting.* The code enforcement program must be concentrated to be effective.

These last two factors are especially relevant to our discussion. Code enforcement is most effective when citizens are involved, because a strong sense of neighborhood identity brings peer pressure to bear on homeowners. When your neighbors say, "Fix up your house," that's a much stronger message than an impersonal directive from city hall. And the program must be concentrated on a neighborhood basis because that is the most effective way to "spin off" one homeowner's improvements for the benefit of a whole block; looking at it another way, scattered fix-up loses the cumulative effect that helps turn a neighborhood around.

Of course, code enforcement is no panacea. It works best in certain kinds of neighborhoods—places with relatively salvageable housing, a reasonable demand for housing, a high level of owner-occupancy, and a strong sense of neighborhood identity, preferably a strong community organization. That is not to say that code enforcement should be ruled out for the most hard-hit neighborhoods: it can be a useful tool, but it must be used wisely and delicately, like a scalpel in the hands of a skilled surgeon.

The key to a successful code enforcement program is that it must reinforce the sense of *confidence* neighbors have about the future of their area. That, of course, is the theme we have been stressing throughout this book. Let's look at some examples of effective code enforcement.

In Cincinnati's Madisonville neighborhood, a house-by-house "flexible" inspection system is an integral part of the local Neighborhood Housing Services (NHS) program. "Madisonville's people have said, 'We want to bring Madisonville back,' and that can only be done on a systematic basis," says Jeanne Davis, the program's assistant director. As in most NHS areas, a team of city housing inspectors visits each house, not only noting violations, but offering advice on hiring contractors, getting home-repair loans, and making additional improvements above and beyond the minimum standards. Says Davis, "The individual inspector has to approach the homeowner with the idea that he's there to *assist*." Code enforcement is thus viewed as a service, not a police operation. ("The key to code enforcement," says Roger Ahlbrandt, "is working *with* neighborhood residents. You need code people who really *sell* code enforcement to the people. If you have insensitive inspectors, they're going to turn off the homeowners.") Homeowners who fail to make the required repairs get a letter from the president of the Madisonville Community Council, followed by a personal visit. If the homeowner still refuses to cooperate, the case is turned over to the city. But that's rare. "Our people know the community so well," says Davis, "we have extremely good entrée to just about anyone in the neighborhood."

Not every code enforcement program is this successful. In fact, code enforcement is plagued with problems. For one thing, people resent any invasion of privacy. A man's home is his castle, Americans believe, and they don't want some city inspector monkeying around with the plumbing and looking under the beds. In some cities, too, it is a widely held belief that the inspectors are on the take. Even honest inspectors get accused of finding "too many" violations. In cities with powerful labor lobbies, such as Chicago, the complaint is that the building trades use their influence to get unusually tough codes approved, on the theory that this creates work for union members.

One of the most frustrating aspects of code enforcement involves cases in which a landlord owns a few buildings in the neighborhood and refuses to maintain them properly. It's difficult to prosecute such a slumlord. First of all, he is hard to find; he rarely lives in the building and may not even live in the same state. Serving legal papers then becomes extremely difficult. Only a few states require property owners to have an agent within the state who is legally responsible for maintaining the building. If the authorities manage to get the owner into court, he can usually get a continuance; he may even make a few minor repairs, to show the judge his "good faith." Or he may choose simply to pay the fine if it is less than the cost of making the repairs. Most likely he won't have to go to jail, because (as Richard E. Starr has noted) criminal intent would have to be proved. If things get bad enough, he may just walk away from the building, leaving the city with a white elephant.

Some jurisdictions have laws that help in the fight against slumlords who abandon their properties. Minnesota, for example, defines "owner" as any person in direct or indirect control of a property. In the case of code violations, the law allows any tenant to file a private lawsuit against the owner (who may be the building manager); the suit must be heard within ten days. If the owner, building manager, or landlord fails to make the necessary repairs, the court may appoint an administrator to carry them out. During this period, the tenants' rents go into an escrow account to pay the cost of the repairs. New York State law also permits the court to appoint a "receiver," or substitute manager, to effect court-ordered repairs, but it is a cumbersome process, since each repair has to be approved by court order. Baltimore has a "quick-takeover" power which allows the city to negotiate the purchase or begin condemnation of any building that has been recently vacated, poses an obstacle to neighborhood growth, or acts as a source of deterioration. New Jersey has a state code enforcement system for multifamily buildings and hotels. Each building must have a resident owner or in-state agent. Alleged violations become accepted as facts if they are not challenged by the owner. The state's housing bureau sets the fine, based on the severity of the violation. If the owner fails to pay, he may be prosecuted in a civil suit.

Despite its drawbacks, code enforcement *can* work, especially if there is a firm commitment to it from city officials and close cooperation with a well-organized community group. The Belair-Edison Improvement Association is a perfect example of the latter.

"At our membership meetings, we'd constantly get these complaints—'This house has a broken downspout,' 'This house needs painting,'" recalls Richard Lelonek, the association's president emeritus. "We'd have an inspector come down, and maybe something would get done, but it usually didn't solve the problem."

Belair-Edison is an almost suburban area in the northeast quadrant of Baltimore's "Outer City," as the fringe area is known. It is a section of brick single-family homes, occupied mostly by whites, and surrounded by largely black neighborhoods. Fifteen years ago, when Dick Lelonek was elected to the first of ten consecutive terms as president of the improvement association, Belair-Edison was in an area whose future was in doubt. "If you tried to sell," notes Lelonek, "you couldn't get your money."

Lelonek approached city officials with the idea of getting a house-by-house inspection performed by city inspectors. "They said they didn't have the manpower, so we said, 'Why can't we inspect the area ourselves?'"

That was the start of the Outer City Program, later called the Neighborhood Cooperation Program. It works like this: First, the city and the cooperating community organization sign a letter of agreement stating which services the city will provide and what the civic group promises to contribute. Then volunteers from the neighborhood go through an intensive training course, similar to what city housing inspectors get. A target area of the neighborhood is then chosen, homeowners are notified of the program, and the volunteers make their inspections of the yards and *exteriors* of the buildings. (They don't go inside anyone's house.) Owners whose properties have minor problems receive a checklist from the community organization, with a friendly note asking them to make repairs. After a reasonable period, some cases with "minor" deficiencies get turned over to the city; a small percentage of hard-core cases get the full treatment from the city's housing department.

"The program has met with fantastic success," says Lelonek. In the first years of the program, Belair-Edison volunteers inspected 561 houses, of which only 30 had to be turned over to the city for action. Families began to feel secure in their investment, putting in new kitchens, redoing basements. Long-time residents who had contemplated moving decided to stay. Not surprisingly, other neighborhoods wanted a piece of the program. By 1977, eleven were active. In that year alone, they inspected 4,755 properties, issued 952 checklists, and got voluntary compliance from 628, or two-thirds, of the owners. Of the 324 turned over to the city, 84 were issued violation notices, 128 got "minor deficiency" letters, and 112 were found to have no cause for action, according to a report by the city. Of the total number of houses inspected in 1977, therefore, the city had to take action in less than 5 percent of the cases. "This program has saved the city millions of dollars," says Lelonek.

Here, then, are some points to remember in developing a code enforcement program for your neighborhood:

1.) *Create a strong neighborhood base.* The neighborhood must be behind the program. People must recognize it as a helpful measure, not a punitive one. A hefty publicity campaign should get the message across, but don't oversell the program before people get a chance to see results.

2.) *Restrict the program to voluntary action.* A citizen-based code enforcement program could run into legal problems. It must be structured so that citizens are not themselves enforcing the law; alleged violations must be turned over to the proper authorities for action. Don't make your volunteers serve as policemen.

3.) *Inspect exteriors only.* Avoid the legal hassle of possible trespassing by inspecting only the outside of the house. From the community's point of view, it's the exterior that counts anyway. Serious code violations that can be determined only from an interior inspection will probably be revealed by tenant complaints or as a result of city action anyway.

4.) *Maintain flexibility.* The program has to allow for hardship cases. The classic situation is the elderly couple who have lived in the house all their lives and have gotten by on 110-volt electricity—only to learn that the code now requires 220 hook-ups. Do what they do in Cincinnati. Mark the report "Sufficient for present use only." When the house changes hands, the new owner will have to bring it up to code.

5.) *Be aware of people's sensitivities.* Don't hurt their feelings. Maureen Hellwig, planning director for Community 21/Northwest Community Organization in Chicago, tells about how one group of surveyors said a certain church needed "minor repairs." When the people from that parish heard about the accusation, they were insulted. To keep peace in the neighborhood, it was decided that the church was indeed "sound."

6.) *Cooperate with city officials.* The ground rules for the program must be firmly established. Citizen volunteers have to be given rigorous training. The community organization must have the city's assurance that the arm of government will be used against delinquent property owners, particularly slumlords. The city's inspectors and other involved public officials must be made aware of the community organization's goals and must agree to uphold them. Finally, the city should provide the necessary backup services (public improvements, subsidized rehabilitation loans, and staff) to make the program work.

If you've completed the field inventory recommended in Chapter 5, you already know where most of your problem properties are located. Developing a code enforcement program to deal with them is the logical next step.

The Automobile Problem

If there is one complaint that many neighborhoods share, it is what to do about that modern-day monster, *automobilus tyrannis.* Transportation should therefore be a major component of your neighborhood plan. How can traffic be made to flow more freely? What limits should be set on truck traffic? What about mass transit? What plans are in the works for new highways and major streets in your area? These are matters that deserve thoughtful consideration by your organization.

Two problems in particular plague community activists: "outsiders" parking their cars on neighborhood streets, and commuters using quiet residential boulevards as raceways to get to and from work. Let's look at the latter problem first.

Cut-through traffic is a headache for any neighborhood where people are concerned about improving the quality of life. Who wants hundreds, even thousands, of extra cars flooding the streets, cars driven by people who don't live in the neighborhood and care little about it? The noise, the air pollution, the increased danger of traffic accidents, the threat to children, pedestrians, and bicyclists—these are conditions that no neighborhood should have to put up with merely for some commuter to save five minutes getting to work.

One way to discourage drivers from cutting through the neighborhood is to have your city's traffic engineers install road signs or other traffic control devices at strategic locations. You could ask to have stop signs installed at every corner, for example. If you find that a certain street is used during rush hour by commuters driving in one direction, have the city install signs making the street one-way in the opposite direction during that period. Or have drivers prohibited from making left-hand turns off the main highway to cut through your neighborhood in the morning—have the city put up a sign saying, NO LEFT TURN, 7–9 A.M., MON.–FRI.

These suggestions may help, but there's no guarantee drivers will obey the signs. They may even drive faster, say, between stop signs to make up for "lost time." And the restrictions are also a nuisance for residents. Plus you'll find that your friendly city traffic engineer doesn't like to install "unnecessary" traffic control devices; and if your city receives certain federal highway funds, the traffic department is almost bound to follow specific guidelines as to where and when they may install such controls.

The newest method for keeping outside traffic off local streets is the traffic diverter—a physical obstruction that either blocks or diverts traffic from the street. Traffic diverting systems can be designed in various ways. A street can simply be closed off with a barricade, barrels, stanchions, posts, or paved landscaping. The cul-de-sac also serves to close off a street, at the same time providing a well-designed turn-around area for drivers. (See Figure 5.) Or a street can be blocked off at both ends and made into a

play area—or even landscaped into a "block park." (See Figure 6.)
The "diagonal divider" forces traffic to turn. (See Figure 7.)
The "star diverter" is a variation of the diagonal, permitting
traffic from all four directions to be diverted. (See Figure 8.)

Still another design is the traffic circle, which slows traffic at
an intersection and allows drivers to either turn or proceed
straight ahead. (See Figure 9.) Devices like these are in use in nu-

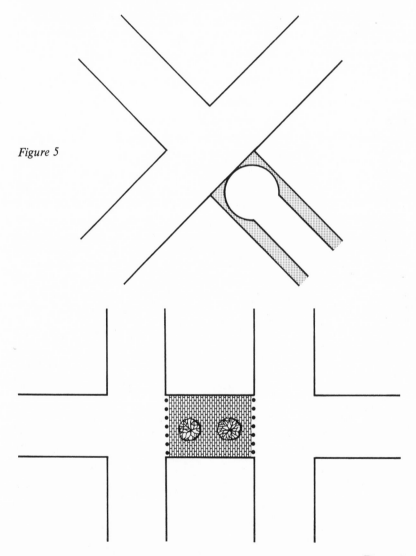

Figure 5

Figure 6

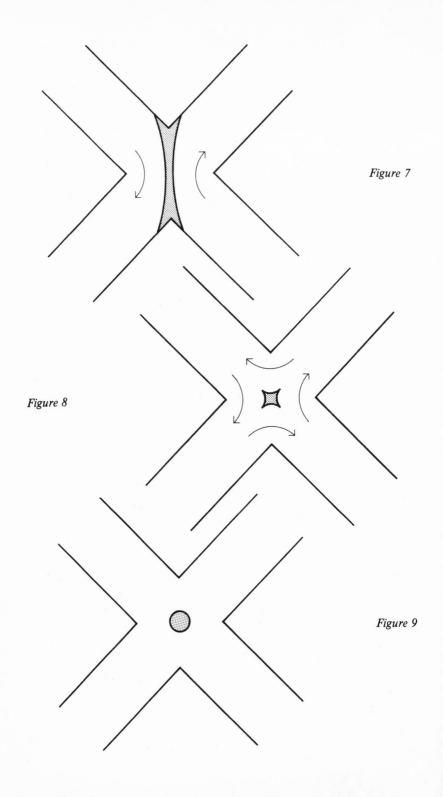

Figure 7

Figure 8

Figure 9

merous communities across the country. How can you get them for your neighborhood?

First, establish the need. Is the cut-through traffic a hazard? How many accidents have occurred there? Is there any other way to control the flow of traffic? You'll have to consult your city's traffic department for their help and advice in determining which intersections should be given priority. When you've established the probable trouble spots, conduct a field survey. Have volunteers from your neighborhood watch the street during the worst periods. (Through such a survey, the Ashton Heights neighborhood in Arlington, Virginia, found that 60 percent of the cars using the neighborhood's most heavily trafficked street were from outside the county.) Then inform the immediate community of your plans. Make up flyers or cards and pass them out to residents and store owners in the areas near where the diverter will be installed. If possible, give the flyers to drivers, too.

Don't construct anything permanent until a test has been made, preferably for at least ninety days. "Demonstration is very important so that changes can be made," says Lloyd Orlob, Seattle's traffic engineer. Orlob's department found that the star diverters tested on Seattle's East Republic Street didn't work and recommended changing them to traffic circles. Temporary diverters can be made of wood barricades, plastic poles, barrels, and metal guard rails.

As a final step, conduct a survey of area residents (and drivers, if possible) to determine the level of support for the traffic diverter. The city of Seattle used a questionnaire like the following example to test public opinion in the Leschi area:

1. How were you affected by the traffic diverters?
   ( ) Not at all inconvenienced
   ( ) Slightly inconvenienced
   ( ) Significantly inconvenienced
2. Do you favor installing permanent diverters?
   ( ) Yes   ( ) No
3. Comments: _____

Incidentally, the vote in the Leschi area was split fifty-fifty, and the traffic engineers recommended against permanent installation.

Do traffic diverters work? In many cases, yes. In one Seattle neighborhood where diverters were installed, the number of traffic accidents was reduced by twelve in one year. In the East Republic area, the city reported that "Traffic diverters are a major contributor to enhancing the traffic safety of the neighborhood." For the Stevens neighborhood, Seattle's traffic engineers reported reduced traffic volumes, fewer accidents, and less street noise as a result of the diverter program. "The residents are convinced that their neighborhood is a more pleasant place in which to live," said the city's report. The cost of the barriers was "overshadowed by the reduction in traffic and associated problems."

Not everyone is crazy about the diverters, however. In San Francisco, voters approved a referendum to remove permanent barriers from one neighborhood, at a total cost of $137,000. In neighboring Berkeley, citizens petitioned to have some fifty diverters removed, but the effort failed. Yet the city of Berkeley has to spend $1,000 a month to maintain the barriers due to vandalism. Sometimes adjacent property owners complain because the city has to take additional right-of-way to build the diverters. In many cities, fire and police officials object to the diverters because, they say, the barriers increase their response time in emergencies. This problem can be solved in a number of ways: by making barriers that can be "smashed" by a heavy fire truck or police car; by installing a gate for emergency vehicles at each barrier and supplying the drivers with keys; or by landscaping the barriers with bushes, shrubs, and grass, again permitting emergency vehicles to crash through. As more neighborhoods feel the impact of heavy traffic from outside their borders, the traffic diverter will grow in popularity.

Another traffic control device that's sure to spread is the special-district parking restriction. It is designed to prevent parking by nonresidents in neighborhoods near shopping areas, offices and workplaces, or mass transit stops—places where commuters or shoppers are likely to park their cars on the neighborhood streets. Arlington, Virginia, uses a sticker system, whereby residents of highly impacted areas are given stickers for their cars. Any car parked in the area without a sticker during weekday business hours is in violation of the ordinance. The idea went unchallenged until a group of commuters took the matter to court.

Ultimately, the case came before the U.S. Supreme Court, which found the ordinance reasonable and not in violation of the equal protection clause. The court also made certain comments of importance to all neighborhoods, not only those affected by commuter parking. I quote the decision at length:

> To reduce air pollution and other environmental effects of automobile commuting, a community reasonably may restrict on-street parking available to commuters, thus encouraging reliance on car pools and mass transit. The same goal is served by assuring convenient parking to residents who leave their cars at home during the day. A community may also decide that restrictions on the flow of outside traffic into particular residential areas would enhance the quality of life thereby reducing noise, traffic hazards, and litter. By definition, discrimination against nonresidents would inhere in such restrictions.
>
> The Constitution does not outlaw these social and environment objectives, *nor does it presume distinctions between residents and nonresidents of a local neighborhood to be invidious.* The Equal Protection Clause requires only that the distinction drawn by an ordinance like Arlington's rationally promote the regulation's objectives. (Emphasis added.)

Thus, not only does this decision ratify restricting parking for nonresidents—leading to similar steps being taken in San Francisco, Chicago, Montgomery County, Maryland, Cambridge, Massachusetts, and numerous other places—but it strongly implies that, where reasonable social and environmental objectives can be adduced, a city or town may put the needs of neighborhood residents over those of nonresidents, even for the use of a public commodity like the streets. This decision, therefore, deserves careful study by any neighborhood faced with a seemingly uncontrollable nuisance from outside. It is, to some extent, the high court's recognition of the right of neighborhood autonomy.

7

NEIGHBORHOOD STABILITY: INTEGRATION AND CRIME PREVENTION

In Chapter 2 we saw how neighborhood decline is to a considerable extent a function of certain social factors. I do not presume to be able to offer solutions for all the problems neighborhoods confront, but I would like to describe the efforts of a number of community groups in attacking two of the worst problems—racial resegregation and neighborhood crime—in the hope that other community organizations can learn from these examples. Let's begin with the problem of maintaining racial stability.

Despite federal open-housing laws and the efforts of civil-rights groups, most American neighborhoods remain racially homogeneous, or at least heavily weighted toward one group. Segregation is to some extent voluntary, particularly among immigrant groups, such as the Puerto Ricans or Vietnamese, who find security in numbers. But there is no denying that it often is imposed, a consequence of racist practices, such as residential "steering" and block busting.

Nevertheless, there are hundreds of communities in cities and suburbs around the country where integration is the norm. Nearly two hundred of them have formed National Neighbors, Inc., a Washington-based nonprofit organization to promote racial integration and stability. Let's look briefly at how two such organizations are achieving integration.

In the early 1970s, changing racial patterns were the primary concern of residents of Beverly Hills–Morgan Park, a suburblike area in the southwest corner of Chicago. By 1971, it was apparent that certain real estate operators in the area were trying to panic white homeowners into selling to blacks, a process that, left unchecked, almost surely would lead to complete racial change. "Very clearly, the issue was race, and how we were going to deal with it," says Mark Franzen, executive director of the Beverly Area Planning Association (BAPA), a coalition of thirteen civic associations and local business groups. Franzen and a number of local residents described the approach the neighborhood took. "We broke the real estate people down into two groups," said Franzen. "Yeah," chimed in the others, "the good guys and the bad guys."

To help control the panic, volunteers manned a rumor hotline, which handled an average of sixty-five calls a day during the worst periods. They also advised homeowners on ways to deal with unscrupulous real estate dealers. BAPA held hundreds of kaffeeklatsches, where neighbors could explore their fears. "If there was any racial problem, people on the block knew that they could call me and we'd talk about it," says Shirley Pickett, a black homeowner.

BAPA also initiated a program of "affirmative marketing," to prevent further resegregation. "We've practiced 'reverse steering' for years," says Joseph Thouvenell, BAPA's treasurer and one of the "good guy" real estate dealers in the area. "We decided to control the market and keep the little fly-by-night operations under control." The responsible realtors in the area agreed to work cooperatively with the community organization to stop panic peddling. BAPA also set up a housing office to guide prospective homeowners and renters. "We counsel both black and white families as to where the demand is and we 'suggest' where they might look," says Ginger Rugai, a homeowner and director of BAPA's housing center. "If they are white, I suggest areas where whites are in demand. If they are black, I show them areas of black demand. I'm very up front with them." Rugai has a personal stake in the housing program. "We were forced to move three times because of resegregation," she said, "and I don't want to have to move again."

What holds for housing goes for the schools. "All of our schools, public and parochial, are of very good quality, and we have a lot of interest from parents," says Sue Delves, BAPA's president. Morgan Park High School is 59 percent black, 41 percent white, but entering classes must be fifty-fifty black and white.

In Philadelphia, the East Mount Aire Neighbors took a decidedly different approach to maintaining racial stability. "We call East Mount Aire 'a community that's integrated,' rather than 'an integrated community,'" says Eversley Vaughan, a portly black state welfare caseworker and the group's first president. East Mount Aire is a two-hundred-block area in northwest Philadelphia made up mostly of single-family homes ranging in value from $10,000 to over $100,000. Twelve years ago, when East Mount Aire Neighbors was started, it was an area beset by racial change. "When I moved in, I got a call from a real estate guy," recalls Vaughan. "He asked me, 'Would you be interested in selling? You know, the coloreds are coming in.' I said, 'That's okay, some of my best friends are colored.'"

Racial tension was no laughing matter in East Mount Aire after the assassination of Martin Luther King in 1968. "We decided to deal with racism, and we deliberately split up into black and white caucuses," says Vaughan. "Then we came together at a final meeting. It was really hot. There was fear that the whites were going to keep a certain percentage of blacks out, and there were all kinds of ridiculous rumors going around. The meeting lasted till two in the morning. But as we talked, we found that we had a lot more in common than what divided us."

The approach East Mount Aire Neighbors adopted was to stop racial steering, but also to strengthen the qualities that made the neighborhood desirable for both blacks and whites. "We got a voluntary ban on solicitation from the board of realtors and the city's human-rights commission," says Vaughan, meaning that real estate operators in the area agreed not to phone people at home asking if they wanted to sell. They also formed committees to deal with everything from mental health to zoning to housing. The group opened its own child-care facility. It operates four homes for the mentally retarded. It got the city to invest some $500,000 in public projects in the neighborhood, even though the area voted nine to one against Mayor Frank L. Rizzo. It developed and won approval of its own neighborhood plan to counter the city planning commission's scheme for the area. It got two of the city's biggest savings institutions to advertise the availability of mortgages in East Mount Aire. When a YMHA building came on the market, the group thought it would make a perfect community center. It raised more than $50,000, but was still $4,000 short. The citizens' group got a loan from a savings and loan to make up the difference. "The loan was for four years," says Vaughan. "We paid it back in two."

From the experience of groups like the Beverly Area Planning Association and East Mount Aire Neighbors emerges a two-pronged approach to maintaining racial stability. The first part is to preserve and improve the overall quality of the neighborhood so that it will continue to be attractive to stable, middle-class families, no matter what their race. Without that strong community base, the panic peddlers are free to chip away at the neighborhood.

The second part is a direct attack on unscrupulous real estate practices. What might such a program entail? Here are some techniques being used by community groups:

LOCAL OPEN-HOUSING LAWS. Discrimination in housing is prohibited under the Civil Rights Act of 1968 and the Civil Rights Act of 1866. But many communities have found it useful to pass their own antidiscrimination laws to prohibit involuntary, negative racial steering, since the federal enforcement mechanism is so time-consuming. Passage of a local law also establishes an "open-housing" climate in the community.

HOUSING MARKET REGISTRATION. Some cities, such as Bellwood, Illinois, require real estate operators to register all housing for sale or rent with city hall. This allows complete monitoring of local fair-housing ordinances.

HOUSING "TESTERS." Bellwood also uses "testers" to enforce its ordinance. Testers are volunteers—some white, some black, some in mixed couples—who pose as prospective tenants or home purchasers to determine if real estate salesmen treat blacks or mixed couples in a discriminatory manner. In 1979, the U.S. Supreme

Court upheld the right of testers to appear as interested parties in a suit involving the village of Bellwood and two real estate firms accused of racial steering. (*Gladstone, Realtors et al.* v. *Village of Bellwood*, No. 77-1493, Decided April 17, 1979.)

VOLUNTARY BAN ON FOR SALE SIGNS. Some communities—including Gary, Indiana, Country Club Hills, Illinois, and Shaker Heights, Ohio—have passed laws prohibiting the posting of For Sale signs because they might cause a real estate panic. The U.S. Supreme Court has ruled such ordinances unconstitutional. (*Linmark Associates Inc., et al.* v. *Township of Willingboro, N.J.*, No. 76-357, May 2, 1977.) A voluntary ban on For Sale signs, however, would seem to fall within the court's ruling.

VOLUNTARY NONSOLICITATION. Instead of forbidding certain practices, the community can enter into an agreement with the local real estate operators to prevent solicitation over the phone or by an equivalent method. Hazelcrest, Illinois, has worked out such an agreement with its real estate dealers.

RUMOR HOTLINES. The BAPA hotline is a demonstration of how such an information device can be used to control unfounded rumors.

HOUSING COUNSELING CENTERS. Besides offering first-time home purchasers general advice about buying a house, or informing prospective tenants about the availability of apartments, housing centers such as the one established by BAPA "sell" the neighborhood to outsiders and publicize efforts to encourage racial stability.

POSITIVE VOLUNTARY STEERING. Through housing counseling centers, the community encourages integration by explaining the organization's long-range goals for maintaining racial stability and informing individual families of housing opportunities that will further these goals—that is, counseling white families about the potential for moving into a minority area, and encouraging black families to avoid resegregation. An important point: this should be done on a *voluntary* basis. Otherwise your group could be in violation of federal fair-housing laws.

AFFIRMATIVE MARKETING. The village of Park Forest South, Illinois, requires all builders, lessors, and sellers who control more than one housing unit to come up with a program to reach minority groups and otherwise affirmatively promote open housing.

Such a program might include advertising in minority-group newspapers, for example, or posting notices in areas of minority-group concentration. The Beverly Area Planning Association holds seminars for real estate agents and community residents to get together to discuss open-housing issues.

HOUSING-EQUITY INSURANCE. This is perhaps the most interesting technique for maintaining racial stability, although it might be limited in application to areas with a strong housing market.

Equity insurance is designed to discourage panic peddling by assuring property owners that if the value of their homes should decline for any reason (but most likely due to racial change), they will still get nearly full value. In Oak Park, a suburb on the western edge of Chicago, the program insures 80 percent of any loss after a five-year enrollment period. Say a house is appraised at $50,000 today. The property owner registers its value with the village's Equity Assurance Commission. Five years from now, if the property owner gets only $40,000 upon the sale of his home, the insurance plan pays him 80 percent of the difference, or $8,000. The program is paid for through local taxes. The only cost to the owner is for the appraisal.

The Oak Park program came about because of increasing fear of racial change. The village wanted to maintain racial stability—its population is 5 percent black and 2 percent other minorities—but on a voluntary basis. Most of all, the village officials wanted to show that their long-range goal of creating a livable community could go hand in hand with maintaining racial stability. "The fact that the municipality is willing to put itself on the line should create an atmosphere in which white families living here will less likely panic in the face of racial change," says Mayor James J. McClure, Jr. Actually, the program may cost the city nothing, since property values in Oak Park have risen 17 percent a year over the last several years—and are rising at an even faster rate in areas of higher minority concentration!

Before leaving the topic of racial integration, I want to address briefly the matter of racial change in white ethnic enclaves. In recent years, it seems to me, such predominantly white areas—and I say predominantly, since many of them do contain an appreciable minority population—have come under undue attack from academics, liberals, and others who can afford to live in neighborhoods where the threat of racial change is not imminent, with little or no sympathy for the real fears and apprehensions of blue-collar families whose homes, neighborhoods, and ways of life are threatened.

In *Neighborhood*, Andrew M. Greeley writes eloquently about the conflict posed by racial succession in white ethnic enclaves:

> Those who write off as racist all those poor benighted white ethnics who are uneasy about neighborhood change simply cannot grasp how the concepts of "defended neighborhood" or "social turf" can be important to anyone. If you are worried about your neighborhood, your street, your block, your property, then by definition you are a racist—a definition usually made by someone living in a fashionable, safe, upper-middle-class suburb. The intellectual and cultural elites of the country simply cannot understand that there are many people who have no objection to racial integration, no resistance to blacks as neighbors or as parents of children who go to school with their children, yet still have very powerful fears of what racial change does to a neighborhood. Neighborhood integration is fine for such people so long as it is real integration, so long as blacks and whites can share the neighborhood; but the peculiarities of redlining, panic peddling, and a dual real estate market usually mean that the integrated neighborhood is merely a transition from an all-white to an all-black neighborhood. And that in turn means that the white people who do not want to move are forced out by social and economic dynamics over which they have no control. When you have been the victim of such dynamics time after time after time, you find yourself beginning to resist. If you are sophisticated, you know that blacks are the victims of the same dynamics; they are not the cause but only the occasion of the devastation of your community. If you are not so sophisticated, you may still not object to having blacks for neighbors and still wish they would stay the hell out of your neighborhood, because when they come in you are inevitably forced to move. Even to suggest that people may think that way and not be racists is to run the risk of having yourself condemned as a racist—again by people who live in safe, comfortable upper-middle-class suburbs or heavily patrolled university communities.

Instead of wasting their time debating whether inner-city white ethnics are racists, it seems to me, neighborhood activists would do well to concentrate on those matters that afflict both whites and minority groups—what Geno Baroni calls the "convergent issues," such as redlining, the dual real estate market, panic peddling, the shortfall of subsidized housing, and so on. There are many opportunities for white ethnic groups and minority-group organizations to work cooperatively on such issues, as the experience of coalitions like the Metropolitan Area Housing Alliance and networks like National People's Action have proved. It may even come to pass that, having successfully cooperated in attacking one of the above "convergent issues," such a coalition or network could begin to address the problem of racial integration. One thing seems certain, however: Only by finding common cause will neighborhood groups, black, white, brown, or red, be able to overcome the many negative problems facing them. As Vance Packard notes in *A Nation of Strangers*, "Urban turbulence will subside considerably when ethnic groups stop shoving each other around and start cooperating to achieve neighborhood stability."

Turning to the problem of neighborhood crime, it should be emphasized that there are certain kinds of crime about which there is little that can be done. Murder, for instance, is for the most part unpreventable, since the murderer usually knows his victim and is determined to kill him, no matter what. Therefore, while people's confidence in the neighborhood may be shaken by such an incident, very little can be done to prevent murder.

There are certain crimes, however, which I shall call "residential crimes," which can be reduced through concerted public action. These would include certain crimes against people and property—theft, burglary, assault, robbery, rape; in other words, what people commonly refer to in using the phrase "crime on the street." Another form of neighborhood crime, in which prostitution, gambling, and drug dealing fall, can also be attacked on a community basis.

There are four ways to reduce residential crime: (1) police techniques; (2) private security measures; (3) environmental design; and (4) community organizing tactics. I will touch on the first two and concentrate on the latter two.

There are limits to what the police can do to prevent crime, short of posting an officer at every corner, which is both a political and financial impossibility. Yet there is no doubt that the police can do more than they have in the past. In New York City, for example, an experiment called the Neighborhood Police Team assigned officers to high-crime neighborhoods on the basis of the relative amount of crime. If one precinct had 20 percent of the crime, it would get 20 percent of the officers on duty. The patrolmen got to know the local merchants and residents better, establishing a trust that resulted in better intelligence gathering. The police also learned a few tricks about how criminals work in city neighborhoods. In the area around New York University, the Neighborhood Police Team cracked down on auto thefts simply by patrolling the east-west side streets more than the wider, north-south avenues. Since most people park their cars on the dimly lit, narrow side streets, not the brightly lit, open avenues, it was easy for auto thieves to operate there—but not after the police stepped up their patrols. As a result of this simple change, which required no increase in manpower, the annual auto theft rate in the area dropped from eight hundred to one hundred. And this is but one example of how innovative police techniques can result in better neighborhood crime protection, at little or no added cost.

While such efforts are commendable, it remains true, as James Q. Wilson and Barbara Boland have said, that the "primary responsibility for public safety will fall on the citizen," not the police. This can begin with private security measures, or what crime experts call "hardening the target." Such measures as the installation of dead-bolt locks, burglar alarms, timers to turn on lights when the family is out at night, and window security bars discourage criminals, particularly amateurs in search of an easy target. Some communities encourage residents to participate in Operation Identification, in which citizens mark their personal belongings with an identifying number so that stolen goods can be traced and criminals prosecuted more easily.

These efforts, too, merit attention, but we should not be sanguine as to their effectiveness. A top-of-the-line security system is expensive, probably beyond the cost most people can bear. Even spreading the cost to all the tenants of a typical apartment building, installation of such a system might force the landlord to raise rents by 38 percent, according to Wilson and Boland. And while Operation Identification has a nice ring to it, it doesn't prevent crime: Professional burglars know how to get rid of the identifying numbers. Nor is it easy to create public enthusiasm for such a program. A 1974 study by the Illinois Law Enforcement Commission showed that only twenty-four thousand of the state's six million residents bothered to join the program. These measures may have a positive psychological effect, which is crucial to restoring that sense of confidence we have been emphasizing. But it should be recognized that their actual effect in deterring crime often is minimal.

The third technique, environmental design, has both considerable promise and serious shortcomings. The idea behind environmental design is to create "defensible space," a term coined by its principal proponent, Oscar Newman, and elaborated upon in his book of the same name. In high-crime neighborhoods, Newman points out, the residents have no sense of proprietorship over their streets. Outsiders, some of them bent on crime, can prowl the neighborhood, unobserved by residents, their activities rarely questioned. In such an open area, criminals are free to scout opportunities for crime, make their move, and escape without anyone noticing them. "Defensible space," writes Newman, "is a model for residential environments which inhibits crime by creating the physical expression of a social fabric that defends itself." It does this by creating physical barriers to crime and by increasing the level of surveillance that neighborhood residents have over their turf.

In Clason Point Gardens, a public housing project of forty-six buildings in the Bronx, New York, Newman put his ideas to the test. The project, he found, had too many entrances, which in terms of crime translates into too many escape routes for criminals; also, some of the public areas were being taken over by addicts and gangs. To create a defensible space, some of the entrances to the project were closed off with fences, pushing all the pedestrian traffic down a central path, where, theoretically, there would be more chance for observation by the project's tenants. As for the public areas, some of these were redesigned with new playground equipment and leisure space to attract families and drive out the addicts. Thus, by increasing the number of "eyes on the street," to use Jane Jacobs's phrase, and by giving residents a sense of territoriality, environmental design seeks to create a defensible space that helps in the fight against crime.

The federal government, through the Law Enforcement Assistance Administration and the Department of Housing and Urban Development, has jumped on the environmental design bandwagon, especially for crime-ridden public housing projects. In Chicago, for example, the notorious Cabrini-Green project has been the target of a $6.3 million program that includes "hardening the target" (stronger locks on apartment doors), education (classes for residents on safety and self-defense), and environmental design. The latter includes fencing off the building grounds to discourage outsiders from entering the complex. In the two-year period after these measures were instituted, the crime rate dropped 24 percent. The vacancy rate also declined, from 20 percent to only 9 percent, which indicates that tenants feel safer, thanks to the new security measures, and are choosing to remain in their neighborhood.

Defensible space certainly has its selling points, particularly as it promotes the eyes-on-the-street approach. Architects and developers seem to be taking it into greater account in their plans for urban residential and commercial projects by, for example, restricting the number of entrances so that these may be monitored by residents or security guards, eliminating first-floor windows, and even building walls around their projects. (Paul Gapp, architecture critic of the *Chicago Tribune*, reports that bulletproof robots capable of chasing intruders out of a housing project are also available.)

Whether the concept of defensible space can be broadly applied to existing structures, particularly the high-crime public housing projects, is another issue. The cost of refitting thousands of such buildings to the extent done in Chicago's Cabrini-Green pilot program would run into the billions. Short of removing the tenants and blowing up the buildings (as was done in St. Louis's Pruitt-Igoe project), the only alternative is for tenants' groups to demand better security—increased police protection, environmental design improvements, tightened security measures. Which brings us back to the point that the responsibility for effective crime prevention must be assumed by the community organization—in this case, the tenants' group—in its overall organizing program.

While better police methods, improved private security systems, and environmental design have their place in making neighborhoods safer, they operate in a vacuum if there is no effective community organization in the neighborhood. Crime prevention, then, can become yet another organizing tactic, an issue around which to build the organization. More important, it develops among neighbors a sense of shared responsibility for each other's safety. In a *New Yorker* article by Richard Harris, a resident of the city's South Village describes his sense of neighborhood security:

> I don't worry about our house being broken into or the boy getting hurt or anything happening to Colette [his wife]. People watch this place too closely. They keep an eye on strangers. This area is self-policed. An addict who wanders down here from Washington Square looking for an easy hit had better be more careful than the people who live here. There's a kinetic feeling about these streets. . . . This is a street-by-street world, and the people on each street look after it. I think that a well-organized block is the whole secret to safety.

Thus, any neighborhood with an organized and effective community association has a leg up in the battle against crime, for it has already gone far to create that sense of neighborly concern so necessary to such an effort.

In terms of crime prevention, however, there is an even more important reason for having a strong community organization: A strong community group can establish a climate of morality in which criminal behavior won't be tolerated. One of the reasons the addicts and pimps and hoods can operate unmolested in a city neighborhood is because there is no opposing force to stand up to them. Individual citizens are powerless to fight the criminals' strong-arm tactics. But united into a strong community organization, those same terrified citizens *can* fight back against crime.

No neighborhood demonstrates this capacity more clearly than Mount Auburn, a predominantly black section of Cincinnati. In the late sixties, Mount Auburn was a haven for dope pushers and drug addicts. Heroin sales were made right out in the open in neighborhood parks and on the street corners. The police did nothing, because no one in the community brought pressure on them to get the pushers out. Then a group of citizens, led by a black activist, Carl Westmoreland, decided to go after the pushers as part of an overall campaign to improve Mount Auburn.

The first thing the group did was to establish a set of standards, a kind of behavioral code, which of course did not include pushing dope. They also convinced the citizens of Mount Auburn to help the police in apprehending the pushers. "We got people to agree to give us the physical descriptions of the pushers, their automobiles, and the license plate numbers," said Westmoreland. With that information, they were able to make a hard-and-fast case against the pushers. "Then we had a big public announcement, in which we gave the pushers a couple of weeks to get out of Mount Auburn, or we would go to the police." It was also made clear that any retaliation against the anticrime organizers, especially Westmoreland, would result in more serious measures being taken against the pushers—*without* the police being involved. In all, sixteen pushers refused to cooperate and were convicted and sentenced to terms of at least five years' duration. Mount Auburn's crime rate fell from third highest among the city's forty-four neighborhoods to twenty-third.

The Mount Auburn story is a dramatic one, and I'm not so Pollyannish as to believe that it could be repeated in every neighborhood beseiged by a criminal element. Yet it does illustrate clearly the point that the community itself must establish the climate for an anticrime program; otherwise there is no hope of success, even if the neighborhood is flooded with police. For the kinds of residential crimes that *can* be prevented—thefts, dope pushing, prostitution, burglary, gambling, and so on—there must first be an attitudinal stance on the part of the community. The community must unite to fight crime, and in so doing give notice to criminals and potential criminals that their activities are not condoned. Without this essential philosophical underpinning, a neighborhood anticrime program necessarily will be flawed.

One other point about neighborhood crime prevention: any community effort that bypasses the police will be tinged with charges of vigilantism. Therefore, it is necessary to work *with* the police, even in those cases, particularly among minority groups, where there is a history of alleged police brutality. To do otherwise is to throw into doubt the legitimacy of your organization's anticrime efforts.

Here, then, are some suggestions for an anticrime program in your community. As with all the suggestions in this book, adapt these to fit your specific needs and goals:

ORGANIZED BLOCK WATCHING. This is the true use of the "eyes-on-the-street" approach to neighborhood safety. Cooperate with the police to get special training for volunteers on what to observe in the case of potential crime activity. Some cities give block watchers a special police phone number, which insures anonymity and protects block watchers from retribution by suspects. The program also provides an excellent opportunity to get elderly citizens involved in the community. They have time and watch the streets anyway.

WHISTLE STOP PROGRAM. Citizens are equipped with whistles or aerosol horns. In the event of a crime in progress, the citizen blows his whistle, alerting others, who call the police. Get the chamber of commerce or business leaders group either to contribute whistles or to defray their cost. A word of caution: make sure your members don't "cry wolf" or the whole program could be jeopardized.

MOBILE PATROLS. Pairs or groups of citizens patrol the neighborhood during peak crime periods. Using citizens' band radios they contact a central communications desk if they see any suspicious activity. Strict rules must govern such operations. Those in effect in Chicago illustrate the kinds of restrictions mobile patrols must adhere to. They are as follows:

1. Citizen patrollers must carry official police department identification cards at all times while on duty.

2. No firearms or other weapons are authorized while in the performance of assigned duties.

3. No member will leave his automobile to investigate suspicious activity.

4. Members will assist a police officer only upon the officer's specific request.

5. No member will represent himself as a police officer to anyone under any conditions.

6. No member will participate in an automobile chase under any circumstances.

7. No member will detain anyone unless ordered to do so by a police officer.

8. No member is authorized to question anyone.

9. No member with a police department radio monitor may respond to police department transmissions.

10. Patrolling members must be at least eighteen years of age. In addition, some programs prohibit the use of sirens or special lights. Volunteers must also obey all regulations of the Federal Communications Commission when making radio transmissions. Vulgar language or inappropriate use of the radio system is cause for dismissal.

WALKING PATROL. A variation of the mobile patrol in which groups of citizens walk the neighborhood.

TENANT PATROL. Another variation, for use in large apartment complexes. Volunteers can also man guard desks at the entrances to high-rise buildings.

TAXI PATROLS. Taxicabs and other vehicles equipped with two-way radio communications are tied into a network to provide additional eyes on the street.

HOUSESITTING OR HOUSEWATCHING NETWORKS. Neighbors live in or watch the homes of families who are away from the neighborhood. They take in newspapers and mail, make sure lights are on at night, and put trash *in* the trash cans so that burglars will think someone is home.

ELDERLY-ASSISTANCE PROGRAMS. Studies have shown that the elderly are among the most fear-ridden members of the city society. Escort services can be developed to accompany elderly residents to the bank on the day they receive their Social Security checks. A similar service should be provided to escort them to and from shopping so that they are not robbed en route.

CHILD-PROTECTION PROGRAMS. A program to provide "safe houses" for children can be put into effect. Adults who volunteer for the program agree to place a sign in the front window: the sign portrays an adult holding the hand of a child, with a roof over their heads. Children are instructed to go to houses displaying the sign in case they are approached or molested on the street by strangers.

POLICE-CITIZENS COUNCIL. An important constituent of any anticrime program is the formation of a council of citizens and local police officers. The council should provide a forum to air grievances by either side, discuss the performance of current programs, investigate new ideas, and create the atmosphere necessary for the police to understand the concerns of citizens, and for citizens to understand the concerns of the police.

The prevention of crime, like the prevention of racial resegregation, is a complex matter. Unfortunately, many community groups have no choice but to get involved in these delicate and occasionally dangerous areas. If the overall purpose of the effort is to improve the quality of life for community residents, reasonable steps, such as those proposed in this chapter, deserve serious consideration.

8

NEIGHBORHOOD REINVESTMENT STRATEGIES

The color that really matters in the city is
not black or white. It's green. Green is
money, and money is power.

—REV. ALBIN CICIORA,
Citizens Action Program,
Chicago

If redlining is the term for the systematic withdrawal of investment from a neighborhood, "greenlining" describes those
techniques and programs that pump money (particularly from
the private market) back into neighborhoods. By working cooperatively with federal, state, and local officials, lending institutions, and insurance companies, community groups around the
country have been able to demonstrate that investing in city
neighborhoods not only has its social rewards, but can be profit-
able to private enterprise as well. But before community groups
can enter into partnership with private enterprise, the people who
hold the money—the banks, the savings and loan institutions, the
insurance companies, even the pension funds—must first realize
their obligation to help revive city neighborhoods: without their
dollars, the task is impossible. This chapter outlines the major efforts being made at the federal, state, and local levels to increase
the total amount of investment in these areas.

There are a number of federal programs to increase the flow
of dollars into urban neighborhoods, including two new ones.
The Community Investment Fund is designed to provide an ad-

ditional $10 billion in urban lending over a five-year period. The money, which is loaned to savings and loan institutions at below-market rates, comes from the Federal Home Loan Bank's coffers, not from Congressional appropriations. It is targeted specifically for low- and moderate-income families. The other newcomer, the Urban Participation Program, allows the Federal National Mortgage Association to purchase 60 to 90 percent shares in a pool or pools of mortgages on properties located in older neighborhoods that have been victimized by redlining in the past.

The agencies that regulate lenders, notably the Federal Home Loan Bank Board (for federally chartered savings and loan associations) and the Federal Deposit Insurance Corporation (for federally chartered commercial banks and mutual savings banks), are also charged with making sure that the lenders engage in practices that promote fair lending. In May, 1978, for example, the FHLBB issued regulations that prohibit member institutions from automatically refusing to lend because of the age or location of a dwelling and that prohibit loan decisions based on discriminatory appraisals. As we saw in Chapter 1, these are among the most common methods of disinvestment. In addition, the Community Reinvestment Act of 1977 requires the four major regulatory agencies—the FDIC, the FHLBB, the Comptroller of the Currency, and the Federal Reserve Board—to assess whether the institutions they regulate are meeting the credit needs of their communities, including low- and moderate-income neighborhoods. These assessments are to be taken into account when considering applications by the lenders for office relocations, mergers, charters, deposit insurance, holding company acquisitions, and branches. (The latter include those new "twenty-four-hour" computer tellers.)

This new law gives community groups another weapon to use against alleged redliners, because it requires lenders to show a "continuous and affirmative obligation to meeting community needs." A community group could use evidence of redlining against a lender that wanted to move, establish a new branch, or merge with or acquire another institution. In Washington, D.C., the Adams-Morgan Organization was able to use such pressure to achieve a "greenlining pact" with a lending institution that wanted to move into the neighborhood. While the law has several weaknesses—for example, lenders are only "encouraged," not "required," to get input from the public—it is another tool in the hands of community organizations.

The Home Mortgage Disclosure Act of 1975 also can be a major resource for community groups. The law requires lenders with more than $10 million in assets and that are located in a standard metropolitan statistical area to report lending activity to the appropriate regulatory agency. The purpose of the law is to give citizens and public officials "sufficient information to enable them to determine whether depository institutions are fulfilling their obligations to serve the housing needs of the communities and neighborhoods in which they are located. . . ." The law states that the lenders must give information by census tract on the number of loans and total dollar amount for FHA, VA, and Farmers Home Administration loans; "conventional" mortgage loans; home improvement loans; loans on absentee-owned buildings; and multifamily mortgage loans.

A useful five-step approach to capitalizing on the disclosure data is offered in *Redlining Revealed: Where to Bank to Save Your Neighborhood.* The steps are:

Step 1: *Identify the area for your study.* Use a map to indicate your neighborhood's boundaries.

Step 2: *Collect the data.* Use the Yellow Pages to find all the lending institutions in your area. Each lender must make his disclosure report available for public inspection and copying during regular business hours. (They can charge for copying, of course.) If the lender refuses to cooperate, you have the right to complain to the appropriate regulatory agency.

Step 3: *Transfer the data.* Make charts and maps laying out all the information you have gathered.

Step 4: *Analyze the data.* Use the information to compare lending practices in your neighborhood with lending practices in other neighborhoods. For example, what is the percentage of federally guaranteed loans to total loans? Is this an indication that conventional loans are unavailable in your area, and that your neighborhood is being "FHA'd"? What is the ratio of home improvement loans made in your neighborhood to the ratio of such loans in the city or region as a whole?

Unfortunately, the law does not require disclosure of deposits.

But the Federal Deposit Insurance Corporation does make deposit information available by branch offices for all banks it insures. Thus, you can determine if your neighborhood is getting a fair shake by comparing loans to deposits, using the following formula:

$$\frac{\text{Total \$ amount of loans for neighborhood}}{\text{Total \$ amount of deposits in neighborhood}} \times 100 = \begin{matrix} \textit{Ratio of loans} \\ \textit{to deposits} \\ \textit{(percent)} \end{matrix}$$

If the latter figure is less than 100 percent, your neighborhood is putting more dollars into the lending institution than it is getting back in loans and mortgages.

Step 5: *Organize.* If you've determined that local lenders are discriminating against your neighborhood, you should be prepared to take action. Later in this chapter, we'll offer specific suggestions as to the kinds of demands that should be made.

In addition to the various federal greenlining programs, there are also various state regulations to encourage neighborhood investment. Illinois led the nation with the first antiredlining laws in 1975. One law requires loan disclosure; another prohibits lenders from discriminating solely on the basis of the location of the property. The state also passed a law banning insurance redlining. Since 1975, several other states have followed suit, many of them improving on the Illinois model. Michigan, for example, has an interesting clause which requires lenders, in considering a mortgage application, to weigh the positive things that are happening in the neighborhood, such as the presence of active community organizations, public-works programs, revitalization efforts, and "any other factors potentially mitigating the effect of physical decline."

Unfortunately, almost all antiredlining laws are flawed. Michigan, for example, prohibits class-action suits, so that neighborhood organizations are forbidden from collectively suing a redlining institution. Illinois requires disclosure of loans, but not deposits, making it difficult for community groups to know how their members' deposits are being used by the lenders.

California has sidestepped these obstacles by using the regulatory process. In 1976 the state's savings and loan department used its existing authority to issue regulations that add up to the toughest antiredlining strictures in the country. (State banks and federally chartered institutions are not covered.) The regulations have three basic strengths:

1. *Burden of proof on the lender.* The regulations prohibit various discriminatory practices, "unless the [savings and loan] association can demonstrate that such consideration in the particular case is required to avoid an unsafe or unsound business practice." For example, the age of the dwelling units in the neighborhood is not sufficient reason to deny a loan; but a study that showed housing abandonment in the immediate area which led to loan defaults might be sufficient evidence to permit denial of the loan. In other words, the lender has to give good reason for discriminating; otherwise, he is prohibited from doing so.

2. *The effects test.* Outright evidence of redlining is not necessary. If an examination of the institution's lending history reveals "patterns and practices" that have the "effect" of discriminating without good reason, that alone constitutes evidence of redlining.

3. *Affirmative action and enforcement.* Savings and loan institutions are required to carry out the regulations actively, particularly with regard to marketing policies and programs for minority groups and women. The state department of savings and loans is authorized to make on-site investigations of the practices of lending institutions and to issue "cease and desist" orders when necessary.

The beauty of the California savings and loan regulations, then, is that they put the redlining issue back in the institutions' court and (to mix sports metaphors) let the state come to bat for citizens and community groups in the antiredlining game.

Besides antiredlining laws and regulations, there are a number of other greenlining techniques of proven use at the state and city level, among them:

LOANS TO LENDERS. The city of Chicago has embarked on a "keep 'em in the city" campaign in which it has sold $100 million in tax-free municipal bonds for low-cost home mortgage loans to middle-income families. The loans, which are administered by local lending institutions (for a 2 percent fee) require only a 5 to 10 percent down payment and have a rate of 7.99 percent, about two points below the rate for conventional mortgage loans. Persons making up to $40,000 a year are eligible. The maximum loan is $80,000.

A friend of mine who got such a loan on a $30,000 two-flat building figures he will save $50 a month for the twenty-nine years of his loan. That doesn't count the $3,000 he saved in closing costs, which he is pumping back into the building in the form of needed repairs. "You can't beat the deal," he says.

DEPOSIT LAWS. State and city governments must keep millions of dollars on deposit in savings institutions to pay the public's bills. Since the depository institutions can use these funds to make loans (earning money on the interest charged), it makes sense for governments to place such deposits in savings institutions that perform a public good with the money.

Chicago, which pioneered the idea, requires savings institutions that wish to act as depositories for city funds to submit information on their deposits of savings and checking accounts, loans made within the city of Chicago, and deposits from Chicago residents. The city comptroller reviews this information and decides which institutions shall be depositories for city funds—but not before each of them pledges "not to arbitrarily reject mortgage loans . . . because of the location and/or age of the property" or "because of the race, color, religion, national origin, age, sex or marital status" of the borrower. In addition, the institution must pledge to make loans available on "low- and moderate-income residential property . . . within the limits of our legal restrictions and prudent financial practices."

The state of Colorado uses a method of figuring an institution's "social lending ratio" to determine if that institution should be a depository of state funds. When an institution has a higher-than-average ratio of loans to students, farmers, small businesses, or low-income mortgage holders, it gets "Brownie points," so named after Sam Brown, the former state treasurer who thought of the idea. The more Brownie points, the more state funds the bank gets to hold.

NEIGHBORHOOD-ASSISTANCE TAX CREDITS. Pennsylvania gives up to $8.75 million a year in tax credits to businesses that contribute money or other resources to qualified recipients. "Other resources" includes such items as computer services, professional staff time, other in-kind services, even day-care facilities. The business gets a 50 percent credit—70 percent for certain "priority" programs—up to $250,000 in any year. For example, a number of banks contribute services to the Old Philadelphia Development Corporation, a nonprofit company that provides technical assistance to developers of subsidized housing.

STATE AID TO NEIGHBORHOOD PRESERVATION COMPANIES. Chapter 852 of the Laws of New York State permits the commissioner of the state division of housing and community renewal to enter into contracts of up to $100,000 a year (for up to three years) with neighborhood preservation companies for planning and administering various housing- and neighborhood-renewal programs. The money may not, however, be used to actually construct buildings.

While the federal and state governments are making inroads, the real action on greenlining is in the neighborhoods. The first job of any community organization involved in a greenlining campaign is to get the suspected redliners to the negotiating table. That will require all the organizing skills described in Chapter 3, plus knowledge of the various disclosure laws described above. You'll also want to have a general picture of the kinds of activities the lending institution is involved in, its assets and profits, and its general financial status. William Batko's *How to Research Your Local Bank (Or Savings & Loan Institution)* is a helpful guide for just such a purpose.

Armed with information about the lender, you are now ready to "educate" the institution's chief officers. Your goal is to change their perceptions of your neighborhood, so that they see it the way you see it—as a place with a positive future. "I reject the view that the banks are monsters," says John Tepper Marlin, the director of the Council on Municipal Performance in New York. "Some of the banks need to be sensitized." The education program begins with the president and chairman of the board of directors. "There must be a corporate will to act based on a conviction that the risks are reasonable, and a responsible business organization should not avoid taking those risks because they are different from historical risks," notes Robert Hecht, president and chairman of Baltimore Federal Savings and Loan Association. The top dogs must be convinced that they will receive the community's backing in any "risky" ventures. They must also have the assurance that the city government and other lenders back the overall program for saving the neighborhood. Thus, it is a smart idea to have representatives from local churches, businesses, civic groups, and city hall at these meetings, to shore up the confidence of the lenders. Finally, any program that is agreed upon must be filtered down to the lender's line people. The chairman of the board may be totally behind the program, but if the loan officer in the local branch hasn't heard about it, it's as good as having no program at all.

Changing the lenders' perceptions is not an easy job. Experience shows that it may take a series of meetings before the bankers understand the citizens' concerns and the citizens understand the bankers' fears. Get the lenders out into the neighborhood: most of them have probably never visited your streets. Show them the results of your organization's efforts, even if it's something as modest as a tree planting. Let them know what the city's plans are (assuming, of course, the plans are positive). Change their negative feelings about the neighborhood to positive perceptions. Strengthen their confidence in the future.

Once the lenders are at the bargaining table, present them with your greenlining action program. What might be included in such a program? The first item, of course, is the lenders' agreement to make loans in the neighborhood. Other elements might be: improved services to neighborhood customers; targeted use of neighborhood deposits; establishment of a mortgage review board; establishment of a lenders' mortgage pool; and lender participation in a community service corporation.

Improved services includes such items as the provision of a full-time specialist to deal only with rehabilitation loans, or advertising the availability of loans in the neighborhood or in a minority-group newspaper. It could even mean setting up a counseling service for prospective first-home buyers. In San Diego, twelve savings and loans have formed a Neighborhood Home Loan Counseling Service in the poorer southeast section of the city. It is staffed every day by two lending officers, who advise and educate families about obtaining mortgages and rehabilitation loans.

Targeting neighborhood deposits means encouraging lenders to use local deposits for local loans. The Citizens Action Program, a Chicago coalition, started the idea in 1975 with its "Save Our City" campaign. CAP solicitors canvassed neighborhoods, seeking pledges to deposit assets in lending institutions that had agreed to make loans in redlined neighborhoods. In a short period of time CAP had more than $100 million in pledges and agreements from several savings and loan institutions. In Baltimore, the state's second largest savings and loan, Baltimore Federal, at one time allowed a new depositor to specify in which of 123 neighborhoods he wanted his money invested. When a loan was made in that neighborhood, the depositor was notified. As a result of this now-defunct "Dedicated Dollars" program, Baltimore Federal made $10 million in city loans in one six-month period—ten times the amount of city loans it had made in all of 1972.

Mortgage review boards have been established in more than a dozen cities. They are usually set up by several lending institutions to review cases where mortgage applicants feel they have been unjustifiably denied a loan. Many of the boards have citizens or public advocates. In Chicago, two trade associations, the Chicago Area Council of Savings Associations and the Federal Savings and Loan Council of Illinois, have set up a two-tiered panel, called the Home Mortgage Opportunity Committee of Chicagoland, to review such complaints. The committee's first-tier panel consists of lending officers from local S and Ls. If they don't approve the loan, it is automatically appealed to a second level made up of the president of the Federal Home Loan Bank of Chicago, the state savings and loan commissioner, and three public members. "It's the busiest mortgage review panel in the country," says William O'Connell, secretary of the Federal Council. "We've processed about one hundred fifty applications, and not one alleged redlining. Almost without exception, the reason for turndown is inadequate collateral or inadequate credit." The Chicago system has even been praised by antiredlining advocates, including the National Center for Urban Ethnic Affairs.

Mortgage pooling occurs when lenders share the risk of investing in a neighborhood. One of the best examples is the Philadelphia Mortgage Plan, a pool formed by nine commercial and four savings banks. The plan has unusual lending criteria. Welfare payments, for example, may be claimed as income; so, too, may the income of a working spouse or co-signer. Appraisals are made on a block-by-block evaluation, not on the basis of the whole neighborhood. If the median value of the housing on the block is at least $6,000, and if the combined vacancy and abandonment rate is less than 10 percent, a loan of up to $15,000 will be made. Insurance is provided for the first 25 percent of indemnity by a private company. Applicants who are refused loans may appeal to a mortgage review board. In the first fifteen months of operation, the plan made nearly fourteen hundred loans totalling nearly $15 million. Only twenty-eight loans were late in payments, and no foreclosures were reported. Says Rev. William Gray, the pastor of Bright Hope Baptist Church in North Philadelphia, "We don't ask them to do business differently, only with an open and rational mind."

The savings and loan service corporation is one of the most promising local greenlining techniques. Under federal regulations, S and Ls may invest up to 1 percent of their assets in separate corporations, called service corporations, which can then engage in certain kinds of speculative activity from which the mother institution might be prohibited. Service corporations allow the S and Ls to get actively involved in neighborhood development, rather than reacting to others' proposals.

A good example of a service corporation with a track record is Chicago's Renewal Effort Service Corporation, known as RESCORP. "The idea for RESCORP began in 1972," recalls Saul Klibanow, an architect and planner who serves as corporation president. "The leadership of the local savings and loan industry, the Chicago Area Council, was wrestling with the problem of what to do about neighborhood decline, because they were being hurt, too—when a neighborhood goes down, the people who hold the mortgage paper have problems."

A service corporation that would pool the efforts of many savings and loan institutions seemed the answer. Forty institutions joined, bringing a half million dollars in capital with them: later, the program expanded to include sixty lenders.

"We established three criteria," says Klibanow. "First, to try to do something about the urban housing problem, and never to lose sight of that objective. Second, to produce real results, not just public relations, and to avoid throwing good money after bad—in other words, to make a real impact and avoid past mistakes. Finally, to make a profit—but to measure profitability in more than one way. If we revitalize a community, we can prevent losses in the community, and *that* can be a profit."

To get the maximum impact, RESCORP decided to work in communities where revitalization was possible, without bulldozing all the houses. The group then settled on the problem of rehabilitating multifamily housing, the typical Chicago six- or twelve-flat walkup, because as Klibanow says, "when mismanaged or abused, they can hurt the whole community. They can also exert a strong positive influence."

After an extended search, RESCORP chose South Shore, a racially changing neighborhood with a good stock of salvageable apartment buildings, strong community leadership, and promise of economic potential (primarily due, as we shall see shortly, to the presence of the South Shore National Bank).

With long-term financing from the Illinois Housing Development Authority, RESCORP has completed two major projects, an $8 million, 302-unit project and a 19-unit building. Some of the units are subsidized by federal housing programs, and rents are kept at moderate levels. Still, the project is being run at a profit.

"It has worked," says Klibanow. "More than six hundred units in South Shore are in the process of rehabilitation. We're also seeing an increased evidence of fix-up, painting, and lawn care." The success in South Shore was such that the service corporation is tackling another 150-unit project in a North Side neighborhood.

Greenlining efforts need not be limited to lending institutions. In addition to helping communities by insuring homes, insurance companies also have billions of dollars in assets to invest; and a few progressive companies are already doing something to end redlining. In Milwaukee, for example, an industry coalition has set up a Community Insurance Information Center, staffed by volunteers from various insurance companies to answer the public's questions about insurance. (It does not sell insurance; it merely provides information.) Three companies are cooperating to insure homes participating in the Philadelphia Mortgage Plan. A number of companies are offering new kinds of policies, geared to the market value of the house, rather than the cost to replace it at today's prices; such policies reduce the insurer's risk, which is then translated into lower premiums for the homeowner. Aetna Life and Casualty has a program to recruit new agents and place them in previously redlined neighborhoods. It has also agreed to increase insurance availability in targeted neighborhoods in the Bronx, Brooklyn, Chicago, Cleveland, and Philadelphia. Applications rejected by agents in these neighborhoods will be reviewed by the regional office.

But community groups want the insurance companies to do more than stop redlining. "There is a great potential within the insurance industry to direct its corporate investments to make the policyholders' premiums work for the benefit of their neighborhoods," said Gale Cincotta, the president of National People's Action. Allstate, the industry leader, donated $1 million in 1979 to beef up the Neighborhood Housing Services Program. And Cincotta's group went into negotiations with Aetna and other companies to get a commitment of their assets for neighborhood projects. Aetna, for example, is already heavily involved in cities: one of its subsidiary companies built the fantastically profitable Water Tower Place high-rise shopping center in Chicago. Cincotta would like to see a similar effort by insurance companies in the neighborhoods.

Such a greenlining action program, coupled with the rehabilitation financing techniques described in the next chapter, should put your neighborhood well on the way to recovery. But what if you have the kind of problem Philadelphia's Southwest Germantown Community Development Corporation had? "We found that the biggest problem was getting small loans—less than a thousand dollars," says Jim Wilcox. The solution was to set up a *community credit union*. With $25,000 in deposits, which average about $100, the credit union is able to make small loans, primarily for home improvements, at a rate of 1 percent a month on the unpaid balance. A community credit union in Pittsburgh has boosted its equity base by getting deposits from corporations like U.S. Steel and local businesses; the group then asks the companies to waive the interest they would normally get. Since the deposits of the credit union are insured up to $40,000 for each account, there is no risk for large depositors. And the credit union makes money by performing other financial services, such as making money orders, accepting utility payments, and selling food stamps.* Two credit unions are specifically involved in housing development. In San Juan, Texas, Amigos Unidos Federal Credit Union, established by migrant workers in 1971, finances rehabilitation loans for its members. In Springfield, Massachusetts, the Casa Credit Union, which has been in operation since 1965, has filled the gap created by alleged redlining practices of local lending institutions. According to Karen Kollias, formerly of the National Center for Urban Ethnic Affairs, Casa is now the largest mortgage lender in the area. It also makes home improvement and small business loans.

The most ambitious greenlining technique by far is to establish a *community-owned bank*. Needless to say, this is a risky venture for any community organization—there are, consequently, only two such banks in the country. One is the state-owned Bank of North Dakota. The other is the South Shore National Bank, which is owned by the Illinois Neighborhood Development Corporation, a bank holding company which will eventually be owned by the community.

The South Shore Bank's history is intriguing. Until the late 1960s, South Shore was a white, heavily Jewish neighborhood fronting Lake Michigan, with excellent schools, a good commuter railroad to the Loop, and homes that ranged from mansions to modest, but well-kept, bungalows. By 1972, the population had changed from practically all-white to 85 percent black. Yet the area still had good housing, convenient shopping, substantial amenities (including the rail line), and even a community-based hospital. But the racial change, accompanied by some signs of social and economic change, scared people.

The most frightened of all were the owners of the South Shore Bank, who in 1972 asked the Comptroller of the Currency for permission to move their assets to a better location, preferably in

---

*Anything you could possibly want to know about credit unions, especially as agents of community development, is contained in *Community Development Credit Unions: A Self-Help Manual,* published by the National Economic Development Law Project. (See Bibliography of Reference Materials.)

the Loop. The bank's deposits had dipped from a high of $80 million to $45 million, and projections showed that they would fall even lower.

Fortunately for the community, a neighborhood group called the South Shore Commission challenged the bank's move. The Comptroller of the Currency agreed with the community group that there was insufficient reason for the bank to be moved. The application was denied.

At about this time, two fortuitous events took place. The first was that Ron Grzywinski, the former president of the nearby Hyde Park Bank, was finishing work on a proposal to develop a neighborhood-based bank. At the same time, government regulations were changing to allow the formation of bank holding companies. A bank holding company is different from a bank in that it can own other corporations, for example, a housing development corporation or a commercial revitalization company. Such a mechanism was essential to Grzywinski's overall plan for his "neighborhood bank." With contributions from foundations and others, Grzywinski was able to raise $3 million to buy South Shore National Bank, using his holding company, Illinois Neighborhood Development Corporation.

In only a few years, Grzywinski and his colleagues have been able to change the bank's policies around completely. Whereas in 1972 the previous owners had made only two mortgages totaling $59,000 in all of South Shore, by 1976 the new owners were pumping 60 percent of the bank's loans—$1.5 million—back into the community. While the previous owners were losing depositors, the new owners pursued an aggressive policy of getting new depositors—not only neighborhood people, but outsiders as well. They solicited "development deposits" from wealthy people and institutions, asking them to deposit at least $1,000 in the bank. Each $1,000 would generate $500 in credit and $25 a year in earnings that could be used for development purposes—saving the local movie theater, reviving the commercial strip, providing better services for bank customers. The first year's deposits were less than $900,000; by 1976, they were $7,300,000.

Nor have the owners forgotten their commitment to community ownership. Right now, they have a "resident advisory council" from the South Shore Commission to advise on bank services, commercial development, housing programs, marketing, and education programs. Eventually, the community will take an increasingly greater role in the bank's affairs, and South Shore National Bank will become the first community-controlled neighborhood-development bank in the country.

It is well on its way to that goal already—and it is making money in the process. Its 1976 earnings were 0.79 percent of total assets, just short of the 1 percent mark that signifies success for a commercial bank. More important than the profit margin, though, is the psychological boost the new South Shore Bank is giving the community. Says Bob Keeley, president of the South Shore Commission, "Ninety-nine percent of what the bank is doing is providing positive juices, what the neighborhood needed most—confidence in itself."

9

SPENDING THE NEIGHBORHOOD DOLLAR WISELY

The only thing that fixes up houses is money.

—ARNOLD ROSEMEYER,
Chief Housing Officer,
City of Cincinnati

If you had a million dollars to revitalize the housing in your neighborhood, how would you spend it? Well, you could build twenty new homes at $50,000 each and give them away to needy families. But that would benefit relatively few families and would have only a minimal effect on the neighborhood. You could give $1,000 to each of a thousand homeowners to fix up their houses, thus spreading the money more widely. But $1,000 doesn't go far these days: the most you could expect at that price is a good paint job and a few other improvements. Instead of giving the money away, you might decide to *lend* the money in, say, $5,000 lumps. In that way, you'd not only be lending enough money to make considerable improvements, you'd be fixing two hundred houses—a sizable number. What's more, as the loans were paid back, you'd be able to use that money to make more loans. As the bankers say, the funds in your loan pool would keep "revolving."

Since you will not have an open spigot pouring money into your neighborhood, your community organization will have to determine its priorities and figure out which financing mechanisms are best suited for your area. Therefore, your community group will have to make a number of choices. For example, will your program be "targeted" to a specific section of your neigh-

217

borhood, or will it be available throughout the area? Targeting creates a great impact on a small area; on the other hand, it eliminates the possibility of aiding those homeowners whose properties happen to be outside the target area. Who shall be eligible for the program? Only the very poor, or middle-income families, too? Only owner-occupants, or absentee landlords as well? Who will have access to the money first? And who shall control the money—the neighborhood organization, the city, or lending institutions? What standards shall be set for improvements? Will all buildings have to be brought up to strict housing code standards, or will "sensitive" code enforcement for hardship cases be permitted? These are but a few of the questions your community group will have to ponder.

Your goal is to stretch the few dollars your community group controls in order to encourage lending institutions to make more loans in your neighborhood than they normally would *and* to encourage private property owners to dig into their pockets for that extra cash to improve their buildings. In other words, you want the community's dollars to "spin off" other dollars—what the financial whizzes call "leveraging." Leveraging occurs when you take $1,000 and get someone to invest $10,000 that he most likely would not have invested in that property—that's a ten-to-one leverage. You want to get the greatest leverage possible out of your scarce financial resources, while at the same time accomplishing your organization's social goals.

In the following pages, we'll look at some of the financing techniques in use around the country, and we'll explore two special programs, urban homesteading and Neighborhood Housing Services. Let's look first at what's available from the federal government.

There are three basic federal programs for housing rehabilitation other than community-development block grants (to which we'll turn momentarily): Section 8, Section 312, and FHA loan insurance.

Section 8 is part of the 1974 Housing Act. Under its provisions, the U.S. Department of Housing and Urban Development (HUD) pays the difference between the unsubsidized "market rent" for an apartment and 25 percent of the family's income in new, existing, or rehabilitated housing, for a period up to twenty years (forty years for publicly financed housing). Each city gets a share of Section 8 units, but there are never enough to meet the demand. Use your organizing skills to get as many units as possible for the neediest families in your neighborhood.

Section 312 provides direct loans from HUD at the rate of 3 percent for a maximum of twenty years. Considering that interest on home improvement loans can run as high as 18 percent, that's a tremendous savings. The maximum loan is $12,000 a unit ($17,400 in high-cost cities), with priority given to low- and moderate-income families. These funds, too, are allocated to each city by Washington and may be used only in areas of the city designated for "community development" or "urban renewal." If your neighborhood is not in such a designated area, your residents are not eligible for Section 312 loans.

As for FHA-insured home improvement loans, under Title I, the lender and the government share the risk of the loan. Loans of up to $10,000 for single-family homes and up to $25,000 for multifamily properties are available, and absentee owners are eligible. The rate is perhaps a little better than what might be obtained on a conventional loan—about 12 percent—hence this program is designed primarily for the middle-income property owner. Under Title II, Section 203(k) loans can be used to make improvements on one- to four-unit properties at least ten years old. Section 220(h) loans can cover buildings of up to eleven units. The maximum loan per unit is $12,000 ($17,400 in certain cities) for both programs, but the total loan under 220(h) cannot exceed $40,000. In addition, 220(h) loans can only be made in FHA-approved areas.

While each of these programs has its merits and should be used as much as possible by your group, they all pale before the big money—community-development block grants.

In January 1973, President Nixon put an embargo on spending for all so-called categorical grant programs—including Model Cities, urban renewal, and federally assisted code enforcement. Nixon viewed the programs as expensive, inefficient, wasteful, and not in keeping with his philosophy of government, "The New Federalism." He had already made a start on his new program with general revenue sharing, which returned federal taxes directly to the states and cities, and was determined to extend the concept to special revenue sharing. This meant replacing the categorical grant programs—which permitted federal money to be spent only in designated areas (Model Cities districts, for example) for defined purposes (housing code enforcement, for example) and specific groups of people (the poor)—with a new system whereby "blocks" of money would be sent directly to the states and cities, with virtually no restrictions on how they could be used. "CD block grants" became a fact with the passage of the Housing and Community Development Act of 1974.

Some 1,443 communities now receive CD money, and it seems every one of them is using it differently. In terms of financing housing rehabilitation, though, there are some thirteen techniques which, with minor variations, encompass most of the programs: (1) direct grants; (2) direct loans; (3) variable-rate direct loans; (4) deferred payment loans; (5) forgivable loans; (6) partial direct grants, or rebates; (7) partial direct loans; (8) interest-reduction subsidized loans; (9) principal-reduction subsidized loans; (10) security-deposit loans; (11) guaranteed loans; (12) tax-exempt credit agreements; and (13) tax-exempt bond financing.

DIRECT GRANTS. The city agency in charge of CD money gives property owners cash to cover the full cost of rehabilitation. This program has no leverage, since no private money is invested. Yet many small cities prefer this method for its simplicity. It is also the most sure-fire way to help hardship cases.

DIRECT LOANS. Here, the city acts as banker and makes loans, usually at low interest rates (zero to 7 percent) for the full cost of rehabilitation for a long term (up to forty years). Baltimore's Rehabilitation Environmental Assistance Loan (REAL) program, for example, provides direct lending from the city at 7 percent interest for up to twenty years, with a maximum of $17,400 a unit. Since direct loans are repaid to the city, that money can be reused to make more loans, thus creating a "revolving fund." The higher the rate of interest and the shorter the term, the faster the money comes back to the city. For example, a zero-interest loan with a twenty-year term takes 14.2 years in borrower repayments to double the amount of money originally loaned by the CD fund; a 6 percent loan over a five-year term takes only 3.3 years in borrower repayments to double the amount of money originally loaned. But the tradeoff for getting money back more quickly is higher monthly payments for the borrower. Thus, a zero-interest twenty-year loan costs the borrower $4.17 a month for each thousand dollars, whereas a 6 percent, five-year loan costs $19.33 a month for each thousand dollars.

VARIABLE-RATE DIRECT LOANS. These loans come directly from the city, but their rate depends on a number of variables, such as family income, family size, or total housing costs. Take the example of the Community Development Service Center Home Rehabilitation Program in Fall River, Massachusetts. Under this program, if a family's income is less than 50 percent of the median income for a family of the same size in the Fall River region, that family pays 4 percent interest on the loan from the city. If the family income is 150 to 180 percent of the comparable median family income for the region, the rate jumps to 8 percent; when income is over 180 percent, loans are made at the market rate. Baltimore's City Housing Assistance Program works in much the same way, giving loans at rates of 1 to 7 percent, depending on family income and size. Minneapolis's Housing and Redevelopment Authority figures in not only family income and size, but also relative housing expenses. For example, a family that would normally pay 6 percent interest pays only 4 percent interest if its housing-related expenses (mortgage, utilities, taxes, etc.) exceed 25 percent of total income.

DEFERRED PAYMENT LOANS. With this variation of the direct loan method, the city lends the full cost of rehabilitation (usually at zero interest) but does not require the property owner to make payments. Instead, the loan is paid off upon the sale or transfer of the property. This technique is especially useful in dealing with elderly homeowners living on fixed incomes, for it allows them to improve their homes without taking money from their Social Security or pension funds. Eventually, the city will be able to recoup its money, thereby enabling it to lend the money again. The Portland, Oregon, Development Commission uses a chunk of its CD funds to make two kinds of deferred payment loans. One is for owner-occupied houses in designated community development areas: it provides a $1,500 "critical maintenance loan" to make the property livable. The other may be used throughout the city, and has a maximum of $4,000 to bring the property up to code.

FORGIVABLE LOANS. Instead of collecting the value of the loan upon the sale or transfer of the property, all or part of the loan is forgiven. But in most cases the property owner who took the original loan must have occupied the house for a certain period before the loan is forgiven. This technique is used in some urban homesteading programs.

PARTIAL DIRECT GRANTS, OR REBATES. The city pays the property owner directly for a portion of the total cost of rehabilitation. Here's how it works: the property owner registers with the program and supplies the city with several estimates of the cost of the job, taking the lowest bid. He then goes to a lender and borrows the money to pay the contractor, or he does all or part of the work himself using what rehabbers call "sweat equity." When the work is completed, the city inspects the job and pays the property owner the agreed-upon percentage of the estimated cost. In Newark, New Jersey, the rebate program operating in the Iron Bound section, a predominantly Portuguese and Spanish neighborhood, pays the owner up to 30 percent of the value of the improvements. Boston's Home Improvement Program uses CD money to provide 20 percent rebates. The maximum grant is $1,000 for a single-family home, $3,000 for a six-unit building. The owner's income may not exceed $16,000.

Several cities have embellished upon the concept. The Old Holyoke (Massachusetts) Development Corporation administers a city program whereby grants are made on the basis of income. A property owner who makes less than $8,000 taxable income a year gets a grant of 30 percent, while those making up to $20,000 get only a 15 percent rebate. Chicago's Financial Assistance to Property Owners program has a similar "sliding-scale" rebate system based on income, but it goes up to a full 100 percent. The grants are available only in designated neighborhoods for one- to four-unit buildings, with a limit of $10,000 a unit. By the way, at least one private rebate effort is known to exist: in St. Louis, The Hill 2000 Corporation rebates 10 percent of the cost of significant exterior repairs and improvements, up to a maximum of $500, the funds coming out of the community organization's kitty.

The problem with rebates is that they are beside the fact. If the property owner is able to obtain a conventional loan anyway, how much incentive does the grant provide? In the Holyoke program the local lenders *do* create an incentive: they give loans to those registered in the program at rates lower than those for conventional home improvement loans.

PARTIAL DIRECT LOANS. These are similar to direct loans where the city acts as banker, but instead of lending the full cost of rehabilitation, the city lends only a portion. Sometimes the percentage is based on a sliding scale of family income—the smaller the income, the greater the percentage of total cost that the city will lend. The rest of the cost comes from the property owner, through savings, sweat equity, or a conventional loan. Partial direct loans may also be deferred or forgiven.

INTEREST-REDUCTION SUBSIDIZED LOANS. These are market-rate loans made to property owners by private lending institutions, which in turn are subsidized by the city to reduce the actual interest rate the borrower pays. Each month the city makes a payment from its CD fund to the lender to reduce the interest to a specified level, usually 3 percent. The borrower's monthly payment is figured at the subsidized rate, not the market rate.

Say a homeowner needs $5,000 to rehabilitate his house. Under this program, he would get a ten-year, 12 percent loan from a private institution. Normally, that would cost him $72 a month. But he pays the loan at a 3 percent rate, or $48 a month. The difference, $24 a month, is the city's subsidy.

Hoboken, New Jersey, is credited with having the first such program, dating to 1972. Interest is reduced to 3 percent on loans up to $6,000, with a maximum nine-year term; priority is given to owner-occupied homes of one to four units. An interesting additional requirement is that participating landlords must agree to a two-year freeze on rents.

PRINCIPAL-REDUCTION SUBSIDIZED LOANS. Such loans have the same effect for the borrower as interest-reduction subsidized loans: he pays the loan back as if the interest rate had been reduced to, say, 3 percent. It is, however, the *principal* that has been reduced, through a city grant of CD funds. Thus the borrower is actually paying the market rate, but he is paying off a reduced-principal amount. On a $5,000 ten-year loan, he still pays only $48 a month (to continue the above example) as if he were paying at 3 percent. In fact, he is paying a full 12 percent, but on a reduced principal—in this case, $3,365—to get his payments down to $48 a month. The difference of $1,635 is made up in a cash grant of CD funds by the city.

SECURITY-DEPOSIT LOANS. These are made when the city deposits CD money in a private financial institution; the city's account may or may not earn interest, depending on the agreement with the lender. The lender then makes home improvement loans at rates below the market rate. The city's deposits may have to equal all or only a portion of the amount loaned by the institution. The city's deposits do not guarantee the loans, do not reduce the lender's risk, and do not subsidize the lender's loss in case of default. The benefit to each side is that the lender gets the city's deposit at little or no interest, while the city gets free loan servicing from the lender.

GUARANTEED LOANS. These are similar to security-deposit loans, in that the city deposits CD money in a private lending institution at little or no interest, while the lender agrees to make loans at a rate below the market rate. However, the city agrees to pay part or all of the unpaid principal if the loan defaults, and it must keep on deposit a part or all of the money necessary to cover such a loss. In some respects, this is comparable to the city insuring local loans the way the FHA does at the national level. In a number of California cities the Bank of America has set up a City Improvement Restoration Program which includes such a guaranteed loan mechanism. In the Housing Rehabilitation Program in San Diego, the city deposits enough CD money to cover the entire outstanding principal on the low-rate (3.75 percent) loans the Bank of America makes. The Greater Indianapolis Housing Development Corporation, on the other hand, insures only between 50 and 90 percent of such loans, keeping the guaranteed portion of the unpaid principal on deposit with the lending institution in case of default. The Chicago Home Purchase and Rehabilitation Plan, a $7 million mortgage/home improvement loan pool established by twenty lending institutions, is insured by three sources: the first 7.5 percent of loss, for which the homeowner pays the cost, is covered by a private insurance company; the next 12.5 percent is covered by the lenders themselves;

and the remaining 80 percent is insured by a $500,000 deposit (spread among the twenty lenders) of City of Chicago CD funds. TAX-EXEMPT CREDIT AGREEMENTS. These got their start in Norfolk, Virginia. The city borrows money from private financial institutions. Because the interest paid by the city to a private lender is exempt from federal income taxation, the city can borrow at a lower interest rate than the average borrower. The city insures the loan either by keeping a reserve fund on deposit with the lender or by obtaining FHA insurance for each loan. The Portland, Oregon, Development Commission uses this mechanism to get a $1.5 million line of credit from eleven lending institutions. It pays 5.5 percent for the money and lends it to homeowners at 6.5 percent. The commission must keep a cash reserve on deposit amounting to 20 percent of the outstanding principal of the loans; these deposits draw interest at a rate 1 percent below regular certificates of deposit. If a loan is ninety days in default, the commission must pay it back in full.

TAX-EXEMPT BOND FINANCING. Bond financing works pretty much the same way as credit agreements except that the city raises the money through the sale of tax-free municipal bonds. Baltimore raises the money for its Rehabilitation Environmental Assistance Loan program through bond sales. So, too, does San Francisco for its Rehabilitation Assistance Program. In most cases, it is easier to get voter approval of the bonds if the loans are insured by the FHA.

This is only the barest sketch of the major forms of rehabilitation finance in use by the hundreds of communities receiving community development funds. Because the program has been in effect since 1974, most cities have already determined the types of programs—direct loan, rebate, guaranteed loan, etc.—and the specific terms and conditions under which they operate. For that reason, and for lack of space, I have merely implied the relative merits of each technique. For those wishing a more detailed discussion, David Gressel's *Financing Techniques for Local Rehabilitation Programs* is an excellent source.

Cities have also come up with other clever ways to stretch their rehabilitation dollars to derive extra benefits out of neighborhood revitalization programs. Milwaukee, for example, has a tool-lending library in its former Model Cities area, where residents can borrow the proper wrench or saw to get the job done right. Battle Creek and Springfield, Michigan, offer an eight-week course in plumbing, electrical repair, interior decorating, and similar home repairs. The cities of Bellevue and Lincoln, Nebraska, hire retired handymen to perform simple maintenance jobs for elderly homeowners and install special devices, such as bath rails, for the crippled. The cost is about 30 percent of what a regular contractor would charge. Many cities and community organizations offer counseling for first-time home purchasers. The City of Chicago's Department of Human Services has a program for making minor repairs and modifications—for example, installation of walking ramps and removal of barriers—for low-income elderly and handicapped homeowners and tenants; up to $150 of the maximum $800 grant may be used for security devices and smoke detectors. In addition, the department has an energy-conservation and weatherization grant to help "working poor" families save money on their fuel bills. There are ways to save on supplies, too. Chicago gives grants to nonprofit housing development corporations for materials used to rehabilitate properties. Charlottesville, Virginia, operates a program to subsidize building material costs for low-income families who are doing rehab work. People's Development Corporation in the South Bronx has a materials-recycling center and a nonprofit hardware and building-supplies distribution center. The city of Vallejo, California, even offers free termite inspection.

Another way cities aid rehabilitation is through property-tax relief. The property tax has suffered considerable adverse publicity recently with the passage of Proposition 13 in California. Yet it remains the workhorse of local government taxation, bringing in billions of dollars to city coffers every year. In the case of rehabilitation, the property tax seems counterproductive to many observers, since an owner who improves his property often has to pay more in taxes. Many cities are trying to get around this problem by granting exemptions or abatements of property-tax increases resulting from sponsored rehabilitation programs. In New York City, for example, Executive Order J-51 allows a twelve-year exemption from an increase in property taxes due to an increase in value caused by certain kinds of rehabilitation. Most of the urban homesteading programs also have some kind of tax abatement system. In most cases the cities figure it is worth foregoing taxes a few years if that will provide an additional incentive to get an abandoned property back on the tax rolls.

One of the most valuable spinoffs is youth employment and training. Title III of the Comprehensive Employment and Training Act (CETA) provides federal dollars for youth programs. The Youth Employment and Demonstration Act of 1977 makes $1.5 billion available for youth employment in the rehabilitation of public properties, the construction and upgrading of parks, energy conservation (particularly solar energy), weatherization of housing for low-income families, and neighborhood revitalization and improvement. Many cities are taking advantage of these programs. In upper New York State, Rochester Jobs, Inc., has employed and trained some two thousand young people over a seven-year period. They work on the repair of houses, at the same time getting special training to encourage them to go back to school. "We take three hundred kids a year and break the failure syndrome, and we put twenty houses a year back on the tax rolls," says project director Don Ginsberg. Portland, Oregon, has a program where youths do home repairs for the elderly and handicapped. In Battle Creek, Michigan, they weatherize houses. In Denver, they install solar collectors. Charlottesville, Virginia, combines money from a number of sources—CETA, community-development block grants, the Older Americans Act—to rehab houses for needy families, particularly the elderly. In a two-year period, some seventy student workmen fixed up seventy-nine homes, at a cost of $52,000. The real cost would have been $244,000. Through youth training programs, therefore, not only are houses being rehabilitated and neighborhoods improved, but young people are being given training that can prepare them for good jobs in the future.

Urban Homesteading

When Daniel Frawley of Wilmington, Delaware, became the nation's first urban homesteader, shortly after that city passed the country's first urban homesteading law in May 1973, he probably had little notion of how sharply attention would be focused upon him and those who would follow in his footsteps. But obviously there was something romantic, something central to the American character, about getting an abandoned house for practically nothing and turning it into a beautiful home. And that was the whole idea behind homesteading—taking worthless property and putting it to good use. It was a tradition that went back more than a century, to the Rural Homestead Act of 1862, which opened the door for the settling of the Great Plains.* Now it was to be used to resettle the great urban wastelands. "Wilmington has two thousand unproductive abandoned homes, so why not give them away?" asked Mayor Thomas Maloney, rhetorically. With a half million abandoned housing units scarring the cities and another 150,000 units being added to the list every year, it seemed like a good idea.

In the few years since Daniel Frawley got the first homestead, some 25,000 homes have been or are being reclaimed through this mechanism. According to a HUD report, the typical homesteader is thirty-five, a minority-group member, and head of a family of three, with an income of $12,000. Nearly half the homesteaders in a demonstration program involving twenty-three cities financed the repairs—which averaged $8,400—without help from the local government. HUD called homesteading "an exciting and promising tool."

For those cities with the most experience in homesteading— Wilmington, Baltimore, Philadelphia, Newark, and Chicago— the process has ten basic steps: (1) select the building; (2) obtain the title (city); (3) choose the homesteader; (4) arrange for financing; (5) choose a contractor; (6) prepare the building for occupancy; (7) move into the building; (8) complete the rehabilitation; (9) occupy the building for stipulated period and pass final inspection; (10) obtain full ownership of the building. Let me explain briefly.

Most of the buildings that come up for homesteading have

---

*Actually, the first homesteading law was the Armed Occupation Act of 1842, which was passed to encourage settlement of Southeast Florida. See Anne Clark and Zelma Rivin, *Homesteading in Urban U.S.A.*

been foreclosed because the owners didn't pay their taxes; in those cases, the city takes ownership. Many others have been foreclosed because the mortgage wasn't paid, in which case the lender takes ownership. But if the mortgage is insured through the FHA, the federal government (HUD) gets stuck with the house. To get rid of its buildings, HUD must first turn them over to the city, which then finds homesteaders for the buildings.

Typically, each city has a central office which works with HUD to purchase the buildings for the city (usually at minimal cost) for eventual sale to homesteaders. A prospective homeowner must be at least eighteen years old and a U.S. citizen or resident alien. He must also show that he has enough income to pay for the rehabilitation. Since there are always more applicants than available homes, the cities hold lotteries to pick homesteaders. Financing is arranged either through special city programs, as described above, or by private lending institutions. The amount of the loan is based on the estimated cost of rehabilitation and the homesteader's ability to pay. All code violations must be removed. Once a contractor has been chosen by the homesteader (sometimes with the required approval of the city), the house is made sufficiently habitable for him to move in. The homesteader must live in the building while the rehabilitation is going on, and the work must pass periodic city inspections. Once the house has passed final muster, the homesteader may be given outright ownership or he may be required to lease the house for a stipulated period before gaining title to the building; this is done to prevent speculation. (During the leasing period, the homesteader pays no local property taxes, since the city still owns the building; in Baltimore, this is considered an added incentive.) After taking title, the homesteader may enjoy certain property-tax privileges. In Philadelphia, for example, the homestead is assessed at its previous value for the first year; every year for the next five years, the assessment goes up in equal increments until it reaches the true value of the improved building. Wilmington allows homesteaders a tax break for five years; after that, the owner must pay his full share of taxes.

Homesteading sounds easy, but it's not. Because homesteaders are usually inexperienced in housing matters, something is always going wrong. They're so fired up with enthusiasm that they often discount how hard it is to save a house that has been abandoned, how uncomfortable it can be living amid plaster dust, and how long it will take to complete the job. They might select the wrong contractor for the job. "We had one contractor who estimated a job at $85,000," recalls Roger Windsor, the director of Baltimore's "Dollar Houses" program. "Somebody else did it, and it came in at $39,000." The worst problem, says Windsor, is "the unexpected"—the unknown added expense that is revealed when the construction crew tears out the floor or pulls down a wall.

There are also serious limitations to what can be accomplished by urban homesteading. Howard E. Mitchell, Jr., who studied Philadelphia's program, said it had only "moderate prospects of success." The program, he said, "has been reduced to a scattered-site, moderate-income rehabilitated-housing scheme for mildly abandoned areas," with "no obvious advantage over existing 'used housing' or rehabilitation programs." James W. Hughes and Kenneth D. Bleakly, Jr., concluded that the programs they studied were not doing the best job possible. "If the sponsoring municipality is truly serious in regard to increased home ownership and homesteading, a sophisticated operational framework is obviously required," they wrote.

A more telling criticism, perhaps, is that homesteading is a "catch-up" program: if there hadn't been all those abandoned buildings in the first place, there would be no need for homesteading. Rarely is there sufficient concentration of homesteads to tie them into an overall plan for the development of a neighborhood. Baltimore, it is true, has been able to cluster homesteads in several areas—Otterbein, Barre Circle, and Stirling Street—with remarkable effect on the surrounding area. In Chicago's West Englewood neighborhood, the Neighborhood Housing Services program is attacking the problem of abandoned houses on a planned basis, using homesteading where appropriate. But the truth is that in most cases, homesteading is a convenient way for the cities and HUD to cover past mistakes that led to abandonment in the first place. It is not a panacea by any means, despite the extravagant publicity it has enjoyed. "There's no way homesteading should be an overall program," says Jan Jaffe, former assistant director of the Philadelphia program. "It's only a part of the solution."

Finally, homesteading is doing little for the poor. Since rehabilitation costs anywhere from $5,000 to $20,000 and up, with monthly housing costs in the $250 to $300 range, the income requirements are prohibitive; consequently, most cities gear their programs toward families in at least the moderate-income range. Thus, the people most likely to have been the victims of building abandonment hardly ever benefit from the solution.

One way to make homesteading work for the poor is nevertheless being put into effect by Milton Street, a community activist in North Philadelphia. Street simply finds an abandoned house, clips off the lock with snippers (his "master key"), and moves a family in. He calls it "walk-in homesteading." So far, he has found housing for three hundred families. "We have a single mother with four children who, with some help from her brothers and her uncle, has been able to put $2,200 of work into her building," says Street. "It has seven rooms, dropped ceilings, and it's all fixed up." To get the utilities turned on, Street makes up a "lease" that the family can present to the gas and electric companies. The lease, incidentally, binds the family to maintain the building properly. Alcoholics, drug addicts, pimps, and prostitutes are screened out.

All this is illegal, of course, but that doesn't faze Street. He calls his families "house sitters," not squatters. Through a volunteer legal staff, he has been able to negotiate the outright sale of most of the buildings from the true owners, who realize that a court fight would cost more than they could ever hope to obtain for the buildings. The program has received at least tacit approval from Mayor Frank L. Rizzo, although there has been criticism of Street's methods. "There are times when he has victimized the victims," said one city hall staffer. "The city has had to take care of families that he has dumped into houses without knowing what to do with them. Not everyone can rehabilitate a house."

But no one denies that Street's scheme does keep the houses occupied and therefore reduces the chances of vandalism or arson. In Providence, Rhode Island, another variation of walk-in homesteading is accomplishing the same thing. A group called Stop Wasting Abandoned Properties, or SWAP for short, keeps a constant lookout for abandoned buildings. When one comes up, they negotiate with the owner to list the building with SWAP at a set price. SWAP then publicizes the availability of these houses and finds potential buyers. Using various loan and grant techniques (see above), SWAP gets financing for the buyer at a price he can afford. Then it is simply a matter of bringing buyer and seller together. So far, "quick-response homesteading," as it is called, has saved nearly a hundred houses from being abandoned during the drawn-out process of tax foreclosure.

Perhaps the most dramatic form of homesteading, though, is under way in New York City, where more than a thousand housing units have been converted through "sweat equity." Neighborhood people, some of them ex-offenders, some of them gang members, most of them just poor people who want a decent place to live, are taking over squalid apartment buildings and rebuilding them with their own sweat.

At 948 Columbus Avenue, Manhattan, six families, including a grandmother and a retired newspaper man, went from illegally squatting in the building to completely renovating it. On the Lower East Side, a group called Interfaith Adopt-A-Building has saved a whole row of houses on East 11th Street, heating them with solar collectors on the roof and powering them with the city's only electricity-generating windmill. (They even sell their excess juice to Consolidated Edison.) In Harlem the Renigades gang became the Renigades Housing Movement, putting street toughs to work with putty knives instead of switchblades. Both Adopt-A-Building and People's Development Corporation, a South Bronx sweat equity group that has successfully rehabbed a twenty-eight-unit building, will take part in a $3 million HUD-sponsored demonstration program of sweat equity in which two hundred units will be renovated.

The buildings are rehabilitated at about half the cost of conventional rehabilitation. How do they do it? According to Howard Burchman of the Urban Homesteading Assistance Board (U-HAB), homesteader groups are able to benefit from a variety of cost-saving devices. Inexpensive site-acquisition costs together with low-cost financing programs (usually twenty-five-year terms at 7 percent), ten-year tax abatements, and lower insurance rates translate into savings of thousands of dollars per unit. Even greater amounts are saved through do-it-yourself repair and construction; a homesteader putting his sweat equity into a two-bedroom apartment, for example, will save about $4,000 in contractor overhead and profit plus $7,500 in contract labor fees. (Additionally, some worker-participants have actually received wages of up to $3.50 an hour through the Comprehensive Employment Training Act or the Criminal Justice Coordinating Council.) Total development costs for such a unit, according to U-HAB, run about $15,163, compared to $31,183 for a conventional rehab.

After physical rehabilitation has been completed, homesteader groups continue to realize additional savings. If the "tenants" own and manage their buildings, serving as security forces, janitors, and repairmen, overhead and maintenance costs are substantially reduced. There may also be significant energy savings if the building has been given heavy-duty insulation (several have even been converted to use solar energy for heat). Taking all of these savings into account, the rent per room is reduced to about half that of conventional rehabilitation—about $47 a room, compared to $102. Thus, a two-bedroom apartment can be rented for less than $200 a month, compared to about $500 a month for rehabilitated apartments under the Section 8 rent subsidy program.

Yet even the sweat equity program is in trouble. The city's Municipal Loan Program collapsed in 1975, leaving homesteaders in the breach. The city has tried to compensate with "participation loans," which are 1 percent loans financed by CD money. They cover only a portion of the debt, however; the rest must be raised from private lenders at market rates, boosting overall costs. Even so, the delays are astounding—at least two years from conception to final loan approval. Then, the federal job-training funds, which can make the difference between success and failure, are supposed to be used for only one year for each trainee. Some federal officials think the money is being wasted, since only one-fourth of the graduates are able to get jobs in the construction trades. Another threat is that the federal Davis-Bacon Act requires construction workers to be paid the prevailing wage in projects involving eight or more units. This has been waived in some of the sweat equity programs, but not others. Thus, sweat equity might have to be restricted to smaller buildings.

Neighborhood Housing Services

While homesteading has been used only in areas with severe abandonment and is encountering serious difficulties, another approach to urban revitalization, Neighborhood Housing Services, is enjoying more widespread success. NHS got its start in 1968 when a group of residents on Pittsburgh's Central North Side, led by a no-nonsense woman named Dorothy Richardson, decided to take on the slumlords in their area. The group, Citizens Against Slum Housing, or CASH, came up with the original Neighborhood Housing Services program.

NHS is a partnership of citizens, financial institutions, city government, foundations, and federal officials whose purpose is to provide mortgage loans and rehabilitation funds in neighborhoods that are on the brink of decay, but still salvageable. At one end is the National Neighborhood Reinvestment Corporation (formerly the Urban Reinvestment Task Force), a body representing the joint efforts of the federal financial regulatory agencies—the Federal Home Loan Bank Board, the Federal Reserve System, the Federal Deposit Insurance Corporation, and the Comptroller of the Currency—and the Department of Housing and Urban Development. The corporation gets funds from HUD and the Federal Home Bank Loan System to oversee the program and develop special applications of the NHS concept. At the local level, the partnership consists of the local lending institutions, the city government, foundations and local corporations, and, most important, an active and responsive community organization. Each partner plays an important role in the development of an NHS program.

The community organization's function is to provide the grass-roots support the program needs. It serves as a watchdog over the program; in its role of NHS advocate, it is responsible for creating a positive climate for the program; it is also charged with educating the community, particularly in convincing homeowners of the need for code enforcement. Finally, the majority of members of the local corporation that runs the NHS program are taken from the community organization's ranks.

The city's involvement in NHS consists of two major tasks: first, to step up the level of services and improvements in the NHS area; and second, to provide a sensitive and systematic housing inspection program for the NHS area. Sometimes this entails special training for the inspectors assigned to NHS projects. In many NHS programs the city is also involved in other efforts, such as urban homesteading or neighborhood planning.

The lending institutions have three key responsibilities. They must first put up the operating costs of running the program, which totals anywhere from $30,000 to $50,000 a year. They must also agree to be active in the planning, development, and execution of the program, providing high-level officers to sit in on meetings and offer the lenders' expertise. Finally, and most important, the lenders must agree to reinvest in the neighborhood by making loans at market rates to all homeowners who meet normal lending criteria.

Local foundations and corporations participate in NHS programs by contributing to the establishment of a high-risk revolving fund, which makes loans to homeowners who cannot meet regular credit requirements. The loans are made at low interest rates, anywhere from zero to 6 percent, but most are expected to be paid back—there are few grants. As the loans are paid back, the money in the revolving fund is loaned again, eventually making it self-sustaining. Incidentally, the National Neighborhood Reinvestment Corporation makes a one-time $50,000 or $100,000 contribution to the fund, which must be matched locally. Increasingly, too, city governments are contributing to these funds, using community-development block grants.

How does a community group start an NHS program? First, of course, it must be certain that the Neighborhood Housing Services method is the right path to take: will NHS do the job, or would some other program be more appropriate? Then there has to be an assessment of whether the neighborhood fits the criteria established by the Urban Reinvestment Task Force. In allocating NHS monies, priority is given to neighborhoods with the following characteristics: (1) the housing is basically sound but shows early signs of deterioration or lack of maintenance; (2) there is a high level of owner-occupancy, preferably more than half; (3) the neighborhood comprises an area with distinct boundaries encompassing one thousand to two thousand houses, most of them single-family; (4) evidence exists that the area has been discriminated against in obtaining mortgages and home improvement loans; (5) the median family income for the neighborhood is no less than 80 percent of the citywide median; and (6) rehabilitation costs should run about $6,000 a unit. Since there is so much competition for NHS programs, a neighborhood that falls short in any of the criteria that applies to NHS may be raising false hopes.

If the neighborhood meets the criteria outlined above, the community group should put together a coalition of those partners—lenders, city officials, foundations and corporations—necessary to the process. Then it is a matter of making a formal application, a somewhat complicated procedure that is made easier with the help of the national corporation in Washington.

When it receives an application, the national corporation reviews it carefully and conducts its own field survey to determine if the basic elements for a successful NHS program exist. If so, the corporation enters into an agreement with the applicant (usually the city) to assist the various local partners in setting up the program. The local partners must put up $30,000 to $50,000 to defray development costs and to pay the salary of a local full-time staff person hired by the task force for six to twelve months. The money also covers the cost of several workshops for local participants, travel expenses (for local people to visit an operating NHS program in another city), and overhead.

During this period, the task-force representative catalogs the local resources—citizen involvement, lender interest, municipal services and programs, foundation and corporate support—and conducts a series of workshops designed to familiarize the local partners with the details of the NHS program. He also assists in the organization, incorporation, and funding of the program and helps select and train the permanent staff. Once he is sure that the program has been launched properly, the task-force representative is dispatched to another project, although he remains available for technical assistance while the permanent staff members get their sea legs.

Once under way, the local NHS program is run by a private, nonprofit, tax-exempt, state-chartered corporation, which is governed by a board of directors a majority of whom must be neighborhood representatives. Customarily, other members include representatives of the lending institutions, city officials, and at-large community members. The board sets policy for the operation of the program and oversees the staff.

The staff members provide numerous services to homeowners. They inform residents about the program and counsel them on the cost of home repairs. They help write up the work specifications, secure bids from qualified contractors, and prepare contracts. If there are special financial problems, they may recommend ways for the homeowner to consolidate bills, obtain personal loans, and budget his money. They also advise the homeowner as to the availability of conventional loans from the lenders, and, in high-risk cases, the revolving loan fund. As the rehabilitation progresses, they make periodic inspections to be certain that the job is being done properly and will, if necessary, act as mediators in case of any dispute between property owner and contractor. In sum, the local NHS staff is there to help the owner improve his home to meet at least the minimal code standards, with as little added financial burden as possible.

That is the minimum they do. Several NHS programs offer other services. Jamaica, New York, has a twelve-week home-maintenance training program to help property owners repair and maintain their homes. Baltimore offers counseling to help tenants become property owners. (See Chapter 10.) Yonkers, New York, is working on the special problem of large apartment buildings. These and other efforts are part of the Neighborhood Preservation Projects program, which is designed to test new ideas in the hope that they—like the original NHS concept—will be transferable to other communities.

Today NHS is one of the hottest housing games in town. As of March 1979, some eighty-seven neighborhoods in seventy-four cities had NHS programs, with the number of participating neighborhoods expected to reach one hundred by the end of 1979. By March 31, 1978, nearly $27 million in new mortgages had been recorded in NHS areas; $13.6 million in conventional rehabilitation loans; more than $2 million in city or state loan programs; and $6.5 million in "high-risk" loans made by the NHS programs themselves. More than 7,500 homes had been brought up to minimum housing code standards, with a total investment of at least $75 million directly attributable to the NHS program. But this $75 million figure represents only the tip of the iceberg, since many homeowners in NHS areas go directly to lending institutions without consulting the local NHS headquarters. Nor does it include the sweat equity that owners put into their homes, or the public improvements made by the cities. The total investment would have to be in the hundreds of millions.

NHS is "a helluva good program," according to Roger S. Ahlbrandt, Jr., research director of ACTION-Housing, Inc., of Pittsburgh, which conducted a nationwide study of NHS programs for HUD. Ahlbrandt said there are a number of reasons why NHS has worked:

NHS is a local program. "The program wouldn't have worked if it had been a HUD or federally run program," said Ahlbrandt. "The only reason the lending institutions got involved was because it was local, with citizen involvement."

NHS is nongovernmental. The local board of directors of the private corporation runs the NHS, not bureaucrats. City officials may be on the board, but majority control rests with the citizens.

NHS is not bureaucratic. The local staffs are small, usually two or three persons. They handle things with a minimum of red tape.

NHS is flexible. "We try to make each loan fit the individual case," said Dorothy Richardson. There are no rules and regulations from Washington to follow.

NHS is a self-help effort. The only outside money is a one-time matching grant from the National Neighborhood Reinvestment Corporation.

NHS is not a giveaway program. Outright grants are kept to a minimum. In cases where the prospect for repayment is risky, the loans can be secured by a lien on the property. Roger Ahlbrandt notes, "The fact that the program is not a giveaway program is an important feature in the eyes of financial institutions and funding sources, and it effectively communicates the program's philosophy that property upkeep is the responsibility of the homeowners."

NHS concentrates on specific neighborhoods. "Spreading it citywide would not work," said William Whiteside of National Neighborhood Reinvestment Corporation. "It's kind of like sewers. You've got to start putting them in someplace and you hope that eventually the whole city gets them."

NHS's impressive record demonstrates what can be accomplished when community organizations and cities replace direct, massive federal programs, such as those popular during the War on Poverty, with less direct, but in some ways more effective, approaches using community-development block grants and other innovative local programs. Nonetheless, NHS is far from perfect. One limitation is that it reaches only moderately deteriorated neighborhoods with a high quotient of single-family, owner-occupied homes—hardly slums. And some of its proponents fear that Neighborhood Housing Services may succumb to its own popularity, if it spreads to neighborhoods where grass-roots support has not truly taken hold. Overall, however, it has to be judged as a remarkably successful program.

PART FOUR

Special Considerations

10

OVERCOMING DISPLACEMENT

At the beginning of this book a distinction was drawn between two kinds of revitalizing neighborhoods, those undergoing "incumbent upgrading" and those experiencing "gentrification." Incumbent upgrading, you will recall, occurs when the current residents and property owners improve their houses and neighborhoods. This process usually occurs in neighborhoods where the real estate market is either stable or improving slightly, but is not yet ripe for rapid redevelopment. Gentrification, on the other hand, occurs when real estate speculators and a new group of property owners—usually wealthier, higher in class and status, and sometimes more politically savvy than the current residents—moves into the neighborhood and starts to buy up many of the properties from long-time owners. As real estate speculation in such neighborhoods begins to spiral, housing costs, for both owners and renters, increase almost geometrically, with the result that many of the current residents can no longer afford to stay in the neighborhood, whether they'd like to or not. The term given to the phenomenon of the forced removal resulting from market pressures of the long-time residents of a city neighborhood is "displacement."

As a city grows and matures, a certain amount of displacement is inevitable and, in some respects, desirable, since it assures that urban neighborhoods will get an infusion of new blood. But it gets out of hand when long-term residents are forced to move against their will, which not even the newcomers to the neighborhood want to happen. In this chapter, therefore, the emphasis is on providing for an orderly succession, without undue hardship being placed on the existing residents.

How widespread is displacement? According to HUD, reinvestment displacement is not a major phenomenon and actually accounts for less than 4 percent of all household moves in 1976. But even the HUD study admits that "very little reliable information exists" on this subject; moreover, since the HUD analysis took a broad approach, instead of looking at how displacement affects specific neighborhoods, its conclusions are of limited use.

One study that fine-tuned its research is *Displacement: City Neighborhoods in Transition*. In it, the National Urban Coalition, a Washington-based civil rights group, reports the results of a survey of 169 neighborhoods. NUC found that "the phenomenon of housing rehabilitation is widespread, regardless of city size or geographic location," according to M. Carl Holman, the coalition's executive director. The revitalization movement is occurring in cities as small as Newburgh, New York (population 25,000), and as large as New York City, from Boston to Oakland, from Houston to Chicago. The "turn-around" is happening much faster than before: it takes only two years, not ten, for a slum neighborhood to change into another Georgetown. The most rapid improvements reported were in neighborhoods either close to downtown areas or those designated as historic districts (in fact, half the neighborhoods reported undergoing revitalization were historic areas—many of which are located in or near the original center of the city). As for displacement, the coalition found repeated instances of dislocation in the revitalizing neighborhoods, particularly in the historic areas, with a consequent growing resistance among long-time residents to speculators, historic preservationists, and "new people" in the neighborhood. There were frequent reports of grumbling about escalating property taxes, skyrocketing rents and housing prices, and the threat to community values and traditions posed by the new wave of residents. In sum, the National Urban Coalition survey came up with ample evidence that displacement is not an imagined problem.

Today, speculation has driven the price of housing in such up-and-coming neighborhoods almost to the point of absurdity. In the Irish Channel neighborhood of New Orleans, a speculator who bought an old hulk of a building a few years ago for $15,000 or $20,000 can sell it with only modest improvements for $50,000 to $100,000. In Atlanta's West End, buildings bought for $20,000 now go for $60,000. Ohio City, a neighborhood in Cleveland, has buildings that were purchased recently for $12,000 to $18,000 selling for $30,000 to $50,000. A brownstone in the Park Slope section of Brooklyn that sold for $20,000 ten years ago could cost $70,000 today—and that would be a good deal. San Francisco's Mint Hill deserves its name, for a "shell" purchased at $40,000 to $50,000 costs a mint after rehabilitation—$175,000 to $200,000.

Or consider the Adams-Morgan section of Washington, D.C., one of the most notorious examples of rampant speculation in the country. "We have experienced an awful lot of speculation. The average sales price of a boarded-up house in the neighborhood is $50,000," said Frank Smith, a fellow at the Public Resource Center and president of the Adams-Morgan Organization. Houses in Adams-Morgan generally double in price after rehabilitation. In one census tract, Smith found, the average selling price of homes went from $15,000 in 1971 to $37,000 in 1976; in another tract, average sales prices for single-family homes went from the low thirties in 1973 to the mid-sixties by 1976. Many of the sales involved "flipping," whereby one speculator buys a property (or merely gets an option to buy the property) and "flips" it to another speculator without making any improvements. The real jump in price occurs when the speculator sells to a family, not another real estate operator; then, profits of 100 percent or more of the original price are not uncommon. Displacement of the original residents is equally common in such cases.

Another cause for alarm is the dramatic jump in property taxes that accompanies reinvestment. Some neighborhoods in the District of Columbia, for example, have been hit with property-tax increases of 18 to 37 percent within a two-year period. In Queen Village, formerly a working-class neighborhood in South Philadelphia, assessments have gone up several hundred percent in the last few years, according to Conrad Weiler, the president of the local civic association. Though the houses may be worth more (leading to the increased assessments), Weiler points out that the increased value doesn't help the current residents until the house is sold—"and many of our residents have no desire to sell now or in the future."

The burden of displacement falls hardest on those whom Reverend Joseph Kakalec, a Catholic priest active in civic work in Philadelphia, calls the *anawim*. In the Bible, the *anawim* were the "remnant" of Hebrews who struggled under the yoke of the Babylonians. "They were the ones who stayed, who fought the hardest and were the most devout," says Father Kakalec. "Today, many of the people who have stayed in the cities—the poor, the blacks, the old-timers, the ethnics—these are the people who have kept our cities alive." They did this, of course, because, like the ancient Hebrews, they had little or no choice. "They were the ones who had to stay in the city during the worst times," notes Frances Phipps, a staff member of the National Commission on Neighborhoods. Instead of being awarded a special certificate for sticking it out, they get an eviction notice.

Like the *anawim* of the Bible, the modern-day remnant have little to say about what happens to them. "Displacement occurs without the advice, without the consent, without even the minimal consideration of the local residents," says Father Kakalec. "In fact, the current residents are looked upon as obstacles." A black woman who used to rent a house on Capitol Hill in Washington had an experience that many of the *anawim* find typical. "I could have bought this place myself if they had given me a chance to buy it at the original price," she said. "But nobody offered it to me. And I sure can't pay what it's going for now."

If the *anawim* are the people being displaced, who are those doing the displacing? For the most part, they are young adults in the baby-boom group, aged twenty-five to thirty-four. They are well-to-do, educated, single, divorced, or newly married with few or no children. In many of these families, both husband and wife work, thus bolstering their total income; that, combined with the fact that many of them have postponed (or ruled out) having children, gives them a relatively high disposable income. Only about one in ten of these families has moved back to the city from the suburbs. Most have moved within the same city or from another city. They are most likely professionals or managers, middle-class in background, and "highly motivated, and concerned about improving their neighborhood." They may be artists or bohemians, and they may be homosexuals. A substantial portion are blacks.

What these "space colonists" are looking for is a neighborhood that is "set apart" from other neighborhoods, one that is or has the potential of becoming somehow distinctive. The housing stock must be interesting. Perhaps one of the buildings is an old spaghetti factory, or a police station, or even a maximum-security prison. (It's happened, believe me!) The houses should have lots of stained glass, oversize rooms, bay windows, high ceilings, elaborate cornices, gingerbread woodwork and other scrollwork, wide porches, maybe a roof-top garden. Plaster, not plasterboard, is preferred; brick, not aluminum siding; and oak and maple, not knotty pine. (One young woman who bought a house in Dorchester, a working-class section of Boston, marveled at the hardwood floors and banisters. "You don't know what that means to someone from California," she said. "All that beautiful wood. I just fell in love with it.") The area itself must have some kind of unusual characteristic—historic value, for instance, or a view of the river, or proximity to a park. The neighborhood must be near the center of things—downtown or near the center of academic, artistic, or cultural activity. Finally, the neighborhood must have a "sense of momentum." There must be enthusiasm and optimism, the feeling that others will soon follow, that together the new group can unite to overcome any negative characteristics the neighborhood might possess (bad schools, poor delivery of social services), and that there will be a steady progression in the quality of life *and* the value of their investment.

The problem with the displacement issue, as with all urban matters, is not only its complexity but also the lack of a clearly identifiable villain with black hat and waxed moustache. In the past, it was possible to blame the displacement of the urban poor on government programs, such as slum clearance and urban renewal. Today, in gentrifying neighborhoods, the only villain is the real estate market itself. How can one blame the young pioneers for seeking the only housing that is available to them at reasonable prices? Unless there is a radical change in the country's economic system toward a socialistic direction (which I doubt will happen soon), it is unreasonable to expect people to behave in a manner that is contradictory to what our system encourages. Many of the "speculators" in these gentrifying neighborhoods, for example, are not monolithic real estate firms, but local businessmen and property owners, small-timers who are cashing in on their good luck. They feel justified in reaping a substantial profit, since they were forced to hold onto the property during the lean years. So strong is this ethic ingrained in our psyche that even many of those who stand to be displaced, particularly the elderly, see nothing wrong with a neighbor benefiting from real estate speculation. Isn't that the way the free market works? they ask.

Nor is the displacement issue essentially a matter of blacks (and other minorities) versus whites. While it is true, for example, that seventeen of the twenty-seven gentrified neighborhoods studied by MIT's Phillip L. Clay had changed from black to white, the surprising thing is that "the principal factor in dislocation is social class, not race," according to Frances Phipps, who in her previous position with the National Urban Coalition directed the group's displacement study. In Atlanta, for example, upper-class whites *and* upper-class blacks are pushing the poor out of certain neighborhoods, a pattern that holds true in New York, Washington, Philadelphia, St. Louis, New Orleans, and other cities experiencing widespread gentrification. Income, not race, is the crucial factor in displacement.

From the point of view of the nation's mayors, gentrification is a mixed blessing. While publicly they may express concern for the poor, the elderly, and the minorities, there is hardly a mayor in the country who doesn't also want to attract as many affluent, white, stable families to his city as possible—and who can blame them for trying? It's not only common sense, but good politics, to seek to attract families who pay taxes (instead of being on welfare), contribute to the city's economy (rather than drawing off more in public services than they pay for), acting as stabilizing forces (as opposed to creating social problems, particularly crime), and so on. There are some who dispute these claims, notably Conrad Weiler, who argues that the new gentry are *not* that great a bonus to city neighborhoods. He points out that the new gentry often demand more in city services and public improvements than they pay back in added taxes. But arguments like these are hardly ever considered by those whose decisions influence the shape of the cities. So, while they continue to express concern for the displaced poor, the power brokers in city hall go on encouraging gentrification in older neighborhoods. Politically, it's the smart thing to do.

Another reason why gentrification is such a confounding problem is that we know so little of its consequences for those who are actually displaced. Gentrification indisputably produces profound reverberations. "If one neighborhood is undergoing severe revitalization pressure, then there must be another neighborhood in the area that's being affected by the migration of the displaced residents," notes Frances Phipps. Precisely such a thing occurred when the Capitol Hill revitalization pushed poor blacks across the District of Columbia line into Prince George's County, Maryland. The pressure for housing in Prince George's got so high that the county was forced to put a tax on apartment dwellers and curtail further apartment construction by imposing a sewer moratorium. Capitol Hill's gain was Prince George's loss. Cui bono?

Finally, gentrification happens so fast these days that the process is hardly ever recognized until it's too late to stop it. By the time a neighborhood starts taking off, housing prices and rents have escalated to the point where it becomes extremely costly to retain any housing for the original residents, especially the poor.

Any solution, therefore, hinges on timing. That is why I urge community organizations to make *housing the current residents* a guiding principle of any neighborhood revitalization effort—*right from the beginning*. "The key to displacement is getting in before it happens," says Jim Wilcox, of the Southwest Germantown Development Corporation in Philadelphia.

What, then, can be done about displacement?

Relieving the Symptoms

One approach to the displacement problem is to relieve the symptoms of the disease—the higher property taxes, higher housing prices and rentals, and so on. For example, some jurisdictions require developers of apartment buildings that are being converted to condominium ownership to pay the moving expenses of tenants who do not buy units. Another technique is to provide housing elsewhere for those displaced by reinvestment. In Philadelphia's North Central ghetto, we have seen how Milton Street and his North Philadelphia Block Development Corporation are moving families displaced from other parts of the city into abandoned houses. Each family then uses its sweat equity to bring the house up to minimal standards, while Street's group haggles with the absentee landlord to get ownership for the new occupants. "We have reversed the legal process," says Street. "We put the people in the house, and let the speculators take us to court."

If property tax increases are a problem for the poor and the elderly living on fixed incomes, a system that would simply defer taxes until the property is sold or otherwise changes hands makes sense. This, after all, is what slumlords do—they simply refuse to pay their taxes, forcing the city to take them to court. This new method would permit elderly and poor homeowners to stay in their homes. Why shouldn't they be treated as well as slumlords?

Another way to short-circuit the soaring property tax in revitalizing neighborhoods is the so-called circuit-breaker technique. This method permits elderly, handicapped, and other eligible homeowners to forego paying all or part of their property taxes, depending on income. New Castle County, Delaware (which includes Wilmington), for example, exempts the first $11,400 of the true value of a home from taxes for qualified persons—disabled homeowners and those sixty-five and over who own and occupy their houses. To qualify, single homeowners may not make more than $3,500 a year ($6,500 for couples), exclusive of Social Security or railroad retirement benefits.

Some states even permit "reverse mortgages" for homeowners age sixty-five and over who own their homes outright. In Illinois, for example, the Senior Citizens Property Relief Act of 1978 allows qualified elderly homeowners to get a new "mortgage" to pay back their property taxes. Other states go even further, allowing reverse mortgages to be used to pay for utilities, insurance, and home maintenance.

A *speculation tax* would also curb the profit taking in real estate and therefore might dampen the market in gentrifying neighborhoods. Such a law went into effect in the District of Columbia in July 1978. The Residential Real Property Transfer Excise Tax Act hits at two kinds of speculators—persons who sell more than three properties within a thirty-month period, and contract buyers who "flip" properties. ("Flipping" is the term for selling property to another speculator at an inflated price.) The law, in effect, puts a tax on "excess profits" from such operations. For example, a dealer who sells a house at a 300 percent profit in less than six months' time from the original purchase is taxed on 97 percent of the profit. If he sells within six months at only an 11 percent profit, only 10 percent of the profits would be taxed. A dealer could avoid the excise tax completely if his profit on a less-than-six-months sale was less than 11 percent. In addition, there are some thirteen exemptions from the law, including sales by owner-occupants, sales on properties with a two-year warranty on major systems, and sales on properties of more than four units. The law requires dealers to register all deeds, so that a strict accounting of sales and transfers can be made; and all dealers must now be licensed. This is the toughest—in fact, the only—law of its kind in the country and bears close watching; at this writing, it is too new to evaluate as to its effectiveness.

Another method of protecting homeowners from forced displacement involves an old device—restrictive covenants—but with a new twist. A restrictive covenant is a clause placed in the deed prohibiting an owner from doing something—for example, selling his house to blacks. Before the U.S. Supreme Court ruled them illegal, such covenants were used mainly to prevent interracial sales of homes. But why not use them to keep down the cost of housing? asks Anne Blumenberg, of Baltimore's St. Ambrose Housing Aid Center. Blumenberg suggests that homeowners in areas of high speculation could be convinced to agree to a restriction on the sales price of their homes—present value, plus a cost-of-living increase and the value of any substantial improvements. In return for giving up the higher speculative value, the property owner would be paid a cash grant by a nonprofit housing group. He would also be granted a lower property assessment than he would normally have at the speculative value of the house.

The idea is not all that far-fetched. In 1976, the National Endowment for the Arts tested the idea for the area adjacent to the historic district of Alexandria, Virginia. The NEA was concerned because homeownership by lower-income families in the historic downtown district had declined from 80 percent in 1940 to only 40 percent in 1976, and 125 more families were being displaced every year. The NEA hoped to set up a nonprofit corporation to acquire an option—the right of first opportunity to purchase—from homeowners in the area around the historic district, where speculation was spreading. In return for granting the option and agreeing to a restrictive covenant limiting the eventual sales price of their homes, the homeowners would get a cash payment of up to $3,000 and a lower property-tax assessment. They would also benefit by not having to pay a realtor's fee upon sale, since the NEA corporation would act as realtor; and they would be eligible for special low-interest loans for rehabilitation. The corporation would sell the homes at the nonspeculative price to a specific class of families—original residents, those displaced by public or private action, the poor, and so on.

Blumenberg says that restrictive covenants should be mandatory whenever public improvements are involved. In Baltimore, she notes, the city takes a loss on certain abandoned properties it rehabilitates and sells to private homeowners. Why, asks Blumenberg, should the new owners be able to get a windfall upon the resale of the house? The public should capture that benefit. Montgomery County, Maryland, for example, requires developers of certain large housing tracts to set aside fifteen percent of the units for sale to moderate-income families at a cost below what the developer is selling his other homes for. The deed for each of these homes contains a covenant of five years' duration restricting the owner from selling the property for more than the price of the house, plus a cost-of-living increase and the value of substantial improvements.

Blumenberg says all housing that benefits from government programs, such as low-cost municipal loans, should have a similar restrictive covenant requiring that such homes be sold to a preferred group of buyers—the poor, families displaced by public projects or private actions (condominium conversions, for example), the handicapped, and others who should receive the primary benefits of public action.

While these proposals are worthy, each has its shortcomings. Walk-in homesteading is often an involuntary reaction to displacement, not a solution to it. Property-tax relief usually benefits only a select group—the elderly and disabled. The speculation tax has proven politically, and perhaps constitutionally, unsupportable—we will have to wait and see what the experience in the District of Columbia will be. Restrictive covenants require property owners to give up the right to sell their homes on the open market, which is contrary to the free-enterprise system (although the idea of restricting the sales price of publicly assisted housing has merit). The NEA proposal, for example, has failed to be approved by the city of Alexandria. In short, these nostrums relieve the symptoms, but they do not cure the disease. A more basic remedy is called for.

Security of Tenure

The only foolproof way to prevent families from being displaced is to have them own their homes, either individually or through a neighborhood corporation. There are a number of ways this can be done. All the methods described previously in this book to help families obtain low-cost home improvement loans and mortgages—rehabilitation financing schemes, revolving loan funds, homesteading programs, sweat equity, low-down-payment mortgages, rebate programs, and so on—serve to keep the original residents in their homes at prices they can afford. (See Chapters 8 and 9.) Obviously, community groups should use such programs in their neighborhoods.* The sooner you start them, the cheaper they will be in the long run, because obviously it costs less to finance a $25,000 home than to finance the same home when its speculative value has increased to $40,000.

Top priority should be given to making tenants into homeowners, for tenants are the group most vulnerable to being displaced. Community groups should pressure their city councils to pass laws similar to Section 301 of the District of Columbia Rental Accommodations Act of 1975, which requires owners of one- to four-unit buildings to make a bona fide offer of sale to their tenants before selling to anyone else. In the meantime, neighborhood

---

*It should be noted that a program introduced in 1978, called the Neighborhood Strategy Areas Program, allocates funds from the Section 8 program to rehabilitate 37,688 housing units in 155 neighborhoods undergoing or threatened by gentrification.

groups can also help mitigate any negative aspects of tenancy. In the Sabine neighborhood of Houston, for example, the Old Sixth Ward Historical Association contacts absentee landlords and offers to renovate their buildings in return for a guarantee that the landlord will not sell the building or raise the rents (thus displacing the tenants) for a stated period of time.

Community organizations can also set up nonprofit housing corporations to purchase a stock of housing in the neighborhood (presumably early enough to get nonspeculative prices) and then rent the properties back to the tenants or to other incumbent residents of the area. Jon Brown, of the Public Interest Research Group in Washington, D.C., takes the idea one step further and suggests that the housing corporation set aside a portion of the tenant's rent (with his consent) for a certain period—say, eighteen months—to be used as a down payment on the house. This is called a purchase-option agreement. The neighborhood housing corporation can then have the new owner agree to a restrictive covenant requiring him to sell the property back to the corporation (at original cost, plus a cost-of-living increase and the value of substantial improvements) if he sells within, say, five years. This clause would prevent tenants from becoming speculators and would keep the supply of low-cost housing available to others in need.

In Minnesota, the St. Paul Housing and Redevelopment Authority is already sponsoring a form of purchase-option tenure. Its Homeownership Opportunities Program enables selected low-income families to rent single-family homes from the housing authority at a maximum monthly cost of 25 percent of family income. The family is responsible for making all repairs and routine maintenance on the home. Each month, a portion of the rent is allocated as equity to the family's Homebuyer's Earned Home Payment Account. This is called the Earned Home Payment Credit, and is based on the value of the maintenance and repair services the homeowner provides, plus the value of the principal being paid back on the housing authority's mortgage. When the amount in the Earned Home Payment Account is twenty times the amount of the monthly Earned Home Payment Credit, the family has the option of purchasing the home from the housing authority. In effect, the Homeownership Opportunities Program is a combination of a purchase-option system with a form of urban homesteading.

An equally ambitious program to convert tenants to homeowners is being conducted by the Baltimore Neighborhood Housing Services program. "We had lots of tenants who had rented for eight or ten years and wanted to buy, and lots of owners who wanted to sell," says Thomas Adams, the local NHS director. The solution was "Project Match," by which the NHS allocated staff to find absentee-owners who were willing to sell and tenants who wanted to buy—preferably, of course, the same building. The program usually works like this: an NHS tenant adviser consults with block captains, clergy, and community leaders to identify interested tenants and landlords, who are then contacted and given information about the program. The NHS adviser then helps speed through the credit check, appraisal, and other paperwork for the sale of the property. The tenant is informed of the various purchasing methods open to him—conventional loan, high-risk revolving fund, and the Maryland Housing Fund. Under the latter program, the tenant need put down only $500 on the house; the fund will insure 100 percent of the mortgage, plus the closing costs and additional costs not covered by the down payment. Finally, the NHS adviser brings the two parties together, smooths the settlement, and provides backup services to the new owner, such as budgeting or loan consolidation.

Adams reports good success with the program. "In just over a year, ninety tenants have bought," he says. Forty-nine of these families purchased the houses they rented, while most of the others bought homes near their former rented ones. Some of the purchasers were able to buy houses even though their only income was from welfare or Social Security.

To some extent the Project Match program is not exactly illustrative of neighborhoods undergoing gentrification, since the area where it was enacted was not undergoing rampant speculation (in fact, the real estate market in the Baltimore NHS area was relatively weak). But Project Match is a good example to follow for communities on the brink of speculative development. It can make a lot of tenants into homeowners *before* the sales prices of houses take off.

Perhaps the furthest refinement of the homeownership concept is land banking. In Baltimore, for example, the Southeast Community Organization has created a subsidiary, Community Holding, Inc., to purchase vacant, abandoned, or absentee-owned houses in areas of potential displacement, particularly Upper Fell's Point, Washington Hill, and SECO's NHS area. With a $650,000 line of credit from the Ford Foundation, Community Holding buys the houses before the speculators can get them and then has several options. It can: (1) rehabilitate the house and rent it to someone under a purchase-option agreement; (2) sell the property as is to someone and arrange financing through such mechanisms as Neighborhood Housing Services' high-risk pool, if necessary; or (3) do a minimal amount of rehabilitation, then sell it to someone who will use sweat equity and home improvement loans to complete renovation, finally obtaining long-term mortgage financing. As Community Holding sells the properties, it pays back the money borrowed from the Ford Foundation, theoretically making it self-sustaining.

The land banking idea is popular with housing activists. In Savannah, for instance, Leopold Adler II, a prominent historic preservationist, hopes to save half of the twelve hundred Victorian homes in one forty-five-block district by having his Landmark Rehabilitation Project purchase the houses, rehab them (using subsidies, such as Section 312 loans, wherever possible), and then rent them back to low-income tenants, piggybacking Section 8 housing subsidies on top of everything. But land banking is essentially new and untested. Even SECO's project, the most advanced in the country, involved only some sixty houses in its first year.

One modest land banking scheme that seems to hold promise is being put together by the St. Ambrose Housing Aid Center in Baltimore. St. Ambrose's director, Vincent Quayle, a former Jesuit priest, tells how the idea developed: "Sometime in 1976 we noticed that blacks in the Harwood neighborhood were being forced out of their homes and whites were moving in," said Quayle. Harwood is a small black pocket of modest row houses adjacent to Charles Village, the posh section of $30,000 and $40,000 townhouses near Johns Hopkins University. Shirley Rivers, one of Quayle's associates and a resident of Harwood, asked her neighbors if they wanted to move. No, they replied, but they didn't know how they could stay. That's when St. Ambrose Center moved in.

Quayle got a $50,000 line of credit from each of four helpful savings and loan institutions, plus additional money from Associated Catholic Charities, the Maryland Jesuits, and a couple of private benefactors. Then he, Shirley Rivers, and the rest of the St. Ambrose staff went after the landlords in Harwood, pressuring them, coaxing them, pleading with them to sell their homes to St. Ambrose (through its subsidiary, Charm City Realty) instead of some speculator. Many landlords were all too glad to get a guaranteed sale, rather than wait for an offer from some outside purchaser or the tenant.

When he gets a building, Quayle uses a chunk of the $125,000 in block grant funds from the city to put in about $4,000 to repair the plumbing, electricity, and roof. He then sells it to the tenant. (The mortgage is insured through the Maryland Housing Fund; the additional cost is 0.5 percent on the interest rate.) Other homes are obtained through tax auctions and abandonment. If the tenant can't make the $500 down payment, he can rent from St. Ambrose Center until he gets the cash. As of the end of 1977, the St. Ambrose Center had made 35 tenant families into homeowners. The goal: to make homeowners of 150 of the 450 families in Harwood.

More recently, Quayle and his associates have begun working in the Barclay neighborhood, just south of Harwood, where three-story apartment buildings are commonplace. Obviously the land banking system that worked for Harwood's single-family homes would be difficult to implement in Barclay. So, Quayle has developed a new concept to secure tenancy for renters in these buildings. He plans to establish a neighborhood cooperative that will purchase the buildings, then rent them back to the original tenants at moderate costs. And where will he get the money to buy the buildings? Quayle has received commitments from a number of well-to-do Baltimoreans who are prepared to loan the money, "in the spirit of St. Ambrose himself," and be paid back as the rents amortize the loan. Once the benefactors have been fully paid back, they will be approached to donate their equity in the buildings to the neighborhood cooperative. In that way, there will always be a stock of low-priced housing for the poorest families in Barclay.

Quayle's plan to create low-equity cooperatives is one that neighborhood groups should look carefully into as a way to provide good housing for displaced families at a relatively low price. The idea behind a cooperative is that each family owns (and pays the maintenance for) a share of the whole complex. The "low equity" part means that the down payment necessary to buy into the co-op is purposely kept low, sometimes as little as $500. On the other hand, a co-op member who sells his share gets back only his original down payment, without any increase in value of the kind that usually accrues in conventional home ownership. More detailed information on the way such co-ops operate can be obtained from the National Association of Housing Cooperatives. (See the List of Organizations and Institutions.)

Displacement is a thorny issue. On the one hand, it is clear that declining neighborhoods can benefit from the money, talent, and energy that the urban pioneers and their successors bring with them. On the other hand, it is necessary to make sure that the original residents of a neighborhood get treated fairly. For those concerned with revitalizing urban neighborhoods, the emphasis must be on finding new, progressive measures that will permit the entry of newcomers into city neighborhoods, while guaranteeing the rights of those already in the neighborhoods. Needless to say, it's not an easy task.

11

HISTORIC PRESERVATION

Cursed be he that removeth his neighbor's
landmark.

—DEUTERONOMY 27:17

Every neighborhood has a history, but not every neighborhood is a historic area. To be truly a historic district or historic landmark area, a neighborhood must be so designated by an official group, such as the National Register of Historic Places or a state or local historical society. There are already a thousand such historic districts around the country; it is likely that hundreds of other neighborhoods qualify. Yet while the official historic districts are few compared to the thousands of neighborhoods in American cities, they exemplify a very active and special kind of revitalization.

One such neighborhood, the Old West Side of Ann Arbor, Michigan, learned belatedly of its history. "The neighborhood borders on the central business district—we're right downtown—yet it's a very residential neighborhood," says John Hansen, a high-school principal and president of the Old West Side Association. "Downtown" is Ann Arbor, home of the University of Michigan. "These homes were built between 1860 and 1920 to house the people of the working class. These are smaller houses than you find around the university." The houses are mostly of wood, with elaborate gingerbread molding, spacious front porches, and gabled roofs befitting the kind of architecture that appealed to the predominantly German working-class immigrants who first settled there. Take away the automobiles, television antennas, and electric streetlights, and it's not hard to imagine yourself in a sleepy, turn-of-the-century village somewhere deep in the Black Forest.

In 1967, however, few people in Ann Arbor appreciated the historic value of the Old West Side, least of all the people who lived there. Real estate operators ravaged the neighborhood, buying up two or three houses on a block, demolishing them, and putting in eight-unit apartment buildings—"lots of students with parking problems" is how John Hansen sums up the result. The final blow was a plan by a local architect to demolish as many as a hundred old houses to put in a row of twelve-story apartment towers. That's when the Old West Side Association was formed. "The whole population-concentration thing, that was the problem," said Robert Huber, OWS's secretary. The residents brought in a local landscape architect who showed the folly of the design, called upon experts from the University of Michigan, and punctuated the attack with volleys from John Hathaway, the preservation-minded city councilman for the area. The architect backed off; and the Old West Side won a temporary reprieve. More important, it dawned on the people of the Old West Side that they had something worth protecting.

That something was a neighborhood of nearly two thousand houses with a remarkably homogeneous texture and flavor (accountable largely to the frame construction of the buildings), yet diverse in detail. "Nearly every style prevalent in the United States during the Gilded Era and its aftermath (1860–1914) is represented in the Old West Side," a historic survey of the area showed. "Represented are Gothic cottages, Romanesque villas, Italian bracket houses, Colonial and Georgian revival mansions, Queen Anne, American picturesque, Tudor, stick, mansard and 'carpenter's delight' houses."

"No one really knew what we had here," recalls Huber. When someone suggested that the group ask the National Trust for Historic Preservation for a grant to do a historical and architectural survey of the neighborhood, however, the research revealed the Old West Side to be "a neighborhood having considerable architectural and cultural value." Upon the publication of that report, the Old West Side was named to the National Register of Historic Places. "That moved us from a castle-and-moat posture to saying, 'Wow, we've got something here!' " says Huber.

The climate has indeed changed. "Property values are going up, spirit is up, people are considering the Old West Side as an alternative to suburban living," says John Hansen. "We have three hundred paid members, and we've never lacked volunteer help. Even the real estate people are our buddies now. They're on the renovation bandwagon. They give out our brochures, and typically they give a one-year membership in the association with every house sale." The next step is the passage of a city ordinance to make the Old West Side a local historic district, an action that will allow the city council to offer the neighborhood even more protection against undue development.

Historic value, then, can be an extra asset that a community should capitalize on. A unique architectural or historical heritage provides an additional source of pride which contributes to neighborhood cohesion and can help in building its organization. It also is an important defensive weapon that bestows special protection from certain types of development, such as the construction of certain federal projects, including interstate highways.

The best way to ascertain your neighborhood's heritage—assuming, of course, that you believe your area to have significant historical or architectural value—is through a survey. First, contact your state historic-preservation officer for advice on putting the survey together, since requirements vary from state to state. (He can be reached by writing the governor's office.) The National Trust for Historic Preservation also has dozens of booklets on the subject, so write the Trust for its latest publications list. To finance your effort, seek funds from the local historical society, the state agency, or the National Trust. Matching grants are also available under the Historic Preservation Act of 1966. It is wise to obtain the services of an architectural historian who can describe the various kinds of architectural styles in your neighborhood.

The survey itself involves making an inventory of every significant building within your boundaries. The National Register of Historic Places, which is administered by the National Park Service, has a form for such surveys. It is best to use either this form or a similar one that will allow the information to be transferred to the Register's form. The information to be gathered includes: the building's age, address, ownership, present use, original use, architect, value, condition, style, and historical, architectural, and community significance. The survey should also list what Judith Waldhorn, a San Francisco preservationist, calls "misguided improvements"—aluminum siding, asbestos shingles, tarpaper brick, and other modernizing touches that have concealed or destroyed the original construction. Each building should also be photographed.

This inventory provides the basis for completing a documented history of the neighborhood—its architectural heritage, social development, and relationship to the city and the region. Here, again, call upon the expertise of your state historical officer, or any local architectural historian or consultant, to help you put together a booklet that, in effect, states why your area should be made a historic district. Then submit it to the National Register and the appropriate state and local authorities, seeking just such designation.

Special Promotions

One of the great selling points of a historic district is the houses themselves. You can raise money for your organization, promote its activities, and get some terrific publicity by showing off the neighborhood. And it can be a great morale booster, too. "People mortgaged themselves to do what they did, and they should be recognized," says Judith Waldhorn. She tells the story of one homeowner who put so much work into restoring his Victorian mansion that he thought the mayor should see it. So he invited the Honorable Joseph Alioto to a ribbon-cutting ceremony for the "new" house. To the man's surprise, Alioto showed up, with the press, and so did the rest of the neighborhood. It was quite a celebration!

Next, try to get free publicity from radio, television, and newspapers by staging the kinds of media events described in Chapter 4. Develop a knockout slide show, too, with lots of before-and-after pictures of renovated buildings; use it to raise money, seek recruits, and publicize your organization at conferences and workshops. Print a one-page brochure about the organization and give it away. Give extra copies of your annual report to the press.

The house tour is a natural opportunity to promote your cause. Open up several of your best houses to the public once a year. Print a handout brochure describing the history of each house, its unique architectural characteristics, and how your organization was involved in preserving it. Charge a fee for the tour, and ask for donations. Try to interest people in joining your organization, too.

Better yet, come up with special house tours. In Charleston, South Carolina, they hold a candlelight tour. Some groups train volunteers to give walking tours or bicycle tours of the exteriors of significant buildings. The Savannah Historical Foundation has two Mercedes buses (the kind with the big side windows) to shuttle groups around. In Brooklyn, the Brownstone Revival Committee tries to offer different programs from year to year. One year they'll have a "What You Can Buy for Under $30,000" tour, the next year it will be a "Work-in-Progress" tour, with lots of scaffolding and ladders and busy renovators all about. Luncheons, cocktail parties, hospitalities, and "at-homes" are excellent ways to show off one or two exceptional houses to a select group of invited guests, such as potential donors. Everett Ortner, the president of the Brownstone Revival Committee, recalled one such party in which the special guests were all bankers. "Every one of the bankers who came to the party had at one time or another turned down mortgages in that neighborhood without ever having been in the neighborhood," he told a "Back-to-the-City" conference in 1974. "They were amazed to discover it was not a slum."

Design Criteria and Financing Mechanisms

Assuming you get your historic district designation, the job is not over. You have to protect the buildings and the district from abuse. In most cases, this is done through the establishment of design criteria, which govern both the construction of new buildings and changes to existing buildings. The purpose of these guidelines is to maintain the character and general style of the historic district without completely closing the neighborhood to change. In Savannah, the criteria apply to the following: building height; relationship of height to width; proportions of openings; relative width of voids and solids; relative width of buildings and spaces between buildings; type, texture, and color of materials; similarity of detailing; type of roof; presence of garden walls or fences; landscaping; paving; scale; and compositional emphasis of verticals and horizontals. In the event of new construction or a change to an existing building, a board of architectural review (usually composed of architects, planners, public officials, historic preservationists, and citizens) reviews the proposal and determines if it conforms to the design criteria. Savannah, for example, requires such proposals to meet at least six of sixteen design criteria. Of course, the design criteria for your historic district may include other restrictions, depending on the unique character and architectural style of the buildings.

In addition to exercising design controls over buildings in the neighborhood, your organization will want to actively promote the preservation and improvement of the structures, too. There are a number of techniques for doing so, which I shall describe briefly here. For a full explanation, with examples from several cities, let me recommend *Historic Preservation in Inner City Areas: A Manual of Practice* and *Revolving Funds for Historic Preservation: A Manual of Practice*. (See Bibliography of Reference Materials.)

Among the preservation techniques that have proven useful are the following: the option; the purchase or sales contract; interim financing with a balloon payment; the easement; the covenant; and the revolving fund. They can be used to get control of a property or to prevent its misuse.

An *option* is the first right of purchase on a building. If your community organization has an option on a historic structure, it means that you have a written and binding agreement with the owner stating that he must offer it for sale to you before he can offer it to anyone else. Usually, you have a specified amount of time to meet the owner's asking price; after that, he is free to sell it. An option may be obtained for free, but more often it is purchased. Arthur P. Ziegler, Jr., a preservation expert from Pittsburgh, recommends that if you pay for the option, you should have it stated in the agreement that the fee be applied to the final purchase price.

A *purchase or sales contract* is an agreement that allows you to buy a building without making any actual payment for a stipulated period, which may run as long as one year. This arrangement allows your organization to get a firm price on a building and, in turn, sell it to someone else. The benefit to your organization is that you don't have to pay any cash immediately.

A *balloon-payment loan* is good to use if you *do* have to lay out cash for a building. This is an interim financing measure, obtained from a regular lending institution, in which you make small payments for a stipulated period (say, twenty-four months), with virtually all the principal being paid at the end of the loan's term. The idea, of course, is to sell the building before the balloon payment is due, so that the new owner, rather than your group, pays it.

An *easement* is a limited right of ownership in a portion of a building (or piece of land). Utility companies, for example, purchase easements to lay their pipes under someone else's land because it's cheaper than buying the land. For historic preservation purposes, easements are sought for the façade or the entire exterior of buildings; that is, whatever can be seen from the street. Under an easement procedure, the owner agrees not to alter the façade or exterior without permission; if he violates the agreement, he can be sued for damages and made to restore the building to its previous condition. Easements can be granted "in perpetuity" or for a stipulated period, usually ninety-nine years.

Sometimes building owners can be convinced to donate easements to a historic preservation society or governmental unit. Besides performing a social good, the owner may benefit by being eligible to deduct the value of the donation from his federal income taxes, under the provisions of the Tax Reform Act of 1969. (His property-tax assessment should also go down, since he no longer "owns" the entire building.) If your group has to pay for the easement, try to get an agreement that the purchase money will be used to improve the building. Some cities, as a matter of fact, use this technique to get around state laws prohibiting them from giving cash grants to individuals. They can say they're obtaining an easement, not making a grant.

A *covenant*, like an easement, is an agreement that restricts the owner from making unapproved facade or exterior changes for a stipulated period or in perpetuity. Whereas easements are generally used when the owner wants cash, particularly when the building needs repairs, covenants usually do not involve cash payments. They are usually employed when the preservation group already has some control over the building; for example, if the group owns the building or has an option on it, it might agree to sell only on the condition that the new owner accept the covenant restrictions. Many covenants also contain a requirement that the owner give the historic preservation group the option of first purchase for a brief period, anywhere from forty-eight to ninety-six hours.

The beauty of both the covenant and the easement is that they give historic preservation groups a chance to limit development along a whole block, not just on the properties they control directly. Say a developer has his eye on a row of townhouses, which he hopes to turn into some use that is incompatible with the community organization's goals for the area. By obtaining a facade easement or covenant on one or two key buildings in the row, the community organization can thwart the developer's plans. The cost (if anything) to the community group is much less than it would be to purchase the whole row of townhouses.

So far the subject of money has been kept in the background. At some point, however, your group is going to have to come up with some hard cash to purchase an easement or an entire building. The method that historic preservationists have found to be the best is the *revolving fund*. This is similar to the high-risk revolving fund used in the Neighborhood Housing Services program (see p. 234). The money for the fund is raised through donations, membership dues in the local historic preservation society, foundation grants, matching grants (where a corporation or foundation puts up a certain dollar figure, which must be matched by the local group), or special fund-raising efforts, such as house tours. The idea behind the fund is to get control or ownership of a building (using the techniques described above), sell it, and then apply the proceeds to other buildings, which in turn are sold. In Charleston, South Carolina, the Historic Charleston Foundation uses its fund to purchase a building and restore only the façade. Then the building is sold, with a covenant put in the deed restricting changes to the façade. Preservationist Arthur P. Ziegler, Jr., recommends that community groups using revolving funds do three things:

1. Charge overhead and promotional costs to the fund;
2. Invest the money in short-term certificates of deposit or similar notes, so that it doesn't sit idle;
3. Don't let the money sit in the bank forever, building interest but not saving buildings. If you don't use the fund to save buildings, you can hardly expect donors to be enthusiastic about donating more money in the future.

Ziegler also counsels community groups not to worry about occasionally having to pay more for a building than it's worth. At times, preserving the historic, cultural, and architectural tradition of the neighborhood and other social and community goals must take precedence over strict fiscal accounting, he says. These financial losses must be measured against the value of saving an important building or perhaps a whole cluster of buildings. If your group has a good record of saving buildings and preserving the neighborhood, you should have no trouble raising money to replenish your revolving fund.

Ziegler's own organization exemplifies how a group can achieve social goals while saving old buildings. In 1964, Ziegler and a colleague, James D. Van Trump, were walking along a street in Pittsburgh bemoaning the loss of the city's architectural heritage to urban decay and urban renewal. They decided to do something about the problem and founded the Pittsburgh History and Landmarks Foundation. By 1966, they had established a revolving fund from donations from foundations, membership dues, and private gifts. The organization had several clearly set principles: (1) to restore buildings inside and out; (2) to retain as many of the original residents as possible; (3) to find good housing for those displaced by renovation; (4) to purchase absentee-owned properties; and (5) to encourage home ownership and other forms of "security of tenure," such as subsidized rentals.

PHLF's record in several neighborhoods shows that it has lived up to these goals. In its "Mexican War Streets" project (the streets are named after battles and generals of that war), PHLF used its revolving fund to purchase houses in poor condition, restore the exteriors to their original condition, and rehabilitate the interiors to meet modern standards. The houses were then made available to three groups: middle-income families, who were encouraged to buy; moderate-income families, who either bought or paid the market rent; and poor families, who for the most part were given subsidized rentals through the city's housing authority, under the old leased-housing program.* Because the Mexican War Streets were also within the bounds of the then-emerging Neighborhood Housing Services area, some tenants were even able to purchase their homes. In addition, PHLF asked its own members to purchase and renovate other homes within the Mexican War Streets area, either for use as their residences or as investments. Old-timers who owned their buildings were also encouraged to fix them up. In short, the goal, says Ziegler, was to "bind together this mixture of people—young, old, well to do, poor, black, white—in the cause of preserving this unique architecture and conducting an experiment in urban neighborhood renewal." Of the first $235,000 the revolving fund put out, each dollar was matched by six dollars' worth of private improvements.

The Pittsburgh example shows that the displacement of current residents can be avoided if the community organization establishes a clear set of goals and principles to that effect *before* the program gets started. Unfortunately, too many historic preservationists forget this message and wind up backing a program that is just as disastrous to the neighborhood as urban renewal would have been. That is a failing historic preservationists must bear in mind. As Andrew Greeley has said, "The point of view that holds physical constructions to be more valuable to preserve than constructions of human networks is irrelevant if not positively dangerous."

---

*The demise of this program casts into doubt the transferability of the Pittsburgh experience, unless other subsidies (Section 8 housing or community-development block grants) can be employed.

12

NEIGHBORHOOD COMMERCIAL REVITALIZATION

As the neighborhood goes, so goes its shopping area. If the neighborhood begins to decline, it is almost certain that the local commercial area that serves it will begin to decline, too, for merchants and store owners are subject to the same kinds of psychological pressures as other decision makers in the neighborhood confidence game. "Their buildings weren't shabby because they didn't have the money to improve them," says Paul Gilbert, a planner with the city of Baltimore, in reference to store owners in one declining shopping area. "It was because they didn't have any confidence in the neighborhood that they didn't put money into their buildings."

Yet there is considerable potential for inner-city commercial revitalization, both downtown and in the neighborhood shopping strips. Boston's rehabilitated Quincy Market is now earning as much as three times the revenue for each square foot of selling area as a typical suburban shopping center, while Seattle's Pike Place Market has prospered so much that it has created two thousand new jobs. Chicago's Water Tower Place, a high-rise shopping center, is so popular it has changed people's shopping habits in the Windy City and has made North Michigan Avenue, not the Loop, the place to go for certain top-of-the-line items. And while these downtown projects point to increased prosperity for city retail operations, there are hopeful signs even in the neighborhood shopping districts, the older commercial strips of fifty to a hundred stores that serve the needs of the immediately surrounding residential areas. Benjamin Goldstein, chairman of the National Urban Development Services Corporation, who counsels small commercial districts on ways to increase sales and profits, says that three-quarters of all urban neighborhoods have a potential for expanded retail activity.

It would seem, therefore, that the sales potential is there, in the neighborhoods. It is also true that the older neighborhood shopping districts have a number of assets on which to build. Many businesses, for example, have a loyal clientele who provide a steady base of sales. The merchants themselves are often experienced and knowledgeable in terms of their products and the needs of their customers. Obviously, too, local businesses have the advantage of convenience for people in the neighborhood. These and other advantages would argue for continued prosperity in most of the neighborhood commercial shopping areas in the country.

And yet we know the facts are otherwise. Many small commercial strips are in trouble. It is hard to pinpoint whether it is the decline of the surrounding residential neighborhood that signals the collapse of the shopping district, or whether the deterioration of the shopping district is the first sign of decay for the residential area. It hardly matters. The important thing for neighborhood leaders to realize is that the commercial area is a vital, integral part of any neighborhood—its backbone, really. Any effort to revive the residential area must, therefore, take into account the need to breathe new life into the commercial strip.

In Chicago Lawn, a working-class neighborhood on Chicago's Southwest Side, that advice was put to the test a few years ago. The neighborhood, divided between poor blacks on one side and blue-collar white ethnics on the other, could easily have become another victim of disinvestment. The commercial center, running along the dividing line between the black and white areas, was slipping. A corner building at the main intersection was 75 percent vacant; one of the steady tenants was an adult bookstore.

To buck the downward trend, the area's six savings and loan institutions set up a service corporation to pump money back into the shopping district, starting with the problem building.

After rehabbing the property, the service corporation, known as the Greater Southwest Development Corporation, got requests for space from the likes of betting services, discount liquor stores, and currency exchanges, but the owners held out till they found the right tenants. Today the building is worth $273,000, compared to $88,000 before. Occupants include a newspaper business office, a fabric store, a restaurant, a delicatessen, and a black-owned jewelry store. After this initial success, the area experienced numerous other improvements, with eleven businesses alone putting in more than $9 million in new investments in their physical plants in 1976. The GSDC also rehabilitated an old furniture factory and converted it into a ten-store mini-mall, and is sponsoring a $690,000 beautification program for the area, $300,000 of which will be paid for by local property owners.

To reverse the decline of neighborhood commercial strips, therefore, it seems necessary to adopt a comprehensive approach that capitalizes on local strengths and overcomes inherent weaknesses, in much the same way that revitalization programs for residential areas operate. In designing such an approach, the community organization or merchants' association might look to the suburban shopping mall as a model.

It may seem incongruous to point to the suburban shopping mall as the archetype for neighborhood commercial districts to emulate, since the malls are usually blamed for causing the decline of the old shopping strips. And while the malls are not perfect in themselves (as the demise of some of the older ones clearly indicates) nor perfect as a model for neighborhood commercial districts, there is still much to be learned from them.

Why have the malls succeeded where the inner-city commercial strips have largely failed? Primarily, of course, because the malls are located where the most affluent market is centered, in the suburbs. Since, in the terms we have been discussing, it is ridiculous for a merchants' association to have as its goal to move to the suburbs, it is necessary to examine the malls' other assets to determine how these might be adapted to the needs of older commercial strips.

The malls' two greatest assets are their physical configuration and business organization. Physically, suburban malls are easily accessible by automobile, have plenty of free parking, are sealed off from the weather, and have a creative and unified design that not only makes shopping pleasant and convenient for the customer but renders the mall easier to police and maintain. On the business side, the typical mall is financed by a single development company, which also either manages the mall itself or contracts with a management company to handle the job. The manager performs several valuable functions. He is in charge of administration, particularly maintenance and security. He handles promotion of the mall, such as joint advertising programs on television and radio and in the newspapers, and he sponsors special events, such as concerts and festivals, to bring people into the shopping center. He is also in charge of business development, including market research to determine the need for new stores or merchandise. The key to the whole system is that the management is paid not on a flat-rate basis, but on a percentage of the tenants' gross receipts: the more the individual stores make, the more management makes, creating an incentive for everyone to increase overall sales. In other words, the form of management in a suburban shopping center acts as an inducement for overall cooperation.

In the typical neighborhood shopping area, the situation is almost exactly reversed. Historically, retail strips evolved piecemeal, with land owners and merchants opening new stores on a one-by-one basis as the need (that is, the market) developed. This is a distinct contrast to the planned, unified development of the suburban mall. The neighborhood merchants themselves are often highly independent and individualistic, content to rely on their own wits and business acumen to solve their problems, rather than listen to the advice of some management company. This fierce independence is what separates the local retail merchant from the big chain-store and franchise operations. It is one of his great strengths, since it can result in the kind of imaginative problem solving that is unthinkable to more monolithic retail operations. In my neighborhood, for example, we have a little family-run grocery store and butcher shop which, by all rights, should have been wiped out of business years ago since it is in direct competition with a couple of chain supermarkets. Yet it is thriving, because it has adapted to its market: not only does it offer free delivery (as the chain stores do), it also takes phone orders, a real convenience for the many elderly people in the neighborhood. By using their talents and business sense, the little store's owners have survived under circumstances that normally should have ruined them.

Yet the very traits that make the small, independent retailer such a fierce battler also can seal his doom when business starts falling off, as in the case when shopping districts decline. His fierce independence in business matters tends to make him close-minded when it comes to acting cooperatively with his neighboring merchants. As business begins to slacken, the small-time merchant takes the approach that he will either cut back on further investment in the hope of salvaging as much of his business as possible, or devote all his energies to finding ways to increase business for his own shop. It usually does not occur to him, as it does to the suburban mall manager, that by finding ways to attract more customers to the shopping district, all the merchants in the area stand to increase their sales.

A program to revitalize a neighborhood commercial district must, therefore, take its initiative from imaginative, visionary merchants and property owners who are able to see that, by acting cooperatively to bring more business into the district, every merchant stands to benefit. Just as in the case of residential revitalization, a commercial revitalization program must operate from a firm "community" base, the community in this case being the merchants, the property owners, and the residential community organization, which represents the merchants' market. Such a program must also be developed in partnership with the city government and with other neighborhood institutions, such as the churches and clubs. The merchants' association must follow an organizing process similar to that for residential community organizations, including the formation of a steering committee, the gathering of data (market research in particular), the identification of strengths and weaknesses, the formulation of goals and principles, fund-raising, publicity, plan development, and plan implementation. In the case of commercial revitalization, however, the final plan must rest (as John Sower, a consultant with the National Development Council, has noted) on a comprehensive, four-point program of public improvements, design standards, financing, and management.

In terms of *public improvements*, the business district has to be made attractive to shoppers. Again, the suburban shopping center serves as a model. It is clean, safe, unified in concept and design, and physically appealing, not to mention convenient. All these factors make it a pleasant experience for the average shopper, thereby leading to increased sales.

Public improvements in the existing neighborhood commercial area should be planned to produce a similar effect. Street furniture—streetlights, parking meters, signs, kiosks, fire hydrants, bus shelters, benches, litter baskets, emergency callboxes, and other hardware in the public's view—should be unified in form, scale, material, and color, and should be conveniently located. In addition, the landscaping, street and sidewalk paving, graphics, and other design elements of the streetscape must display a sense of unity. It is not enough just to pretty up a few storefronts; the whole physical environment must be upgraded. This may also necessitate a step-up in city services, particularly trash collection and police protection.

A major aspect of the physical planning concerns whether to close any streets to traffic, particularly the main street, to create a pedestrian mall. (Due to the configuration of most neighborhood shopping areas, it is usually not economically feasible to cover or enclose such a mall.) Many shop owners resist the idea of closing a street, since they believe that vehicular traffic is good for business. They become particularly vexed if the street closing results in any loss of parking spaces, especially those in front of or near their stores. One solution is to build parking lots or parking structures on nearby vacant land or in back of the stores, so that customers have a view of the stores when they park their cars.

A good example of how these problems were handled is the Old Town Mall in Baltimore. The original area, known as Gay Street, was a strip of more than a hundred stores, but by the late 1960s nearly a quarter of them were vacant and the strip was showing unmistakable signs of decay. The plan for Gay Street called for creating a pedestrian mall by closing the street to cars and recirculating the through traffic around the shopping area. Moreover, the district was shortened by a third, making the shopping area more compact and convenient for shopping (many of the shop owners whose buildings were demolished moved into vacant stores in the new mall). Finally, the city used public funds to build some three hundred parking spaces around the mall (without tearing down any housing, incidentally, thereby satisfying the demands of the local community organization). Though the parking lots operate at a loss, city officials are satisfied that the increased stability and growing tax base of the shopping district more than compensate the public for its investment. Today, Old Town Mall is virtually fully occupied, with many stores reporting increases in sales.

How can these public improvements be paid for? There are, of course, the usual sources of money—community-development block grants, city bonds, and capital-improvement bonds, for example. Another technique is the special assessment district, whereby the city finances the public improvements by levying extra taxes on property owners in the shopping area. Needless to say, this method is not very popular with store owners, although it does have the effect of taxing those who benefit directly from the expenditure of public money. Tax-increment financing is a similar concept, in which the city finances the improvements from the expected increase in revenue from property and sales taxes that result from the revitalization of the shopping area. Needless to say, there is some risk to the city in using tax-increment financing, because if the additional tax revenues do not cover the cost of the improvements, the city loses money.

In addition, the U.S. Department of Commerce, through its Economic Development Administration, has several programs to finance public improvements in commercial districts. Title IX, a 1974 amendment to the Public Works and Economic Development Act of 1965, created a Special Economic Development and Adjustment Assistance Program, which provides up to 75 percent of the cost of both development and implementation of public improvements for commercial areas. The Technical Assistance Program of the 1965 act provides grants to cover up to 75 percent of the cost of "investment-related" technical assistance, such as feasibility studies, planning reports, or market analyses, as well as development grants to help a merchants' association create the proper organizational structure to be able to receive such grants. Finally, the EDA's Office of Special Projects makes grants of up to 80 percent of the cost of construction, renovation, or repair of public facilities. Such grants must be made to a nonprofit organization, such as a merchants' association, not to a municipality or other government jurisdiction.

The second element in the four-point program calls for the creation of mandatory *design standards* for the storefronts themselves. Just as the suburban shopping center has a theme or motif that unifies and structures its overall design, while allowing for the individuation of stores, the neighborhood commercial district must also project an orderly, harmonious image to the public. Shoppers prefer to patronize a shopping area that is clean, safe, pleasing to the eye, and uplifting to the spirit. But commercial strips are more often than not a visual cacophony of unsightly buildings with ill-conceived façades, forming a wholly disunified street pattern, and, worst of all, a barrage of glaring neon signs and billboards. The latter evolve because every shop owner wants to attract customers from the passing automobile and pedestrian traffic, and he believes that by erecting the largest, most ostentatious sign on the block he will be able to do so. Actually, it works—until the guy down the block builds a bigger, brighter sign. When every store on the block has such signs, the competitive effect is lost. The same thing happens with other accretions to the store's basic design.

The solution to this problem lies in what Baltimore's Paul Gilbert calls "architectural subtraction"—removing the projecting signs, pulling down the false metal façades to expose the underlying brick or stone, unboarding upper-story windows, and removing all other unnecessary additions and "misguided improvements," to recall Judith Lynch Waldhorn's phrase, that cover up the basic materials of the building. With the elimination of these extraneous accretions, the building is ready for rehabilitation to restore it to a functional, attractive structure in harmony with the other buildings on the strip.

The establishment of design standards must be made with the cooperation of a high percentage of property owners and shopkeepers in the district; at least 80 percent agreement is necessary, since peer pressure plays an important role in determining whether the design standards are adhered to. If one shop owner thinks that another shop owner is going to be able to build a sign bigger than his, the whole design scheme is threatened.

The best way to get widespread approval for proposed design standards (which, incidentally, usually must be approved by the city council) is for a design specialist to draw or photograph existing buildings in the shopping district, and then redraw them as they would look under the design guidelines. In this way, building owners and merchants can see the actual effect of complying with the design standards. Since most merchants and building owners are not architects or designers, they need this "before and after" treatment to be able to visualize not only how their own stores will look, but also to be assured that neighboring stores are being treated in a similar way. In Milwaukee, for example, the city hired a designer to come up with exactly such a treatment for the storefronts along Mitchell Street. The publication of these drawings, along with other material about the proposed improvements (in the *Mitchell Center Storefront Improvement Manual*), greatly enhanced the acceptance of the design standards and led to the successful completion of the rehabilitation project.

The design standards should cover the basic exterior aspects of the building. Signs should be regulated as to size, placement on the building (projecting or flat), and lighting. Billboards should be prohibited, and existing ones removed or amortized for future removal. Exterior lighting should be designed to enhance the storefront without marring the visual field in the rest of the shopping district. This might require shielding or recessing lights to prevent glare. Landscaping should conform to an overall landscaping plan for the district. As for the treatment of the buildings' façades, every effort should be made to emphasize the original style and character of each building. Where necessary, distinctive architectural features that have been destroyed should be repaired, while inappropriate façade improvements (such as aluminum siding, artificial brick or stonework, or plastic, asbestos, or asphalt) should be removed. New buildings, or additions to old buildings, should be constructed in a style that, while possibly contemporary, is in conformance with the overall architectural style of the district. Of course, design standards should be made to fit local conditions, but Milwaukee's *Mitchell Center*

Storefront Improvement Manual and Emanuel Berk's *Downtown Improvement Manual* offer some good suggestions for getting started.

Once the large majority of businessmen in the shopping district approve the guidelines and the city has passed an ordinance making them mandatory, the design standards must be enforced. Without a strong enforcement mechanism, they become a mockery—there is no longer any compulsion for store owners to live up to the standards, with the probable result that at least some of them will not do so, thereby ruining the whole plan for the others. Strict enforcement of mandatory design standards has the salutary effect of forcing recalcitrant property owners to either renovate their buildings or to sell or lease them to someone who will make the necessary improvements. In Baltimore, for example, shopping-district design standards are enforced through city inspections of every property within the commercial area's boundaries. Violators are first issued notices of noncompliance, then prosecuted if the repairs are not made within a specified period. In addition, the city has the power (though it is rarely used) to acquire a building through condemnation if the owner cannot or will not rehabilitate his property according to the design standards. In drafting a set of design standards for a commercial revitalization program, therefore, it is wise to keep the enforcement process in mind at all times. Otherwise the design standards are not worth the paper they're printed on.

The third step in the four-point program of commercial revitalization is *financing*. A commercial district where the climate is such that lenders are reluctant to take reasonable risks is a shopping area that will soon be dead. It is crucial, therefore, to get money flowing back into these areas before they are beyond salvation.

At the local level, cities can use the kinds of financing techniques employed in housing rehabilitation programs—low-interest direct loans, interest-subsidy loans, guaranteed loans, various forms of grants, and so on, financing them through community-development block grants, bond sales, or tax receipts. (See Chapter 9.) Some places have come up with special financing mechanisms. In *Neighborhood Commercial Rehabilitation*, Adrienne Levatino reports that Hudson, New York, uses community-development block grants to purchase façade easements from store owners, much as is done in historic preservation districts, with the money being applied to rehabilitate the exteriors of the buildings. In Detroit, she notes, the city has set up special assessment districts in areas where the majority of commercial property owners are agreeable and makes loans of up to ten years' duration to store owners for both exterior and interior improvements. Baltimore has taken the homesteading concept and applied it to stores, coming up with "shopsteading." For $100 a businessman can purchase an abandoned, tax-delinquent store and obtain full ownership of it, provided he brings it up to code standards within a stipulated period. To make things easier, the city offers federal and local loans to the shopsteaders. Finally, there is the savings and loan service corporation, a mechanism which allows these institutions to invest a small percentage of their assets in riskier-than-normal ventures, including commercial rehabilitation. (The Greater Southwest Development Corporation, described earlier in this chapter, is an example of such a corporation.) And the neighborhood-development holding company, of which the South Shore National Bank is the preeminent example, is another device for commercial rehabilitation.

There are also a number of federal loan and grant programs for use in commercial rehabilitation. That old workhorse, Section 312, may be used for commercial revitalization in designated areas. It provides direct 3 percent loans, with a maximum term of twenty years. The U.S. Small Business Administration has three programs of interest to commercial rehabbers. The Section 7(a) program permits the SBA to make loans directly to small businessmen or to guarantee loans made by others to small businessmen. For direct loans, the maximum is $150,000, with a maximum interest rate of 6.625 percent, up to twenty years. Most Section 7(a) loans have a term of six or seven years. The SBA will guarantee up to 90 percent of private loans or $350,000, whichever is less. The second SBA program, Section 502, is similar to Section 7(a), except that loans must be made to local development companies, or LDCs, which are nonprofit development companies set up to improve a commercial area. (A merchants' association would be one example.) Loans of up to $500,000 may be made for each eligible property; the interest rate is around

6.625 percent, for a maximum term of twenty-five years. Only store owners or long-term lessees may apply; absentee owners are not eligible. Section 502 loans may be used not only to rehabilitate the property, but also to pay for fixtures, decorations, expansion, and the purchase of extra property. Finally, there is the Economic Opportunity Loan Program, which is designed to help relatively poor people become businessmen, particularly if the person has been unable to acquire business financing through normal channels at reasonable terms. The program provides direct loans of up to $100,000 for a maximum period of fifteen years.

It is in the area of *management,* the fourth ingredient in the four-point approach to commercial revitalization, that neighborhood shopping strips fall far short of their suburban competitors. The malls, as we have seen, have professional management companies which administer the shopping centers, promote them, and develop them, using the latest business techniques to find ways to bring in new business. Most older business districts lack this kind of professional management, with a few exceptions. In Baltimore, for example, the city maintains the public part of the Old Town Mall, while in Trenton, New Jersey, and Brooklyn, New York, revitalized shopping strips are managed by a corporation jointly controlled by the respective city governments and the merchants and shop owners, with the city assessing the property owners for the maintenance. Some neighborhood shopping areas hire private security guards, as do individual stores, of course. But few, if any, have the kind of unified management program that is the hallmark of the suburban shopping center.

Since the city has a stake in the growth and development of its neighborhood commercial areas, it should be in the forefront of activity to prod the merchants and store owners toward some form of unified management. John Sower has suggested a number of management systems that have merit in these situations. The city could, for example, encourage the merchants' association to contract with an existing real estate management and development company or with an advertising and public relations firm to operate on behalf of the neighborhood business district. Or the city could provide a matching grant or other funds (perhaps through a special assessment district) so that the merchants' association could hire staff to perform the same function as a suburban mall manager. Another approach would be for the city to create a new management organization to work under contract with the merchants' association and the city.

The method with the best track record, however, seems to be for the city to take over the job of managing the revitalized shopping district by providing management and promotional staff to perform these tasks. This is a special form of technical assistance which has proved to be immensely useful in overcoming particular roadblocks. One of the major problems in commercial-district rehabilitation, for example, is the tremendous amount of paperwork that has to be completed in order to get federal grants. Most shop owners and property owners don't have the time, energy, or ability to complete all the necessary forms in the proper manner. Baltimore has overcome this problem by assigning one member of its community development staff to the job of packaging loans. He interviews the merchant, determines his needs and financial situation, gathers all the necessary data, gets appraisals and construction bids, and puts all this information into one package that requires only the merchant's signature before going on to Washington for government approval. Other cities are getting into the game of helping commercial districts with management problems, either by assigning staff or creating whole new departments to offer technical assistance in such areas as security (the procurement of federal crime insurance, the development of internal security systems, the improvement of street lighting), employment and training programs, transportation studies (vehicular and pedestrian traffic, parking impact), as well as management training, business counseling, marketing studies, accounting and other services, group promotions, loan procurement, and numerous other "software" programs.

Neighborhood commercial revitalization can work, as Baltimore's Old Town Mall and Milwaukee's Mitchell Center demonstrate. Nor are the success stories relegated to those two cities. In Toledo, the River East Development Corporation has attracted a forty-thousand-square-foot supermarket to a rundown business district, sparking a whole new development initiative which will ultimately create a $2 million shopping center. In Rhode Island, the Providence Business Development Organization's program in the Federal Hill neighborhood has brought in twenty-nine new businesses, with another fourteen stores expanding. Chicago has a whole string of local development companies working on the revitalization of older shopping areas.

In these cities, the merchants and property owners, public officials, and community organizations have adapted the kinds of management tools and comprehensive planning programs of the suburban shopping center to fit the particular needs and characteristics of their local areas, piecing them together for the maximum effect. "Bricks and mortar alone will not solve the problem, nor will software programs alone," says David Wright, the director of the Neighborhood Revitalization Unit of Chicago's Department of Human Services. The hardware programs have to be mixed with financing, marketing, and management programs.

As the experience with successful programs has shown, commercial revitalization is a painstaking task, often requiring years of effort before it starts to pay off. But no program for residential revitalization would be complete without it. The local shopping strip is the backbone that supports the rest of the neighborhood. If it begins to weaken, it is only a matter of time before the whole structure succumbs. That is why it is essential to make commercial redevelopment an integral component of neighborhood planning.

CONCLUSION: A LOOK AHEAD

What must be done to save America's neighborhoods? Much of the agenda should be apparent from what already has been said in this book. At the top of the list is the need to expand those programs that produce results—Neighborhood Housing Services, the various rehabilitation financing schemes, urban homesteading, commercial development programs, historic preservation, and so on through the catalogue of successful revitalization efforts described in the preceding pages. We should keep in mind, of course, that not every program is transferable from one situation to another; that not every program will have equal success in all places; and that programs, concepts, and institutions must be tailored to fit local conditions, if they are to work at all.

At the same time, we must remove the barriers to neighborhood revitalization. First among these is redlining, the withdrawal of financial support to a neighborhood. Other obstacles include legal barriers, such as overly stringent building codes or outdated zoning regulations. Some cities, for instance, have laws prohibiting housing in certain industrial areas. Yet the SoHo district in New York City is a perfect example of how underused industrial areas can be converted to special residential uses—in this case, studios for artists in need of open spaces. Roadblocks like these have to be knocked down to open up new avenues of support for neighborhood development.

283

We need to establish a modern, efficient rehabilitation industry in this country. At present, there is no organized, systematic means for accomplishing rehabilitation. The existing rehabilitation industry is diffuse, unsystematic, and often chaotic. In some respects that's good, because a disorganized rehabilitation industry is less prone to indulge in the kinds of abuses that are evident in the regular (new-construction) building trades, where an electrician is not allowed to knock in a nail because he isn't in the carpenters' union. But this free-for-all system will not prove workable over the long run. We need rehabilitation experts who appreciate old buildings and old neighborhoods, and programs to train workers in rehabilitation industrial arts. We need an industry that uses the wrecking ball as a last resort, not the standard solution, as well as supply systems that are geared to small-scale, conservation-oriented reconstruction. And the rehabilitation industry must become competitive with new construction.

We also need better ways to share information about saving neighborhoods. In the bureaucrat's jargon, that's called "T.A."—technical assistance. Mechanisms for the transfer of ideas and techniques—workshops, seminars, conferences, and training programs to get the information out and let others benefit from it—are essential. We need a system of talent exchange, similar to that used by industry and government, whereby staff or indigenous experts from one neighborhood group can advise other neighborhood groups on technical matters. This should be enacted at the federal level, with the government training experts in neighborhood problem solving and dispatching them to communities in need—but only at the community's request, and under the community's control.

We also need to think more about the various special groups that comprise a neighborhood—tenants and the elderly, for example, and small-time apartment-building owners. Concerning the latter, most of the programs in support of housing are geared either toward the owner of a single-family home or the large-scale developer. The owner of a typical three-story walk-up building is left in the breach. Yet in many older cities, these smaller apartment buildings, many of them occupied by the owners, are the backbone of the housing industry. New financing schemes designed to shore up this crucially important segment of the housing stock must be found.

It is vital, too, for the nation to develop a neighborhoods policy. Happily, a step in the right direction has been taken with the establishment of a National Commission on Neighborhoods. At this writing the commission, a blue-ribbon panel appointed by President Carter in December 1977, had submitted a thousand-page reexamination of national policies and priorities toward neighborhoods. It is too early to tell what success the commission will have in implementing its many recommendations, but the very fact of its having been formed is evidence of a growing awareness of neighborhood concerns in Washington.

The most politically delicate issue in such a neighborhood policy is bound to be the problem of how best to use the scarce resources available. With every city clamoring for more funds from Washington, and with the inflation fighters in the Nation's Capital holding firmly to the belief that more government spending is inadvisable, how can the limited funds available for neighborhood revitalization be used most efficiently and effectively to save urban neighborhoods?

This is not an idle or rhetorical question. The shortfall of money with which to rebuild city neighborhoods has already prompted some startling pronouncements from urban affairs experts, beginning with Anthony Downs, now a senior economist with the Brookings Institution in Washington, D.C. During the mid-1970s, while serving as a top-level consultant to HUD, Downs expounded his "triage" theory of neighborhood revitalization.

The triage theory uses a medical analogy to explain how best to use scarce urban dollars, particularly community-development block grants. Triage is the method doctors use after a disaster. They divide the survivors into three groups—those who will live even without immediate medical attention; those who will probably die even with such care; and those who will live only if treated immediately—and then concentrate their efforts on the last group to save the most lives possible.

According to Downs's analogy, the healthiest neighborhoods should get as little money as possible—just "showcase" projects, such as beautification programs, which don't cost much. The very worst neighborhoods, the ones that in medical terms are likely to "die" no matter what is done for them, should get a small share of community development money—perhaps one-third of the city's allocation—to be used for human service programs and the demolition of condemned buildings. "The largest part of the money," says Downs, "should go into those neighborhoods where it will have the greatest effect"—the gray-area neighborhoods, which are just beginning to decline but are not beyond salvaging.

The triage proposal has made Downs something of a *bête noire* with community activists, particularly in minority neighborhoods, where it is felt that if his proposal were put into effect, whole neighborhoods would be written off as unsalvageable. In his defense, let me say that Downs's most virulent critics seem less interested in arguing about what he actually says than in interpreting what they think he means. They neglect to mention that his theory does not apply to many cities, such as Minneapolis or Seattle, where there are no terribly bad neighborhoods; that Downs acknowledges the political difficulty of implementing his proposals; that he is opposed to the wholesale abandonment of neighborhoods; and that his theory is contingent upon the production of a surplus of housing in the suburbs, so that through the "filtering" mechanism, those families who can afford to leave the worst-off neighborhoods may do so.

Whatever Downs's original intentions, triage has been latched onto by conservative housing experts. In an article entitled "On the Death of Cities," for example, William C. Baer argues that "twenty years of chasing slums around the city have demonstrated to urban renewal specialists the futility of devoting all of its resources to its most blighted areas." He says that a modified form of triage, tempered by what D. Neuhauser and A. M. Lewicki call "ethical inefficiency," is necessary. Ethical inefficiency is a function of the power struggles inherent in city politics, with the worst-off neighborhoods getting a small share of community development funds as a palliative, the best neighborhoods getting a chunk of city money because they are the "squeaky wheels," and the remainder going to the gray-area neighborhoods, which can benefit most from such support, much as in Downs's formulation. "This may not be the optimum use of aid in a technical sense, but it is a strategy at least superior to that of single-mindedly assisting the worst first," says Baer. "The worst neighborhoods should be allowed to suffer a painless death."

A variation of Baer's proposal has been made by Roger Starr, the former director of the New York City Housing and Development Administration. Starr calls for massive internal resettlement of city populations, including the *deliberate* abandonment of whole neighborhoods. "If the city is to survive with a smaller population," said Starr, "the population must be encouraged to concentrate itself in the sections that remain alive." To this end, Starr suggests that "public investment be hoarded for those areas where it will sustain life." In those areas where population is destined to shrink, the city should "cut back on city services accordingly, realizing considerable savings in the process." This is a far cry from Downs's original concept of triage—such a perversion, in fact, that it was bound to infuriate people in the worst-off neighborhoods that presumably would be the victims of Starr's final solution.

It is my view, however, that the triage concept *can* be modified so as to make it a valid policy for city neighborhoods. To do so, it is necessary to adopt an approach that I have labeled humane Darwinism. This approach advocates the survival of the fittest neighborhoods. It measures fitness not in physical or social terms, however, but in terms of the level of citizen involvement and organization within the community. It is also tempered by a humane attitude, so that no neighborhood will be left twisting in the wind.

Under this approach, every neighborhood would receive a basic share of city services and programs necessary to assure a decent quality of life. Beyond that, however, city investment would be based upon neighborhood type. For stable neighborhoods that are sure to thrive with or without city support, additional or incremental services and programs would be kept to a minimum, such as showcase beautification programs. As for those neighborhoods that are so poorly organized, so disunified, and so socially torn that there is little immediate hope of recovery, it would appear that the wisest investment the city could make is to alert the residents to their plight. For example, the city could hire trained organizers to go into these neighborhoods and attempt to locate and stir up indigenous leaders, who would then move the neighborhood to action. (A warning: The experience of the community action program of the War on Poverty showed that bringing in "outsiders" to organize the community seldom produced long-lasting results. Perhaps conditions have to have become intolerable before local people will act on their own.) In any case, I don't think it a wise or fruitful policy for the city to give up on ill-organized neighborhoods. Instead, the city must make a conscientious attempt to organize them, so that their residents can begin to take action to improve their neighborhoods.

The bulk of any "extra" money—and most cities, I admit, will be hard-pressed to find any leftover cash—should go into a third group of neighborhoods, where indigenous community organizations are hard at work for the local residents. It is my belief that such well-organized but needy neighborhoods, particularly those with a predominance of low-income, elderly, or minority families, can benefit most from an extra infusion of public funds; in fact, their very survival may depend on just such support applied at the right time. If we are to avoid the mistakes of the past, especially our predilection to throw good money after bad, we should invest our money where it will have the greatest payoff. Without it, the neighborhoods in this third group are sure to suffer a loss of confidence that could thrust them into a downward spiral. That would be an almost unconscionable loss, since these are the very neighborhoods on which we must pin our hopes for the future survival and rebirth of the cities.

I realize that my argument has many holes in it. Politically it could prove unworkable: How would politicians decide which neighborhoods fall into each group? Even if they were able to decide the groupings, would the politicians in fact be able to make the hard-nosed allocations necessary to make such a scheme work? Certainly there would be intense pressure from the "squeaky wheels" to get as much money as possible for their neighborhoods. But given the relative scarcity of dollars for neighborhood development, it seems to me that a humane approach, but one that also faces the realities of urban politics, is the most workable tack for city governments to take. It gives every neighborhood a basic level of services and programs and therefore guarantees decent treatment for all residents. But it also recognizes that public programs work better in some neighborhoods—well-organized ones—than others.

We are today at a crossroads in solving the urban crisis. We know enough about the problem to know that the old ways of fighting urban decay—throwing money at problems without helping the people in greatest need; using massive but insensitive approaches that do more harm than good; believing the "bigger is better" fallacy—have not worked. We need an approach that recognizes that small can be beautiful. We need programs that are moderate in scale, flexible, and truly effective. What we need less of are gimmicky programs that waste money and fail to affect people's lives for the better.

It is also crucial that we renew the citizen's faith in his government and restore his place in that government. The average American feels government has let him down, and our nation's city dwellers feel this disappointment the most. City people, especially those who are active in neighborhood revitalization, are demanding greater responsiveness from government, but they also want a greater degree of autonomy in the handling of local affairs. The federal establishment certainly has had its opportunity to try to reverse urban decay through such grandiose schemes as urban renewal and the War on Poverty. Washington's efforts can hardly be termed successful. Neither can those of the mayors and city councils, when the Nixon and Ford administrations turned control of federal urban dollars over to them under the community-development block grant program. Perhaps now it is time, as John McClaughry has suggested, to give the people a chance to run their neighborhoods.

I am not advocating the wholesale turnover of power to the neighborhoods, for I believe that there is a proper role for government at the federal, state, and municipal levels. Nor do I wish to imply that, should neighborhoods be given greater autonomy over their own affairs, all urban problems suddenly would disappear. One thing I hope I have made clear in this book is that urban problems do not lend themselves to such easy solutions. But giving neighborhood people greater autonomy over local affairs is crucial to the success of urban policy. Norton E. Long has, I believe, put his finger on the crux of the matter. "We have learned that the new states of the world require nation building," he wrote. "We have to learn that this also applies to us: Our cities and their citizenship require renewing, as well as brick and mortar. This will require city builders whose job is as important as the nation builders in new countries. In fact, the rebuilding of our cities is the rebuilding of our nation—though, incredibly, we do not realize it." The neighborhood movement must *not* be measured solely by physical standards—number of housing units repaired, total dollar investment, and so on. It must also be judged by a higher political, social, and moral standard: Will it restore the citizen to his proper role in government? The physical rehabilitation of a neighborhood is worth little if the people have no tangible role in its renewal. A neighborhood renewal effort cannot be considered a success without there having been a rebirth of spirit, hope, and self-determination among the people who live there.

At one time in our nation's history, public decisions were made at such a level. The New England town meeting is a perfect example of that intimate form of government. Today, our cities and government have grown so large and impersonal that the average citizen feels overwhelmed by them. The neighborhood movement is crucial, therefore, not only because it may provide a better environment for people to live in, but because it offers the hope of restoring control over at least one aspect of our lives.

Writing in *The New Yorker*, Richard Harris aptly described the change in attitude necessary for our survival: "If the American people are to survive even as shadows of their ancient independent selves, they will have to return to the ways that simpler days made a necessity, and solve their own problems themselves in the smallest and most manageable form of human society—the neighborhood community."

If the neighborhood movement can achieve that, it will have done far more than fix up a few buildings. It will have rekindled the pioneering American spirit.

NOTES

Whenever full publication data has not been supplied for books and periodicals mentioned in the notes below, it may be found in the Bibliography of Reference Materials. Addresses of organizations are listed in the List of Organizations and Institutions.

Introduction/The Neighborhood Renaissance
The material on "trends" is taken from the surveys by Phillip L. Clay, the Urban Land Institute, and the National Urban Coalition. The Gallup Poll results are contained in the *Christian Science Monitor* reprint, *A Nation of Neighborhoods*. The figures on savings and loan investments are from Norman Strunk, executive vice-president of the U.S. League of Savings Associations, as reported in the *Wall Street Journal*.

For further reading on decentralization, the following are recommended: Howard W. Hallman, *Neighborhood Government in a Metropolitan Setting* (Beverly Hills: Sage Publications, 1974); Milton Kotler, *Neighborhood Government: The Local Foundations of Political Life* (Indianapolis: Bobbs-Merrill, 1969); David Morris and Karl Hess, *Neighborhood Power: The New Localism* (Boston: Beacon Press, 1975); Robert K. Yin and Douglas Yates, *Street Level Government: Assessing Decentralization and Urban Services* (Santa Monica: The Rand Corporation, 1974).

For information on Canadian revitalization programs, see "Neighborhood Improvement: What It Means in Calgary, Vancouver, and Toronto," *City* magazine, August/September 1975, vol. 1 no. 5–6, pp. 15–28. For British programs, see "Conserving Urbanity in Norwich," *Urban Land*, June 1976, pp. 17–28.

Information on housing preferences is taken from the 1978 Consumer-Builder Survey on Housing, conducted by National Family Opinion, Inc., for *Professional Builder* magazine, as reported by Jack Houston, "When It Comes to Houses, They'll Buy That Dream," *Chicago Tribune*, December 18, 1977.

I am indebted to William Alonso's paper, *The Population Factor and Urban Structure*, for much of the material in the section on changing demographic patterns.

The quotation by Franklin W. James is from the *National Journal*, July 17, 1977, p. 1006.

The two papers by Dennis Gale are *The Back-to-the-City Movement . . . Or Is It?* (1976) and *The Back-to-the-City Movement Revisited* (1977). Available from the Department of Urban and Regional Planning, The George Washington University, Washington, DC 20006.

A lengthy account of Southeast Baltimore's struggles can be found in *SECO History*, a June 1977 monograph by Lee Truelove (SECO, 10 S. Wolfe St., Baltimore, MD 21231).

1/The Money Drain

The Allen K. Pritchard quotation is from Calvin Trillin's "U.S. Journal: Houston," *The New Yorker*, January 6, 1975, pp. 57–60. The George E. Peterson quotation is from "Impact of Federal Tax Policies on Cities," *CUED Commentary*, vol. 1 no. 1, August 1977, pp. 7–8.

An excellent account of the failure of the new-towns-in-town program is contained in Martha Derthick's *New Towns in Town: A Federal Program that Failed* (Washington, D.C.: The Urban Institute, 1972).

The figures on professional and managerial workers living outside central cities are adapted from Peter Libassi and Victor Hausner, *Revitalizing Central City Investment* (Columbus, Ohio: Academy for Contemporary Problems, 1977).

The article by Gurney Breckenfeld is "It's Up to the Cities to Save Themselves," *Fortune*, March 1977, pp. 194–201.

The figures on population change are from U.S. Senate, Com-

NOTES **293**

mittee on Banking, Housing, and Urban Affairs, *Neighborhood Diversity*, 95th Cong., 1st Sess., July 7, 1977, pp. 14–34. The job-shift figures are from Henry S. Reuss, *To Save Our Cities*.

The story of the Sholar family is based on the testimony of Mary Bates, Greater Roseland Organization, before the U.S. Senate Committee on Banking, Housing and Urban Affairs, July 14, 1975 (Chicago, Illinois).

The "several observers" of the mortgage banking industry are the authors of *Opportunities for Abuse*.

The material on post-foreclosure abuse by mortgage bankers is from *More Hole Than Net*.

The case of bureaucratic bungling in Park Slope is told in "How One New York Neighborhood Was Destroyed: A Case for Community Boards," *COMP Newsletter*, vol. IV no. 3, June 15, 1977.

The story of the Jamaica Plain redlining victim is cited in an article by Harriet Tee Taggart, "Red-lining," *Planning* magazine, vol. 40 no. 11, December 1974, pp. 11–16.

The ten-point list of discriminatory lending practices is adapted from "Methods of Redlining," published by the National Training and Information Center.

The section on redlining is based on the following reports: *Redlining: Discrimination in Residential Mortgage Loans* (1975), Illinois Legislative Investigating Commission, 300 W. Washington St., Chicago, IL 60606; *Home Mortgage Lending Patterns in Metropolitan Boston* (1977), Carol S. Greenwald, Commissioner of Banks, Government Center, 100 Cambridge St., Boston, MA 02202; *Neighbors*, vol. 7 no. 1, February–March 1977 (for Dallas); Thomas S. Andrezejewski, "Mortgageville's a Suburb" and "City Branches Provide Money Invested in Suburbs," *Cleveland Plain Dealer*, January 2–3, 1977; Richard Ratcliff, *Mortgage Lending in the St. Louis Area: An Examination of the Second Year of Mortgage Lending Disclosure Data*, Missouri ACORN, 3177 S. Grand., St. Louis, MO 63118; *Final Report of the Governor's Task Force on Redlining*, Richard J. Francis, Commissioner, Department of Commerce, Financial Institutions Bureau, Lansing, MI 48913 (for Flint); *Journal of Housing*, September 1975 (for Baltimore); and *Strategy for Change: Housing Finance in Washington, D.C.* (1975); Final Report of the D.C. Commission on Residential Mortgage Investment, Suite 459, Munsey Bldg., 1329 E St., N.W., Washington, DC 20004.

The quotation from *The Saver* magazine is from the reprint in "Red-lining Problem Blown Out of Proportion," *Chicago Daily News*, July 12–13, 1975. The Thygerson-Jacobe quotation is from "Better Housing Alone Won't Do Away with Urban Decay," *Savings & Loan News* (Chicago: U.S. Savings and Loan Association), December 1976. The Marshall quotation is from "The Urban Disinvestment Dilemma," *Savings & Loan News*, June 1974. Perhaps the most public attack on the antiredliners comes from George J. Benston, in "The Persistent Myth of Redlining," *Fortune*, March 13, 1978, pp. 66–69. Benston's figures on housing patterns in Rochester, New York, are disputed, however, in an article by Rinker Buck, "Politics: The Redlining Myth," *New York*, April 10, 1978, pp. 10–11.

The Michigan insurance report is entitled *Essential Insurance in Michigan: An Avoidable Crisis; A Report to the Governor*, Insurance Bureau, Michigan Department of Commerce, P.O. Box 30220, Lansing, MI 48909 (1977). The Valukas Report is called *An Investigation of Discrimination in the Sale of Homeowners Insurance in Illinois*, Illinois Department of Insurance, Springfield, IL 62706 (1978). The General Accounting Office report is entitled *Arson-for-Profit: More Could Be Done to Reduce It* (Washington, D.C.: Comptroller General of the United States, May 31, 1978).

The appraisal "conformity" guidelines are cited in an article by Harriet Tee Taggart, "Appraisal Practices Need a Thorough Reappraisal," *Planning* magazine, vol. 43 no. 7, August 1977, pp. 17–18.

2/Social Factors in Neighborhood Decline

The figures on poverty are adapted from "The American Underclass," *Time*, August 29, 1977, pp. 13–27. The school racial-composition figures come from the *Statistical Abstract of the United States* (Washington, D.C.: U.S. Bureau of the Census, 1972).

The story of the Park Slope family is by Michele Cusumano, "A Middle-Class Family Leaves the City: Who's Deserting Whom?" *The Village Voice*, November 21, 1977.

The 1977 Gallup Poll is cited in *A Nation of Neighborhoods*, the *Christian Science Monitor* reprint. The 1975 Gallup Poll is reported in the *Washington Post*, September 26, 1975, as cited in an unpublished paper by Lawrence O. Houstoun, Jr. The Harris Survey of Baltimoreans is from "The Cage of Fear on Cities Beset by Crime," *Life*, July 11, 1969.

For a full account of the chilling effects of the cliques in the South Bronx, see the series by Martin Tolchin in *The New York Times*, January 15–18, 1973. The figures on Chicago's gangs are from Lynn Emmerman, "North Side Story," *Chicago* magazine, October 1977, pp. 211ff.

The Kansas City police study is described in "Police to Cut Back Patrol Duty," *Kansas City Star*, September 29, 1974. The Attorney General's report on the LEAA is cited in the *Wall Street Journal*, July 7, 1978, p. 30.

The government-commissioned report is entitled *Arson and Arson Investigation: Survey and Assessment.* The Illinois Legislative Investigating Commission statistics are from "Urge Fire Dept. Arson Probes," *Chicago Tribune*, March 26, 1978.

3/From the Grass Roots Up

In the section on negotiating sessions I am indebted to Shel Trapp's *A Challenge for Change: Selected Essays on Community Organizing, Leadership Development, and Citizen Participation.*

For the section on tenant organizing, I am indebted to Michael McKee of the People's Housing Network, New York City; Woody Widrow, Shelterforce Collective, East Orange, N.J.; Barry Brodsky, South End Project Area Committee, Boston; Catherine Galvin, Brockton Legal Services, Brockton, Mass.; Anni Waterflow; and the Cambridge (Mass.) Tenants Organizing Committee, publishers of *Legal Tactics Handbook,* from which the material on rent-strike agreements is adapted.

4/Money and Publicity

The quotation by the Jacquettes is from "What Makes a Good Proposal?", *Foundation News*, January–February 1973.

The National Trust for Historic Preservation has devised a "Do-It-Yourself Press Kit" with sample press releases, a thirty-second television announcement, a sample radio spot, and a tip sheet of pointers for gaining media recognition.

5/How to Complete a Neighborhood Plan

For a detailed explanation of how to get a random sample, consult any standard statistics textbook, such as *Fundamental Statistics for Business and Economics* (third ed.), by John Neter and William Wasserman (Boston: Allyn and Bacon, 1966).

The material for the sample questionnaire was based on the following: "Neighborhood Survey," Atlanta Bureau of Planning, Atlanta, Ga. (1974); "Survey of Whittier Neighborhood" (1976) and "Goss-Grove Neighborhood Association Survey" (1976), City Planning Department, Boulder, Colo.; "Neighborhood Conservation Committee Questionnaire," Arlington Ridge Civic Association, Arlington, Va. (undated); *Community Needs in the San Jose Model Cities District: A Report on a Survey of Attitudes*, prepared for the San Jose Planning Department and the San Jose Model Cities Agency by Barton-Aschman Associates, Inc. (W. V. Rouse, Ltd.), Evanston, Ill., November 30, 1972.

An excellent guide to the use of alleys is *Alleys: A Hidden Resource*, which is available from the author, Grady Clay, 1190 E. Broadway, Louisville, KY 40204.

6/Three Neighborhood Planning Problems

The largest city with no zoning is Houston, which uses a system of restrictive covenants to control land use. See Bernard J. Frieden, *Land Use Without Zoning* (Cambridge: MIT Press, 1975).

For a review of the fast-food franchise problem, see Antoinette McCallister's *Zoning for Fast-Food and Drive-In Restaurants*, PAS Report No. 320, 1976. For more on adult-sex-business problems, see William Toner's *Regulating Sex Businesses*, PAS Report No. 327, 1977. Both are published by the American Planning Association, Chicago.

The Wisconsin group-facility law is Wis. Stat., Chapter 205, Laws of 1978. Other state laws on this subject are Minn. Stat. Ann. Section 252.28; Calif. Welf. & Inst. Code Section 5116; N.J. Stat. Ann. Section 40:55-32.2; N.Y. Soc. Ser. Law Section 371; Mich. Comp. Laws Ann. Section 125. See "Legal Digest," *Planning* magazine, September 1978, p. 9.

For more on advisory planning powers, see Ephraim Gil's *Neighborhood Zoning: Practice and Prospects*, PAS Report No. 311 (Chicago: American Planning Association, September 1975).

The Cincinnati ordinance on sensitive areas (No. 357-1976) is available from the City Planning Department, City Hall, Cincinnati, OH 45202. The Pyramid Density Concept proposal (GG-X District, August 19, 1977) is available from Dena Wild, Boulder Department of Community Development, Municipal Bldg., Boulder, CO 80302.

The citation for Richard E. Starr is "Sensitive Housing Code Enforcement Needed in Neighborhood Preservation," *Practicing Planner* (American Institute of Planners), June 1976, pp. 31ff.

Baltimore's quick-take-over power is cited in John S. McClaughry, *Obstacles to Neighborhood Revitalization.* . . . The New Jersey law is cited in Karen Kollias, *Neighborhood Reinvestment: A Citizen's Compendium for Programs and Strategies.*

For more information on the Neighborhood Cooperation Program, contact the Baltimore Department of Housing and Community Development, 222 E. Saratoga St., Baltimore, MD 21203.

For copies of Seattle's reports on traffic diverters, contact the Traffic and Transportation Division, Seattle Municipal Building, 600 Fourth Ave., Seattle, WA 98104. For another view of diverters, see "The Bumpy Road to Traffic Diversion," *Planning* magazine, vol. 43 no. 4, April/May 1977, pp. 7–8. The emergency-vehicle issue is discussed in "Traffic Control Devices and Emergency Services," Appendix D of *Liveable Urban Streets: Managing Auto Traffic in Neighborhoods.*

A copy of Arlington's parking sticker ordinance may be obtained by writing the Zoning Administrator, Arlington County Court House, Arlington, VA 22201. See also County Board of Arlington, Virginia v. Rudolph A. Richards, U.S. Supreme Court, No. 76-1418, Decided October 11, 1977.

7/Neighborhood Stability: Integration and Crime Prevention

For a thorough review of residential integration techniques, see Dudley Onderdonk's "Achieving Stable, Attractive Integrated Housing Markets," *Innovations*, vol. 2 no. 3, April 1978 (Springfield, Ill.: Illinois Department of Local Government Affairs).

The Neighborhood Police Team concept, reported in the January 2, 1978, *The New Yorker* ("The Team") pp. 16–18, fell victim to New York's budget crunch.

The Wilson/Boland quotation is from "Crime," in William Gorham and Nathan Glazer, eds., *The Urban Predicament* (Washington, D.C.: The Urban Institute, 1976).

The statistics on Cabrini-Green are taken from Sheila Castillo *et al.*, "Working Against Crime in the City that Works," *Planning*, vol. 43 no. 10, November 1977, pp. 14–15. Paul Gapp's article, "To Some City Dwellers, Security is an 11-Foot Wall," appeared in the *Chicago Tribune*, November 11, 1978.

There is no better source of case histories on community crime programs than George J. Washnis, *Citizen Involvement in Crime Prevention*. The list of guidelines for mobile patrols is adapted from his book. For a packet of materials on how to start a neighborhood radio watch program, write: Program Director, Community Radio Watch, Room 4420, 1301 E. Algonquin Road, Schaumburg, IL 60196.

8/Neighborhood Reinvestment Strategies

The regulatory agencies are: The Comptroller of the Currency, Consumer Affairs Division, Washington, DC 20219 (for national banks); the Federal Reserve Bank serving the area (for state member banks in the Federal Reserve System); the Office of Bank Customer Affairs, Federal Deposit Insurance Corporation, 550 17th St., N.W., Washington, DC 20429 (for all other FDIC-insured banks and mutual savings banks); the Office of Housing and Urban Affairs, Federal Home Loan Bank Board, 320 First St., N.W., Washington, DC 20552 (for savings and loans associations and FHLB System members, except savings banks insured by the FDIC); and the National Credit Union Administration, 2025 M St., N.W., Washington, DC 20456 (for credit unions).

For more information on the California regulations, contact the Department of Savings and Loan at either 600 S. Commonwealth Ave., Los Angeles, CA 90005, or 350 Sansome St., San Francisco, CA 94104.

For more information on the Pennsylvania program, contact the chief of the Human Resources Division, Bureau of Human Resources, Pennsylvania Department of Community Affairs, 529 South Office Bldg., Harrisburg, PA 17120.

For a good review of mortgage review boards, see "Mortgage Review Boards: The Second Chance," *Savings & Loan News*

(Chicago: U.S. Savings and Loan Association, September 1977). For a brochure on the Chicago HMOC, write HMOC, P.O. Box 516, Chicago, IL 60690.

The statistics on the Philadelphia Mortgage Plan are from Fran Odyniec, "The Banks Become Good Citizens," *Planning* magazine, vol. 43 no. 3, March 1977, pp. 6–7.

For the brochure *The Rebuilding of an American Neighborhood*, write the South Shore National Bank, 7054 S. Jeffery Blvd., Chicago, IL 60649 (undated).

9/Spending the Neighborhood Dollar Wisely

HUD has published two booklets that sort out the use of community development funds. *Directory of Program Characteristics of Community Development Block Grant (CDBG) Property Rehabilitation Financing Activities* (HUD-CPD-258-2) tabulates the financing techniques, number of units approved, the rehabilitation budget, and related data for every CDBG recipient. A companion booklet, *Directory of Localities with Community Development Block Grant (CDBG) Property Rehabilitation Financing Activities* (HUD-CPD-258-1) gives the name, address, and phone number of every program director. The booklets, published October 1977, may be obtained from: HUD, Publications Service Center, Room B-237, 451 Seventh St., S.W., Washington, DC 20410.

The information on the Charlottesville program is from Carl C. Chancellor, "Aid Volunteer Rehabilitation Program," *Journal of Housing*, June 1976, p. 271.

Among the techniques for turning HUD properties over to municipalities, Chicago has three special programs. The Mayor's Home Rehabilitation Program identifies abandoned HUD-owned properties and conveys them to homesteaders. The Property Release Option Program permits the city to purchase HUD houses at minimal cost and "pass through" ownership to nonprofit housing corporations for sale, rehabilitation, or demolition. The Assistance for HUD-Owned Properties Program provides zero-interest interim financing to nonprofit housing groups, who identify HUD-owned properties, prepare plans and specifications for rehabilitation, and apply to the city for title to the buildings. The city obtains the title from HUD and "passes through" title to the nonprofit group, which then sells the property to a qualified homesteader. For more information: Department of Urban Renewal, 320 N. Clark St., Chicago, IL 60610.

For further information on quick-response homesteading, contact SWAP, 434 Pine St., Providence, RI 02907.

The figures on NHS's accomplishments are from a letter to the author from Myra Peabody, National Neighborhood Reinvestment Corp., August 15, 1978.

10/Overcoming Displacement

In his survey of gentrified neighborhoods in thirty cities, Phillip L. Clay found results similar to the National Urban Coalition study. Besides proximity to downtown and historic designation, Clay lists "attractive topographic features" (hills, parks, bodies of water) and "recent nonresidential upgrading (including new construction)" as factors that attract the gentry. He also lists four kinds of neighborhoods where gentrification is likely *not* to occur: (1) neighborhoods with lots of big apartment buildings (hard to finance, unattractive to the new gentry); (2) areas distant from the "action" (away from downtown or some other hot real estate node); (3) areas with mixed land uses that are perceived as being nuisances—gas stations and drug clinics, for example; and (4) areas with small houses.

An excellent source for information on speculation in Washington, D.C., is Frank Smith's *Rip-Off and Reinvestment: A Report on Speculation and Evictions in Washington, D.C.*, Public Resource Center, 1747 Connecticut Ave., N.W., Washington, D.C. 20009 (1977). The statistics on property tax in the District of Columbia are from "Assessments to Rise Sharply in Many D.C. Neighborhoods," *Washington Post*, February 23, 1977. The quotation from the black woman in Washington is from Carol Richards and Jonathan Rowe, "Restoring a City: Who Pays the Price?" *Working Papers for a New Society*, Winter 1977, pp. 54–61.

The quotation from the Dorchester woman is taken from *Young Professionals and City Neighborhoods*, published by the Parkman Center, 33 Beacon St., Boston, MA 02108 (August 1977). This booklet is perhaps the most cogent statement in favor of gentrification.

The data on New Castle County's circuit-breaker program was supplied by Betty Swoboda of the county's finance department.

For further information on the Washington antispeculation tax, contact the District of Columbia City Council, Committee on Finance and Revenue, District Bldg., Washington, DC 20014.

The Alexandria program is described in *Final NEA Study Report to the City of Alexandria, Virginia, March 26, 1976*, prepared by Hammer Siler George Associates, 1140 Connecticut Ave., N.W., Washington, DC 20036. The Savannah program is described by Neal R. Peirce in "Savannah Shows Way for Inner Cities," *Oregonian*, March 20, 1977.

Complete information on the St. Ambrose Housing Aid Center may be obtained by writing for the group's annual report: 319 E. 25th St., Baltimore, MD 21218.

11/Historic Preservation

For more information about the Old West Side, contact OWS at P.O. Box 405, Ann Arbor, MI 48107.

The Tax Reform Act of 1976 provides incentives to owners of *commercial* or *income-producing* historic structures. The act allows the owner of a "certified historic structure" to deduct for federal income-tax purposes over a five-year period the costs of "certified rehabilitation," even if the expected life of the improvements exceeds five years, in lieu of otherwise allowable depreciation deductions. A good explanation of the new law is contained in "Preservation and the Tax Reform Act of 1976," *Preservation News* Supplement (November 1977), available from the National Trust for Historic Preservation. For a critique of the law, see Robert L. Nessen, "Treasure Houses," *Harper's*, December 1978, pp. 16–18.

The Ziegler quotation is from a reprint of his article, "Renovate, Don't Relocate," *Museum News*, December 1972.

12/Neighborhood Commercial Revitalization

In this chapter I am particularly indebted to John Sower of the National Development Council.

For a short but useful look at the principles behind street furniture design, see Harold Lewis Malt, "Street Furniture and the Urban Environment," *Practicing Planner*, June 1977, pp. 31–34. (*Practicing Planner* was published by the American Institute of Planners, which is now part of the American Planning Association.)

Bibliography of
Reference Materials

General Reference

Building Neighborhood Confidence: A Humanistic Strategy for Urban Housing. Rolf Goetze. Cambridge, Mass.: Ballinger Publishing Co., 1976.

The Death and Life of Great American Cities. Jane Jacobs. New York: Random House, 1961.
Must reading for anyone who hopes to understand neighborhoods.

"Housing and Central Cities: The Conservation Approach." Kenneth F. Phillips and Michael A. Agelasto, II. *Ecology Law Quarterly,* vol. 4 no. 4, 1975, pp. 796–880.

A Nation of Neighborhoods. Stewart Dill McBride. *Christian Science Monitor,* PO Box 527, Back Bay Station, Boston, MA 02117.
Reprint of series published in 1977 on various self-help neighborhood efforts. Well-written, inspirational.

Neighborhood Conservation: Lessons from Three Cities. Phyllis Myers and Gordon Binder. Washington, D.C.: The Conservation Foundation, 1977.
A look at Cincinnati, Seattle, and Annapolis by two incisive researchers.

Neighborhood Revitalization: Theory and Practice. Roger S. Ahlbrandt, Jr., and Paul C. Brophy. Lexington, Mass.: Lexington Books, D.C. Heath and Co., 1975.

"Neighborhood Revitalization: The Recent Experience in Large American Cities." Phillip L. Clay. Cambridge: Department of Urban Studies, Massachusetts Institute of Technology, April 1978.

People, Building Neighborhoods: Final Report to The President and The Congress of the United States. Washington, D.C.: National Commission on Neighborhoods, March 19, 1979. Order from: USGPO, Washington, DC 20402. Stock No. 052-003-00616-2.

The Population Factor and Urban Structure. William Alonso. Center for Population Studies, School of Public Health, Harvard University, 9 Bow St., Cambridge, MA 02138. Working Paper No. 102, August 1977.

"Recycling Declining Neighborhoods: Give the People a Chance." John McClaughry. *The Urban Lawyer,* vol. 10 no. 2, Spring 1978, pp. 318ff.

Reviving an Inner City Community: The Drama of Urban Change in Chicago's East Humboldt Park. E. Marciniak. Dept. of Political Science, Room 601, Loyola University, 820 N. Michigan Ave., Chicago, IL 60611. 1977.

Good case study of the planning problems in Chicago's Polish district.

To Save Our Cities: What Needs to Be Done. Henry S. Reuss. Washington, D.C.: Public Affairs Press, 1977.

Urban Community Development: Case Studies in Neighborhood Survival. Daniel V. Folkman, ed. University of Wisconsin Extension, 929 N. Sixth St., Milwaukee, WI 53203. 1978.

Neighborhood Decline

The Abuse of Power: The Permanent Government and the Fall of New York. Jack Newfield and Paul Dubrul. New York: Viking Press, 1977.

The American Nightmare. Chicago: National Training and Information Center, 1976.

Brief review of the Federal Housing Administration scandals.

Bum Rap on America's Cities: The Real Causes of Urban Decay. Richard S. Morris. Englewood Cliffs, N.J.: Prentice-Hall, 1978.

Cities Destroyed for Cash: The FHA Scandal at HUD. Brian D. Boyer. Chicago: Follett Publishing Co., 1973.

Disclosure and Neighborhood Reinvestment: A Citizen's Guide. Karen Kollias, *et al.* Washington, D.C.: National Center for Urban Ethnic Affairs, October 1976.

The Dynamics of Neighborhood Change. Public Affairs Counseling. Washington, D.C.: U.S. Department of Housing and Urban Development, May 1975.

An interesting document because it presents the "official" view of neighborhood decline from HUD's vantage point.

Essential Insurance in Michigan: An Avoidable Crisis; A Report to the Governor. Insurance Bureau, Michigan Dept. of Commerce, P.O. Box 30220, Lansing, MI 48909. March 1977.

Housing Abandonment in New York City. HOMEFRONT, P.O. Box 269, Peter Stuyvesant Sta., New York, NY 10019. 1977.
A social appraisal of the abandonment problem.

How to Research Your Local Bank. William Batko. Washington, D.C.: Institute for Local Self-Reliance, undated.

How to Use the Home Mortgage Disclosure Act of 1975. Chicago: National Training and Information Center, 1976.

The Lifeblood of Housing: A Report on Housing Investment and Conservation. Center for Community Change. Harrisburg, Pa.: Pennsylvania Department of Community Affairs, October 1976.

Measuring Neighborhood Confidence. Robert M. Hollister, et al. Cambridge, Mass.: Dept. of Urban Studies and Planning, Massachusetts Institute of Technology, 1978.

More Holes than Net: A Critical Evaluation of HUD's System for Catching and Deterring FHA Lender Misconduct. Peter L. Maier, Courtland J. W. Troutman, and Thomas H. Stanton. Washington, D.C.: Center for the Study of Responsive Law (Housing Research Group), July 1977.

Obstacles to Neighborhood Revitalization Posed by Laws, Ordinances, and Governmental Practices in Five Cities. John McClaughry. Concord, Vt.: Institute for Liberty and Community, January 1975.

Opportunities for Abuse: Private Profits, Public Losses and the Mortgage Banking Industry. Jeffrey Zinsmeyer, Judith Turnock, and Andrew Mott. Washington, D.C.: Center for Community Change, October 1977.

Redlining. Office of Corporate Relations, Federal National Mortgage Assoc., 1133 15th St., N.W., Washington, DC 20005. January 1976.
Contains two papers: Gordon E. Nelson, "Some Perspectives on Redlining"; Hilbert Fefferman, "The Redlining of Neighborhoods by Mortgage Lending Institutions and What Can Be Done About It."

Redlining Revealed: Where to Bank to Save Your Neighborhood. Ron Finney, Greg Jackson, and Sheridan Sonne. Los Angeles: Center for New Corporate Priorities, 1977.
Good general information on redlining, and excellent section on using disclosure data.

Understanding Neighborhood Change: The Role of Confidence in Urban Revitalization. Rolf Goetze. Cambridge, Mass.: Ballinger Publishing Co., 1979.

Urban Disinvestment: New Implications for Community Organization, Research and Public Policy. Arthur J. Naparstek and Gale Cincotta. Joint Publication of the National Center for Urban Ethnic Affairs and the National Training and Information Center, February 1976.
"The Urban-Suburban Investment-Disinvestment Process: Consequences for Older Neighborhoods." Calvin P. Bradford and Leonard S. Rubinowitz. *Annals of the American Academy of Political and Social Sciences,* vol. 422, November 1975, pp. 77–86.

Community Organizing
About Foundations: How to Find the Facts You Need to Get a Grant. Judith B. Margolin. New York and Washington, D.C.: The Foundation Center, 1975.
Census Data for Community Action. U.S. Bureau of the Census, Washington, DC 20233. November 1972.
How to use census reports, examples of census material, where to get more information.
A Challenge for Change: Selected Essays on Community Organizing, Leadership Development, and Citizen Participation. Shel Trapp. Chicago: National Training and Information Center, 1976.
A collection of essays by one of the nation's outstanding organizers; full of good ideas.
The Community Activist's Handbook: A Guide to Organizing, Financing, and Publicizing Community Campaigns. John Huenfeld. Boston: Beacon Press, 1970.
Strong on organizational techniques, such as running a meeting, with lots of good, solid advice.
Dynamics of Organizing. Shel Trapp. Chicago: National Training and Information Center, 1976.
A brief step-by-step description of how to build a community organization.
Everypersons's Guide to Neighbourhood Defense or Rape of the Block. Missy Parnell, Verna Semotuk, and Joan Swain. Edmonton Social Planning Council, 10006 107th St., Edmonton, Alberta. 1974.
A helpful guide to the Canadian scene.
The Foundation Directory. Edited by Marianna O. Lewis. New York: The Foundation Center, 1979 (seventh edition).
The Grass Roots Fundraising Book: How to Raise Money in Your Community. Joan Flanagan. Chicago: Swallow Press, 1977. May be ordered from: The Youth Project, 1000 Wisconsin Ave., N.W., Washington, DC 20007.

Everything from Bingo to Haunted House parties—one of the handful of indispensable books for community groups.

The Grassroots Primer. James Robertson and John Lewallen. San Francisco: Sierra Club Books, 1975.

A Guide to Fundraising and Proposal Writing. Joan Kennedy, Earl Anthes, Jerry Cronin, and Carolyn Strong. Hampton, Ark.: Independent Community Consultants, Inc., 1975.

A Guide to Funding Sources Research. Hampton, Ark.: Independent Community Consultants, Inc., 1974.

Help! I Have to Write a Report. Scholarship, Education, and Defense Fund for Racial Equality (SEDFRE), 164 Madison Ave., N.Y. 10016. April 1971.
A short pamphlet that covers the basics of report writing.

How to Do Leaflets, Newsletters, and Newspapers. Nancy Brigham. Boston Community School (1975). Order from: New England Free Press, 60 Union Square, Somerville, MA 02143.
If you're going to send out any written material, get this booklet first. Highly recommended.

How to Gather Data About Your Neighborhood. Margaret L. Lotspeich and John E. Kleymeyer. Chicago: American Planning Association (Neighborhood Technical Information Service, vol. 1 no. 10), undated.

Lend a Hand and Improve Your Block. Citizens Committee for New York City, 630 Fifth Ave., New York, NY 10020.
Small booklet on how to start a block association.

Lend a Hand for a Cleaner New York. Citizens Committee for New York City, 630 Fifth Ave., New York, NY 10020.
Recyling, litter baskets, graffiti removal, doggy poop elimination—it's all here. A good little booklet, particularly for New Yorkers.

The Neighborhood Organizer's Handbook. Rachelle B. Warren and Donald I. Warren. South Bend, Ind.: University of Notre Dame Press, 1977.

New York's City Streets: A Guide to Making Your Block More Lively and More Livable. Mary Grozier and Richard Roberts, Council on the Environment of New York City, 51 Chambers St., New York, NY 10017. 1973.
Handbook for citizens interested in neighborhood improvement; particularly useful for New York City residents.

New York Self Help Handbook: A Step by Step Guide to Neighborhood Improvement Projects. Karin Carlson, Project Director. Citizens Committee for New York City, 630 Fifth Ave., New York, NY 10020. 1978.
An encyclopedia of things community groups can do to improve

neighborhoods, with details on resources. Especially good for New York City.

The People's Guide to Urban Renewal and Community Development Programs. Leslie Shipnuck and Dennis Keating, with Mary Morgan. Berkeley Tenants Organizing Committee, 2022 Blake St., Berkeley, CA 94704. 1974.
Somewhat dated (it focuses on old urban renewal programs) but still generally useful.

Planning and Producing Slide Programs. Publication No. S-30. 1975. Kodak Motion Picture and Audiovisual Markets Division, Rochester, NY 14650.
Thorough guide to putting together a slide show to promote your organization.

Where the Money Is! Federal Funding Guide for Community Action Agencies and Non-Profit Organizations. National Center for Community Action, 1711 Connecticut Ave., N.W., Washington, DC 20009. September 1975.
Lists federal programs that have potential benefits for low-income persons served by community-action agencies.

Neighborhood Planning

Citizen's Action Manual: A Guide to Recycling Vacant Property in Your Neighborhood. Washington, D.C.: Heritage Conservation and Recreation Service, U.S. Dept. of the Interior, February 1979.

The Citizen's Guide to Planning. Rev. ed. Herbert H. Smith. Chicago: American Planning Association, 1979.
A helpful, sympathetic, digestible book on a difficult subject.

The Citizen's Guide to Zoning. Herbert H. Smith. West Trenton, N.J.: Chandler-Davis Publishing Co., 1965.
A sympathetic, nonscholarly primer written by an experienced planner.

Citizen's Guide to Zoning Series. Department of Community Development, 306 Cherry St., Arctic Bldg., Seattle, WA 98104. February 1977.
No. 1—*Zoning in Seattle*
No. 2—*Variances*
No. 3—*Conditional Uses*
No. 4—*Rezones*
No. 5—*Special Review Districts*
No. 6—*Short Plats or Short Subdivisions*
No. 7—*How to Make Zoning Work for You*

Why every city doesn't have excellent booklets like these to explain the zoning process to citizens is incomprehensible. Clearly written, well-illustrated, helpful.

Citizen's Handbook on Neighborhood Land Planning. John Platt *et al.* Northwest Environmental Defense Center, 11015 S.W. Terwilliger Blvd., Portland, OR 97219. 1973.

Excellent book for laymen on the complexities of land planning, with an emphasis on the situation in Portland, Oregon.

Everything You Always Wanted to Know About Planning, Zoning, Subdivision in Montgomery County, Maryland, But Were Afraid to Ask. Montgomery County Planning Board, 8787 Georgia Ave., Silver Spring, MD 20907. October 1973.

Answers forty-four questions, from "What is downzoning?" to "What is site plan review?"

Flexible Code Enforcement: A Key Ingredient in Neighborhood Preservation Programming. Roger S. Ahlbrandt, Jr. Washington, D.C.: National Association of Housing and Redevelopment Officials, 1976.

General Information: Neighborhood Conservation Program. Arlington Planning Division, 2100 No. 14th St., Arlington, VA 22201. 1973.

A Guide to Citizen-Based Planning for Suburbs, Small Cities, and Towns. Citizen Involvement Network, 1211 Connecticut Ave., N.W., Washington, DC 20036. July 1977.

Helpful guide to small-area planning, with an excellent bibliography and resource section.

Guide to Neighborhood Planning. Dena Wild, Project Coordinator. Department of Community Development, City of Boulder, Municipal Bldg., 1977 Broadway, Boulder, CO 80302. 1975.

How to Do Neighborhood Planning. Atlanta Bureau of Planning and ABC Management Consultants, Inc. Atlanta Bureau of Planning, 68 Mitchell St., S.W., Atlanta, GA 30303. June 1974.

Liveable Urban Streets: Managing Auto Traffic in Neighborhoods. Donald Appleyard. Federal Highway Administration, Washington, DC 20590. 1976. Report No. FHWA/SES-76-03. USGPO Stock No. 050-001-00111-0.

Manual of Housing/Planning and Design Criteria. Joseph DeChiara and Lee Koppelman. Englewood Cliffs, N.J.: Prentice-Hall, 1975.

Lots of illustrations in this how-to manual for city planners.

Neighborhood Land Use Workbook. Bureau of Planning, 424 S.W. Main St., Portland, OR 97204.

Provides a detailed checklist of points to ponder in studying a land-use change.

Neighborhood Notebook. Dallas Department of Urban Planning, 500 S. Ervay, Suite 200B, Dallas, TX 75201. 1976.
Dozens of small "notebooks" on physical maintenance, solving neighborhood problems, organizing, city services, historic preservation.

Neighborhood Planning: Who, Where, What, When, Why & How. Lakewood Department of Community Development, 1580 Yarrow St., Lakewood, CO 80215. January 1975.
Citizens' planning guide, particularly useful for a city of less than 100,000 people.

Planning and Zoning Administration in Utah. Herschel G. Hester, III, ed. Utah Bureau of Community Development, University of Utah, and Utah League of Cities and Towns. Available from Utah League of Cities and Towns, 10 W. Broadway, Suite 304-307, Salt Lake City, UT 84101. April 1977.
Focuses on Utah, but is actually a detailed book on planning, zoning, subdivision, with lots of illustrations.

Planning the Neighborhood: Standards for Healthful Housing. American Public Health Association, 1960. Order from: Public Administration Service, 1313 E. 60th St., Chicago, IL 60637.
Lists standards for housing, parks, transportation, community facilities, health services, and schools.

The Practice of Local Government Planning. Frank S. So, Israel Stollman, Frank Beal, and David S. Arnold, eds. Chicago and Washington, D.C.: The American Planning Association and the International City Management Association, 1979.
In previous editions, this book, the Bible of city planning, was known as *Principles and Practice of Urban Planning.* Order from ICMA.

Urban Planning and Design Criteria. Second ed. Joseph DeChiara and Lee Koppelman. New York: Van Nostrand Reinhold Co., 1975.
If you need to know the proper turning radius for a cul-de-sac, this is the book to turn to.

Financing Techniques

A Citizen's Guide to the Housing and Community Development Act of 1974. Antoinette McAllister. NTIS Report, vol. 1 no. 9. Chicago: American Planning Association, 1975.

Community Development Credit Unions: A Self-Help Manual. Brad J. Caftel. National Economic Development Law Project, 2150 Shattuck Ave., Berkeley, CA 94704. 1978.

Developing a Local Housing Strategy: A Guidebook for Local Govern-

ment. U.S. Conference of Mayors, National Community Development Association, and the Urban Land Institute. Undated. Order from: HUD, Room 8124, Washington, DC 20410.

An Evaluation of Pittsburgh's Neighborhood Housing Services Program. Roger S. Ahlbrandt, Jr. and Paul C. Brophy. ACTION-Housing, 2 Gateway Center, Pittsburgh, PA 15222. May 1975. HUD-PDR-97.

Financing Techniques for Local Rehabilitation Programs. David Gressel. Washington, D.C.: National Association of Housing and Redevelopment Officials, 1976.
An excellent synopsis and analysis of the basic financing programs.

A Guide to Housing Rehabilitation Programs. Washington, D.C.: U.S. Department of Housing and Urban Development, November 1978. HUD-NVACP-320[3].
Outlines the major HUD programs.

Homesteading in Urban U.S.A. Anne Clark and Zelma Rivin. New York: Praeger Publishers, 1977.

Housing Rehabilitation: A Guidebook for Municipal Programs. A. William Benitez. Washington, D.C.: National Association of Housing and Redevelopment Officials, 1976.
A thorough book for rehabilitation specialists, particularly those working in city government.

Housing Rehabilitation Loan Programs in Minnesota. James D. Fitzsimmons, Julia A. Nutter, and Kathleen A. Gilder. Center for Urban and Regional Affairs, 311 Walter Library, University of Minnesota, Minneapolis, MN 55455. May 1975.

How to Research Your Local Bank (Or Savings & Loan Institution). William Batko. Washington, D.C.: Institute for Local Self-Reliance, 1976.
Explains how to use the disclosure laws to determine whether lenders are redlining your neighborhood.

Local Housing Assistance Tools and Techniques: A Guidebook for Local Government. U.S. Conference of Mayors, National Community Development Association, and the Urban Land Institute. Undated. Order from: HUD, Room 8124, Washington, DC 20410.

The Neighborhood Housing Services Model: A Progress Assessment of the Related Activities of the Urban Reinvestment Task Force. Roger S. Ahlbrandt, Jr., Paul C. Brophy, and Jonathan E. Zimmer. ACTION-Housing, Inc., 2 Gateway Center, Pittsburgh, PA 15222. September 1975.

Neighborhood Reinvestment: A Citizen's Compendium For Programs and Strategies. Karen Kollias *et al.* Washington, D.C.: National Center for Urban Ethnic Affairs, 1977.

The Planner's Role in Facilitating Private Sector Reinvestment. Dennis R. Marino, Lawrence B. Rosser, and Andrea R. Rozran. PAS Report No. 340. Chicago: American Planning Association, 1979.

The Private Development Process: A Guidebook for Local Government. Washington, D.C.: U.S. Department of Housing and Urban Development, February 1979. HUD-PDR-352-2.

Urban Community Development: Case Studies in Neighborhood Survival. Dan Folkman, ed. Center for Urban Community Development, University of Wisconsin Extension, 929 N. Sixth St., Milwaukee, WI 53203. 1978.

Urban Homesteading. James W. Hughes and Kenneth D. Bleakly, Jr. New Brunswick, N.J.: Center for Urban Policy Research, Rutgers University, 1975.

General description of neighborhood decline, with detailed review of programs in Baltimore, Wilmington, Philadelphia, and Newark.

Urban Homesteading: The Philadelphia Experience—A Technical Report. Howard E. Mitchell, Jr. Department of Management, The Wharton School, University of Pennsylvania, Philadelphia, PA 19174. May 1975.

Crime

Arson and Arson Investigation: Survey and Assessment. John F. Boudreau, Quon Y. Kwan, William E. Faragher, and Genevieve C. Denault. Law Enforcement Assistance Administration, Washington, DC 20531. October 1977. USGPO Stock No. 027-000-00600-1.

A Call for Citizen Action: Crime Prevention and the Citizen. National Advisory Commission on Criminal Justice Standards and Goals. Order from: National Criminal Justice Reference Service, Washington, DC 20530. April 1974. USGPO Stock No. 545-414/582 1-3.

General study of activities citizens can get involved in, such as parole system, youth work, anticorruption efforts, plus some neighborhood-based programs.

Citizen Involvement in Crime Prevention. George J. Washnis. Lexington, Mass.: Lexington Books, D.C. Heath and Co., 1976.

A Community Guide to Crime Prevention. Citizen Involvement Network, 1211 Connecticut Ave., N.W., Washington, DC 20036. August 1977.

Good outline of community crime-prevention planning, with examples and case studies of successful groups.

Defensible Space: Crime Prevention Through Environmental Design. Oscar Newman. New York: Collier Books, 1973.

How to Protect Yourself from Crime: Everything You Need to Know to

Guard Yourself, Your Family, Your Home, Your Possessions, and Your Business. Ira A. Lipman. New York: Atheneum, 1975.
Tips for apartment dwellers, inside/outside security, defenses against rape—it's all here, in big type, with illustrations.
Lend a Hand for a Safer New York. Citizens Committee for New York City, 630 Fifth Ave., New York, NY 10020.
Lists a variety of methods community organizations can use to deter crime.
Manageable Space: Proposals for Crime Prevention in Subsidized Housing. Donald J. Perlgut. Sedway/Cooke, 325 Pacific Ave., San Francisco, CA 94111. April 1979.

Displacement

Displacement: City Neighborhoods in Transition. Washington, D.C.: National Urban Coalition, 1978.
Survey of displacement in forty-four cities.
Displacement Report. Washington, D.C.: U.S. Department of Housing and Urban Development, February 1979. HUD-PDR-382.
NAN Handbook on Reinvestment Displacement: HUD's Role in a New Housing Issue. Conrad Weiler. Washington, D.C.: National Association of Neighborhoods, May 1978.
Neighborhood Conservation and the Elderly: A Consideration of the Impacts of Neighborhood Conservation on the Elderly in Cities. Phyllis Myers. Washington, D.C.: The Conservation Foundation, 1978.
Neighborhood Diversity. U.S. Senate. Hearings before the Committee on Banking, Housing, and Urban Affairs, United States Senate, 95th Cong. 1st sess., 7–8 July 1977.
New Opportunities for Residential Development in Central Cities: Case Studies of Private New Construction and Rehabilitation. Washington, D.C.: Urban Land Institute, 1976.
Private-Market Housing Renovation in Older Urban Areas. J. Thomas Black, Allan Borut, and Robert Dubinsky. Washington, D.C.: Urban Land Institute, 1977.
Descriptions of various neighborhoods where private-market renovation is occurring.
Queen Village: The Eclipse of Community. Paul R. Levy. Philadelphia: Institute for the Study of Civic Values, 1978.
A case study of gentrification and displacement in South Philadelphia.
Seattle Displacement Study: Executive Summary. July 1979. Seattle Physical Planning Division, 400 Yesler Bldg., Seattle, WA 98104.

Historic Preservation

Historic Preservation in Inner City Areas: A Manual of Practice. Rev. ed. Arthur P. Ziegler, Jr. Ober Park Associates, 701 Allegheny Square West, Pittsburgh, PA 15212. 1974.

Return to the City: How to Restore Old Buildings and Ourselves in America's Historic Urban Neighborhoods. Richard Ernie Reed. Garden City, N.Y.: Doubleday & Co., 1979.

Revolving Funds for Historic Preservation: A Manual of Practice. Arthur P. Ziegler, Jr., Leopold Adler II, and Walter C. Kidney. Ober Park Associates, 701 Allegheny Square West, Pittsburgh, PA 15212. 1975.

Neighborhood Commercial Revitalization

Downtown Improvement Manual. Emanuel Berk, principal author. Chicago: American Planning Association, 1976.

Good handbook on reviving small commercial areas, particularly in small towns.

The Mitchell Center Pedestrian Mall: A Case Study of Neighborhood Commercial Redevelopment in Milwaukee, Wisconsin. David H. Laughrey. Washington, D.C.: National Council for Urban Economic Development, November 1975.

Detailed case study of one commercial rehab project.

Mitchell Center Storefront Improvement Manual. Mitchell Center Development Corp., 1717 S. 12th St., Milwaukee, WI 53204.

A primary resource manual. Contains examples of the actual storefront survey, the statement of design principles, and an artist's conception of proposed solutions to several design problems. Excellent.

Neighborhood Commercial Rehabilitation. Adrienne M. Levatino. Washington, D.C.: National Association of Housing and Redevelopment Officials, January 1978.

Neighborhoods in the Urban Economy: The Dynamics of Decline and Revitalization. Benjamin Goldstein and Ross Davis. Lexington, Mass.: Lexington Books, D.C. Heath and Co., 1977.

Proceedings of the Second National Conference on Neighborhood Commercial Revitalization, September 1976. Contains papers and commentary by several experts.

Catalogs and Sourcebooks

Community Preservation Synopsis. Planning Branch, National Register of Historic Places, National Park Service, Washington, DC 20240. August 1977.

Lists sixty-five special programs, most of them involving historic preservation, with brief outline of each program.

Directory of Community Crime Prevention Programs: National and State Levels. James L. Lockard, J.T. Skip Duncan, and Robert N. Brenner. December 1978. Order from: National Criminal Justice Reference Service, Washington, DC 20531. Stock No. 027-000-00817-8.

Directory of Community Development Information Sources. Hampton, Ark.: Independent Community Consultants, 1975.
Good listing of helpful agencies.

Federal Programs for Neighborhood Conservation. Advisory Council on Historic Preservation, 1522 K St., N.W., Washington, DC 20005. 1975.
Useful listing of federal programs.

Human Work for Human Needs: A Catalog of Community Action Programs. National Center for Community Action, 1711 Connecticut Ave., N.W., Washington, DC 20009. December 1975.
A catalog of some 171 of the more innovative and effective antipoverty programs.

Neighborhood Conservation: A Source Book. Stephen A. Kliment, ed. New York: Whitney Library of Design, Watson-Guptill, 1976.
Presents a summary of the Neighborhood Conservation Conference, New York City, September 24–26, 1975. Contains sketches of numerous conservation programs.

The Neighborhood Housing Movement. Robert Schur and Virginia Sherry. New York: Association of Neighborhood Housing Developers, January 1977.
A survey of ANHB's members—nonprofit community-based organizations in low-income NYC neighborhoods.

Neighborhood Preservation: A Catalog of Programs. Washington, D.C.: U.S. Department of Housing and Urban Development, February 1975, HUD-PDR-75. Order from: USGPO, Washington, DC 20402, Stock No. 023-000-00285-0.
Describes one hundred programs in detail: code enforcement, comprehensive programs, focused public services, neighborhood control, historic preservation, NHS, and financing programs.

PAS Memo 76-9. Chicago: Planning Advisory Service, American Planning Association, September 1, 1976.
An excellent compendium of historic preservation sources, including audio-visual materials, legal aspects, and sample surveys.

Source Catalog: Communities/Housing. Chicago: Swallow Press, 1972.
A kind of Whole Earth Catalog for community groups, particularly strong on tenant problems.

Periodicals

American Preservation, P.O. Box 2451, Little Rock, AR 72203.

Catalyst, Center for Community Change, 1000 Wisconsin Ave., N.W., Washington, DC 20007.
Focuses on CETA involvement.

Chicago Rehabber, 218 Prudential Plaza, Chicago, IL 60601.

City Limits, Association of Neighborhood Housing Developers, Inc., 29 E. 22nd St., New York, NY 10010.

Communities: A Journal of Cooperative Living, P.O. Box 426, Louisa, VA 23093.

Community Development Digest, 1319 F St., N.W., Washington, DC 20004.

COMP Newsletter, Council on Municipal Performance, 84 Fifth Ave., New York, NY 10011.

Conserve Neighborhoods, 1735 Massachusetts Ave., N.W., Washington, DC 20036.

CUED Commentary, National Council for Urban Economic Development, 1730 M St., N.W., Washington, DC 20006.

Disclosure, National Training and Information Center, 1123 W. Washington Blvd., Chicago, IL 60607.
A citizen-action newspaper.

The Elements, 1901 Q St., N.W., Washington, DC 20009.

Environmental Action Magazine, 1346 Connecticut Ave., N.W., Washington, DC 20036.

Foundation News, Council on Foundations, 1828 L St., N.W., Washington, DC 20036.

Grantsmanship Center News, Grantsmanship Center, 1031 S. Grand Ave., Los Angeles, CA 90015.

Historic Preservation, National Trust for Historic Preservation, 1735 Massachusetts Ave., N.W., Washington, DC 20036.

Humanizing City Life (formerly *doing it!*), P.O. Box 303, Worthington, OH 43085.

Impact, P.O. Box 23126, Washington, DC 20024.

Journal of Housing, National Association of Housing and Redevelopment Officials (NAHRO), 2600 Virginia Ave., N.W., Washington, DC 20037.

The Monitor, Center for Community Change, 1000 Wisconsin Ave., N.W., Washington, DC 20007.

National Center Reporter, National Center for Community Action, 1328 New York Ave., N.W., Washington, DC 20005.
Information on community-action agencies.

Nation's Cities, National League of Cities, 1620 Eye St., N.W., Washington, DC 20006.

Neighborhood Conservation and Reinvestment, c/o Preservation Reports, Inc., 919 18th St., N.W., Suite 624, Washington, DC 20006.

Neighborhood Ideas, Center for Governmental Studies, 1010 16th Street, N.W., Washington, DC 20036.

Neighborhoods, Institute for the Study of Civic Values, 401 N. Broad St., Philadelphia, PA 19108.

The Neighborhood Works, Center for Neighborhood Technology, 570 W. Randolph St., Chicago, IL 60606. Clearinghouse on appròpriate technology.

Neighbors, National Neighbors, Bowen Bld., Suite 611, 815 15th St., N.W., Washington, DC 20005.

Network, People's Housing Network, 29 E. 22nd St., New York, NY 10010.

Network Notes, National Self-Help Resource Center, 2000 S St., N.W., Washington, DC 20009.

The Old-House Journal, 199 Berkeley Pl., Brooklyn, NY 11217.

Planners Network, 360 Elizabeth St., San Francisco, CA 94114.

Planning, American Planning Association, 1313 E. 60th St., Chicago, IL 60637.

Preservation News, 1735 Massachusetts Ave., N.W., Washington, DC 20036.

The Public Works, Community Ownership Organizing Project, 349 62nd St., Oakland, CA 94618.

Rodale's Environment Action Bulletin, Rodale Press, Emmaus, PA 18049.

Rehab Notes, P.O. Box 5067, Tampa, FL 33675.

Rain: Journal of Appropriate Technology, 2270 N.W. Irving, Portland, OR 97210.

Self-Reliance, Institute for Local Self-Reliance, 1717 18th St., N.W., Washington, DC 20009.

Shelterforce, 380 Main St., East Orange, NJ 07018.

Small Town, P.O. Box 517, Ellensburg, WA 98929.

Street: Magazine of the Environment, c/o PICCED, 240 Hall St., Brooklyn, NY 11205.

USA, 523 W. 15th St., Little Rock, AR 72202. Published by ACORN.

Voluntary Action Leadership, P.O. Box 4179, Boulder, CO 80302.

Voluntary Action News, National Center for Voluntary Action, 1785 Massachusetts Ave., N.W., Washington, DC 20036.

List of Organizations
and Institutions

ACORN (Arkansas Community Organizations for Reform Now)
523 W. 15th St.
Little Rock, AR 72202
A network of citizens' and community groups, particularly strong in the environmental field.

ACTION
Washington, DC 20525
The federal umbrella agency for volunteers. Provides volunteers to help local efforts and supplies technical assistance and materials to volunteer projects.

Alliance for Volunteerism
1214 16th St., N.W.
Washington, DC 20036
Coordinates national volunteer efforts.

American Institute of Architects
1735 New York Ave., N.W.
Washington, DC 20036
Professional association of architects; provides regional/urban design assistance teams to give technical assistance to cities and community groups.

American Planning Association
1313 E. 60th St.
Chicago, IL 60637

Combines the American Society of Planning Officials and the American Institute of Planners; issues books, technical reports, research, and monthly magazine, *Planning* (incorporating *Practicing Planner*).

Association of Neighborhood Housing Developers, Inc.
29 E. 22nd St.
New York, NY 10010
Provides technical assistance to groups involved in housing rehabilitation; publishes monthly newsletter, *City Limits*.

Back to the Cities, Inc.
12 E. 41st St.
New York, NY 10017
Loose network of neighborhood groups; sponsors annual conference.

Brownstone Revival Committee
230 Park Ave., Room 1825
New York, NY 10017
Sponsor's annual conference.

Campaign for Human Development
U.S. Catholic Conference
1312 Massachusetts Ave., N.W.
Washington, DC 20005
Allocates $1 million a year to community groups.

Center for Community Change
1000 Wisconsin Ave., N.W.
Washington, DC 20007
Provides technical assistance to local groups, publishes reports, and issues newsletter, *The Monitor*.

Center for Community Economic Development
639 Massachusetts Ave., Room 316
Cambridge, MA 02139
Focuses on economic development corporations.

Center for Community Organization
1214 16th St., N.W.
Washington, DC 20036

Center for Neighborhood Technology
570 W. Randolph St.
Chicago, IL 60606
Conducts research and publishes newsletter, *The Neighborhood Works*.

Center for New Corporate Priorities
1801 S. La Cienega, Suite 208
Los Angeles, CA 90035
Conducts research and publishes reports on consumer issues related to
neighborhoods, particularly redlining.

Center for the Visual Environment
1525 New Hampshire Ave., N.W.
Washington, DC 20036
Publishes booklets and pamphlets.

Center for Urban Encounter
3410 University Ave., S.E.
Minneapolis, MN 55414

Chicago Rehab Network
343 S. Dearborn, Suite 1508
Chicago, IL 60604
Network of 15 Chicago rehab groups.

Citizen Involvement Training Project
138 Hasbrouck
Division of Continuing Education
University of Massachusetts
Amherst, MA 01103
Provides workshops, training materials, and consulting services for
neighborhood groups.

Civic Action Institute
1010 16th St., N.W.
Washington, DC 20036
Publishes books and studies on neighborhood issues, plus monthly
newsletter, *Neighborhood Ideas.*

Coalition for Human Needs
Executive Council of the Episcopal Church
815 Second Ave.
New York, NY 10017

Community Action Training
128 W. State St.
Trenton, NJ 08608
Publishes books and reports on organizing techniques and provides
training to help public employees involved in community work.

Community Services Administration
1200 19th St., N.W.
Washington, DC 20506
For information on federal community action programs for low-income people.

Conservation Foundation
1717 Massachusetts Ave., N.W.
Washington, DC 20036
Conducts research and publishes books and reports; issues monthly newsletter.

Economic Development Administration
U.S. Department of Commerce
Washington, DC 20230
Provides grants for local development, particularly commercial revitalization.

The Foundation Center
888 Seventh Ave.
New York, NY 10019
Also: 1001 Connecticut Ave., N.W.
Washington, DC 20036
A principal source of information on grants.

Grantsmanship Center
1031 South Grand Ave.
Los Angeles, CA 90015
Excellent fund-raising resource, comparable to the Foundation Center.

Heritage Conservation and Recreation Service
U.S. Dept. of the Interior
440 G St., N.W.
Washington, DC 20243
Publishes numerous booklets of use to community groups; write its Information Exchange for details.

Highlander Center
Rural Route Box 370
New Market, TN 37820
Particularly helpful to rural-based groups.

Independent Community Consultants
PLANNING AND TRAINING OFFICE:
P.O. Box 141
Hampton, AR 71744
RESEARCH OFFICE
304 S. 18th St.
West Memphis, AR 72301
Research and training institute for community organizers; publishes research reports.

The Independent Foundation
1028 Connecticut Ave., N.W.
Washington, DC 20036
Provides specialists, mostly former VISTA and Peace Corps volunteers, through a computerized skills bank.

Industrial Areas Foundation Training Institute
12 E. Grand Ave.
Chicago, IL 60611
The formal successor organization to the Saul Alinsky legacy.

The Institute
c/o ACORN
523 W. 15th St.
Little Rock, AR 72202

The Institute
3814 Ross Ave.
Dallas, TX 75204

Institute for Local Self-Reliance
1717 18th St., N.W.
Washington, DC 20009
Provides technical assistance to groups interested in self-help programs, ecological matters, and economic development; publishes newsletter, *Self-Reliance.*

League of Women Voters of the United States
1730 M St., N.W.
Washington, DC 20036
Publishes excellent booklets of use to community groups.

Mid-Atlantic Center for Community Concern
554 Bloomfield Ave.
Bloomfield, NJ 07003

Midwest Academy
600 W. Fullerton Pkwy.
Chicago, IL 60614

National Alliance for Safer Cities
165 E. 56th St.
New York, NY 10022
Network sponsored by the American Jewish Committee.

National Association of Housing and Redevelopment Officials
(NAHRO)
2600 Virginia Ave., N.W.
Washington, DC 20037
National membership group of professionals involved in government
housing and redevelopment programs; publish books and monthly
newsletter, the *Journal of Housing*.

National Association of Housing Cooperatives
1522 K St., N.W., Room 1036
Washington, DC 20005

National Association of Neighborhoods
1612 20th St., N.W.
Washington, DC 20009
National network of some 150 neighborhood groups; sponsors annual
conference.

National Center for Community Action
1328 New York Ave., N.W.
Washington, DC 20005
Support group for community-action groups.

National Center for Urban Ethnic Affairs
1521 16th St., N.W.
Washington, DC 20036
NCUEA is one of the foremost nonprofit institutions aiding community
groups; issues publications and a newsletter. Good resource for community organizations, particularly in low-income, ethnic areas.

National Citizen Participation Council
1620 Eye St., N.W.
Washington, DC 20006
Provides information and training for low-income groups.

National Commission on Neighborhoods
2000 K St., N.W.
Washington, DC 20006
Blue-ribbon panel investigating ways to improve neighborhoods.

National Committee on the Self-Development of the People
United Presbyterian Church
475 Riverside Dr., Room 1260
New York, NY 10027

National Conference of Catholic Charities
1346 Connecticut Ave., N.W., Suite 307
Washington, DC 20036

National Congress of Neighborhood Women
1-29 Catharine St.
Brooklyn, NY 11211

National Corporation for Housing Partnerships
1133 15th St., N.W.
Washington, DC 20005
A private organization created by Congress in 1968, this group is the
largest private developer of low-income housing in the country.

National Council for Urban Economic Development
1730 M St., N.W.
Washington, DC 20006

National Development Council
1421 29th St., N.W.
Washington, DC 20007
Nonprofit group providing technical assistance to cities and community
groups pursuing commercial revitalization.

National Endowment for the Arts
Architecture + Environmental Arts
Washington, DC 20506
Makes grants to individuals and groups in the area of urban conserva-
tion and improvement of the man-made environment.

National Hispanic Coalition for Better Housing
810 18th St., N.W.
Washington, DC 20006

National Information Center on Volunteerism
P.O. Box 4179
Boulder, CO 80302

Information on volunteer efforts; co-publishes quarterly magazine, *Voluntary Action Leadership*.

National League of Cities/U.S. Conference of Mayors
1620 Eye St., N.W.
Washington, DC 20006
A coalition of cities and towns representing the bureaucracy of local government.

National Neighborhood Reinvestment Corp.
1120 19th St., N.W.
Washington, DC 20036
Formerly the Urban Reinvestment Task Force. Funds Neighborhood Housing Services and other programs.

National Neighborhood Watch Program
(Community Involvement in Burglary Protection)
National Sheriffs' Association
1250 Connecticut Ave., N.W.
Washington, DC 20036

National Neighbors, Inc.
Bowen Bldg., Suite 611
815 15th St., N.W.
Washington, DC 20005
Network of 180 integrated communities working for integration.

National People's Action (see National Training and Information Center)

National Self-Help Resource Center
2000 S St., N.W.
Washington, DC 20009

National Training and Information Center
1123 W. Washington St.
Chicago, IL 60607
NTIC publishes books, booklets, and a newsletter (*Disclosure*) and sponsors training programs for organizers.

National Trust for Historic Preservation
1785 Massachusetts Ave., N.W.
Washington, DC 20036
The national clearinghouse for information on historic preservation.

National Urban Coalition
1201 Connecticut Ave., N.W.
Washington, DC 20036
Civil-rights activist group; publishes research on housing-related matters.

National Urban Development Services Corp.
1211 Connecticut Ave., N.W., suite 310
Washington, DC 20036
A nonprofit division of the National Council for Equal Business Opportunity, Inc. Provides technical assistance to neighborhoods and cities on commercial revitalization and center-city work.

National Urban League
500 E. 62nd St.
New York, NY 10021
Provides numerous programs for low-income and minority-group families; in the crime-prevention area, sponsors the Administration of Justice Division.

Neighborhood Information Sharing Exchange
1028 Connecticut Ave., N.W.
Washington, DC 20036

New England Training Center for Community Organizers
19 Davis St.
Providence, RI 02908

Opportunity Funding Corporation
2021 K St., N.W., suite 701
Washington, DC 20006
A private, tax-exempt corporation established in 1970 by the federal Office of Economic Opportunity to conduct projects designed to test new methods of attracting capital into low-income communities.

Organize, Inc.
814 Mission St.
San Francisco, CA 94103

Organizers Book Center
P.O. Box 21066
Washington, DC 20009
Bookstore for organizers; free catalog, *Books for Organizers.*

People's Housing Network
29 E. 22nd St.
New York, NY 10010
Network of tenants' groups, particularly strong in New York State.

Pratt Institute Center for Community and Environmental Development
240 Hall St.
Brooklyn, NY 11205
Provides technical assistance to low-income community organizations, particularly in New York City.

Rehab: The Housing Resource Center
53 W. Jackson Blvd.
Chicago, IL 60604

Small Business Administration
1441 L St., N.W., Room 1025
Washington, DC 20416
Provides grants to small businessmen; useful in commercial-revitalization programs.

Small Town Institute
P.O. Box 517
Ellensburg, WA 98926
Resource agency for those interested in improving small towns.

Suburban Action Institute
257 Park Ave. South
New York, NY 10010
Conducts research on suburban planning issues and serves as advocacy group for suburban poor.

United Methodist Commission on Religion and Race
Minority Group Self-Determination Fund
Box 48–49
110 Maryland Ave., N.W.
Washington, DC 20002

Urban Homesteading Assistance Board (U-HAB)
1047 Amsterdam Ave.
New York, NY 10025
Provides technical assistance to persons and community groups interested in homesteading through "sweat equity."

The Urban Institute
2100 M St., N.W.
Washington, DC 20037
Conducts research and issues books and reports.

Urban Land Institute
1200 18th St., N.W.
Washington, DC 20036
Membership organization with development emphasis; conducts research, issues reports and books, publishes monthly newsletter.

Urban Planning Aid, Inc.
2 Park Square, room 305
Boston, MA 02116
Provides technical assistance to community groups; publishes booklets.

Urban Reinvestment Task Force
(See National Neighborhood Reinvestment Corporation)

U.S. Department of Housing and Urban Development
Washington, DC 20410
Besides its function as the government's chief housing agency, HUD also publishes an informative monthly magazine, *HUD Challenge*.

Voluntary Action Leadership
P.O. Box 4179
Boulder, CO 80306

Youth Project
1555 Connecticut Ave., N.W.
Washington, DC 20009
Supports community development work of young (under-thirty) organizers.

Index